SMARTStart series

Entrepreneur Press

THE #1 RESOURCE FOR STARTING A BUSINESS

HOW TO START A BUSINESS IN UTAH

AF807700

Includes:

• *current state and federal start-up information* • *contracts* • *statistics and legislation* • *business organization* • *business plans* • *financial management* • *sales and marketing tips* • *tax strategies* • *office procedures* • *company policy* • *and licensing information*

Editorial Director: Jere L. Calmes
Cover Design: Beth Hansen-Winter
Composition: Eliot House Productions

This publication is designed to provide accurate and authoritative information in regard to the subject matter covered. It is sold with the understanding that the publisher is not engaged in rendering legal, accounting, or other professional services. If legal advice or other expert assistance is required, the services of a competent professional person should be sought.

Library of Congress Cataloging-in-Publication Data

How to start a business in Utah/by Entrepreneur Press.
p. cm. — (SmartStart series)
"The #1 resource for starting a business."
ISBN 1-932531-07-6
1. New business enterprises—Utah. 2. New business enterprises—Utah—Management. 3. New business enterprises—Law and legislation—Utah. I. Entrepreneur Press. II. SmartStart series (Entrepreneur Press)

HD62.5.H68563 2004
658.1'1'09792—dc22 2004045435

Printed in the United States of America

10 09 08 07 06 10 9 8 7 6 5 4 3 2

Contents

Preface

The zipper, the helicopter, and the artificial heart valve. What do these inventions have in common? They came to us through small business ventures—not major corporations. In fact, small businesses are responsible for more than half of all the innovations developed during the 20th century. Today, small businesses play an integral role in our daily lives as Americans, whether we are directly involved with one or not. According to a recent study by the House Committee on Small Business, small businesses represent more than 99 percent of all employers. They employ 51 percent of private-sector workers, 51 percent of workers on public assistance, and 38 percent of workers in high-tech jobs. The study also found that 85 percent of Americans view small businesses as a positive influence on American life.

Another factor contributing to the move towards small business in this country is the erosion of public confidence in large, established corporations. From the fear of falling victim to downsizing, to a perceived lack of concern for employees' well-being, former corporate workers are turning away from big business and embracing the opportunities and rewards offered through entrepreneurship. In turn, these entrepreneurs are bringing new sources of innovation and creativity to the marketplace.

Given the current social and economic climate in the United States, there has never been a better time to start your own business.

Support for entrepreneurship at the federal, state, and local levels is at an all-time high—further evidence that the time is right for starting your own business. Many government agencies understand the import role small business plays in America's stability and economic future, and are acting accordingly when it comes to funding various ventures. In fact, the House Committee report concluded that small businesses receive one third of all federal prime and subcontract dollars.

Yet with all this potential success and personal fulfillment comes the risk of failure and disappointment, so it is crucial for you to understand the ins and outs of small business ownership, from what it takes to fund, open, and manage your company through how to make the right decisions when times turn difficult.

SmartStart Your [State] Business is a state-specific, start-up book designed specifically for entrepreneurs. The following is a sampling of what you'll find:

- State and federal information on specifics for starting your business from choosing the right legal forms to filing taxes and incorporating.
- Tips for operating your business once you have officially conquered the start-up phase. There are helpful hints regarding proper accounting methods, how to market your product or service, and how to choose and keep quality employees.
- Guidelines for developing a business plan—possibly the most important step in forming and operating a profitable business.
- Statistical information about your state to help you anticipate trends and give you the ability to compare economic and social factors affecting your business.
- Several appendices filled with addresses, phone numbers, and Web site addresses for the agencies and resources you will probably need to contact for licenses, permits, business registration, financing alternatives, workers' compensation, unemployment taxes, and more.

It's all here, in one helpful, easy-to-use volume. If you find errors, or if changes to existing laws are not reflected, please let us know so we can better help others who will be using this information in the future. Thank you for choosing *SmartStart* and we wish you much success in your new enterprise.

CHAPTER 1

Initial Business Considerations

smart (smärt) *adj.* 1) characterized by sharp, quick thought: intelligent; 2) shrewd in dealings: canny

start (stärt) *v.* 1) to begin an activity or movement: set out; 2) to have a beginning: commence; 3) to move suddenly or involuntarily; 4) to come quickly into view, life, or activity: spring forth

---

A smart start—this phrase certainly has a ring to it. In fact, it sounds like what all burgeoning small business owners and entrepreneurs strive to achieve. And, yet, the statistics show that only one out of 20 new ventures will survive to celebrate its fifth anniversary. So what is it that will give you the edge on starting your new venture? The answer involves knowledge and preplanning.

Look back at the definitions of smart and start. These two words imply action—action on your part. You have a dream—starting your own business. You are the one responsible for making that dream come true. You won't be working for a boss; you will be the boss. You won't have a set nine to five schedule; you will work whatever hours are necessary to stay on course.

Of course, with any dream comes inherent challenges. A study published by Dun & Bradstreet lends some insight into the common challenges faced by today's small business owners. The top ten challenges include:

1. *Knowing your business.* This aspect entails indepth industry knowledge, market savvy, and a certain practical knowledge.
2. *Knowing the basics of business management.* The basics include accounting and bookkeeping principles, production scheduling, personnel management, financial management, marketing, and planning for the future.
3. *Having the proper attitude.* Realistic expectations coupled with a strong personal commitment will carry you through.
4. *Having adequate capital.* From establishing a good relationship with a bank to maintaining a business credit report, sufficient capital is vital to surviving the first year.
5. *Managing finances effectively.* In a phrase . . . cash flow. Cash flow entails ongoing capital, inventory management, extending credit to customers, and managing accounts receivable.
6. *Managing time efficiently.* A combination of discipline, delegation, and planning (your business plan has already set the priorities) is essential for effective time management.
7. *Managing people.* Finding and keeping qualified personnel is critical to building a successful business.
8. *Satisfying customers by providing high quality.* You will establish and maintain credibility with your customers when you constantly deliver the best possible product or service.
9. *Knowing how to compete.* New ways of selling, knowing the marketplace, a clear understanding of your niche, and sticking to your original plan all qualify as things you must do for the stiff competition that may lie ahead.
10. *Coping with regulations and paperwork.* Welcome to red tape central—where you may be required to file anything from quarterly tax payments to withholding taxes, from employee manuals to profit-sharing and pension plans, from sales tax records to industry-related reports.

Working smarter means overcoming these ten challenges by knowing what lies ahead of you.

You have heard the phrase "work smarter, not harder." Working smarter means overcoming these ten challenges by knowing what lies ahead of you. A smart start for your business means understanding the course, possessing the skills to overcome the obstacles, and knowing the right way to clear the hurdles. Whether you've competed in athletics, academics, or in a simple game of cards, if you are starting a small business then you're in for the race of a lifetime. Before you run out and buy a pair of the best and fanciest running shoes, take a moment to consider what it takes to be an effective and profitable small business owner.

The Entrepreneurial Archetype

entrepreneur (än´tr pr nur´) *n.*: One who organizes, operates, and assumes the risk in a business in expectation of gaining the profit.

Today more than ever entrepreneurs are playing a vital role in America's diverse economic structure. According to the John F. Baugh Center for Entrepreneurship at Baylor University, the number one course of new jobs in the United States will continue to be entrepreneurial ventures and emerging firms. Even large corporations are beginning to recognize the value and importance of the "entrepreneurial spirit." Numerous books have been written on this so-called entrepreneurial spirit and the subject is the focus of many research groups at business colleges throughout the world. A cursory look at what many believe to be the entrepreneurial archetype may help you discover if owning your own small business is right for you.

Even large corporations are beginning to recognize the value and importance of the "entrepreneurial spirit."

Some Serious Self-Evaluation

What lies within you? Today's researchers believe some of the necessary traits for successful entrepreneuring are drive, commitment, passion, energy, leadership, and pride of ownership. As a fledgling entrepreneur, it is important to understand your strongest talents and skills and realize your areas of weakness. Successful business owners choose a business that allows them to do the things they love to do. Ask yourself questions, such as:

- What kinds of things do I most enjoy doing?
- What do I like to do on my day off?
- What have I always wanted to do but have never had time to do it?
- What do other people compliment me on?
- Do I enjoy interacting with others?
- What types of things do I not enjoy?

These types of questions and many others are listed in self-assessment worksheets in the small business development centers (SBDCs) throughout the nation. SBDC counselors are located in various communities of all 50 states and the District of Columbia to help you plan your business startup. (See Chapter 5 for more details on how SBDCs can assist you.) As you identify your strengths and weaknesses you become more aware of what business type will compliment your personality. Once you have done some self-assessment, you will need to ask yourself some more practical questions related to four major areas of concern:

- Your experience and motivation
- Your product or service
- Your customer
- Your competition

Your Experience and Motivation

You may have all the drive and ambition in the world. But without some experience or way to gain experience in the type of business you plan to start, you may be facing some major hurdles. If you don't have direct experience in the business you want to start, don't be discouraged. Start now by plugging in to the right resources for your industry or trade. For instance, you can join one or more of the trade associations that represent your industry. By joining an association you will get information about legal and other issues of interest to your industry. Membership or affiliation with these associations will also help you support lobbying efforts to represent your interest in the state legislatures and Congress.

As you identify your strengths and weaknesses you become more aware of what business type will compliment your personality.

Other types of assistance and support you will receive from membership in an association include:

- Periodic newsletters or magazines that keep you abreast of important changes occurring in your industry;
- Seminars and meetings that you can attend to get information from other business owners and experts; and
- A network of small business owners like yourself to help you stay in touch with what others are doing in their communities.

Your local library should have association directories. If you prefer, you can access information and oftentimes direct links to the associations via the Internet.

Your Product or Service

Nearly all businesses fall into one of two categories: selling products or selling services. If you have an innovative product and the know-how to produce it cost-effectively and know a distinct market for it exists, then you have the basis for a successful venture. In addition, if you want to start a service business you may be looking at quicker start-up and lower start-up costs due to reduced or no inventory.

Have you clearly identified what you will be selling? In attempting to answer this question, make sure you know how your product or service is different from that of your competitors. Determine what is unique about your product—is it less expensive or of better quality than your competitor's? Maybe it is the same price as your competitor's but you offer guarantees and place warranties. Does it have more options at the same price? You will need to know (not to mention be able to convince) your customers that your product or service is better than the competition's. Further, you will need to know how to measure the demand for your product or service.

Your challenge, among many, will be to establish your product or service upfront—that is, before you open your doors for business. The true test of whether you have clearly identified what you will sell will be sitting down to write your business plan. Your business plan will guide your business to achieve its purpose, its product's or service's purpose, and its long and short-term goals. You will learn more on this critical aspect of business planning in Chapter 7. A sample business plan for a service-type business is at the end of Chapter 7 to help you create your own plan.

Your business plan will guide your business to achieve its purpose, its product's or service's purpose, and its long and short-term goals.

Your Customers

Part of knowing your product or service is knowing who will buy it. To smartstart your business you must have a clear idea of who your customers are and where they are located. You should understand the demographic and psychographic makeup of your customer base. Make sure you know the answers to questions, such as:

- Which age group, income range, and gender will my product or service target?
- Will my product or service appeal to a specific ethnic group?
- Do I know the marital status, education level, and family size of the people I will be selling to?
- Do I know the lifestyles and buying preferences of the target market I've identified?

In addition, you must determine such things as the number of potential customers that exist in your geographic market area and how you will attract and retain buyers. You will want to understand the purchasing patterns and buying sensitivity of your potential customers. It is important to understand the current size of your market and its growth rate. Things like social values and other concerns will influence your customers' buying habits.

As a prospective business owner, your top priority goals should be establishing a strong sales and marketing plan and a smart business plan. As you gain a thorough understanding of your target market you will begin to reap the benefits of repeat business from loyal and satisfied customers. Customer loyalty is a challenge for all businesses; but with the right sales and marketing plan and quality control measures, you can establish a solid customer base.

Your Competition

As important as knowing your customers, you will be one step ahead of the game if you have clearly identified your competitors. Make sure your start-up efforts involve researching your competitors. Who are your major competitors? What advantages and disadvantages do you have compared with the existing competition? Does your business face any barriers for entry? How do customers perceive your competitors? For instance, do their customers remain loyal because of perceived quality, image, or value? Further, determine how you will gain a sufficient share of the market. For the most part, unless you are part of a new industry, your market is probably already served by one of your competitors. Your goal is to carefully plan how you will snatch some of this market share and show that you will continue to reach new markets.

> Your top priority goals should be establishing a strong sales and marketing plan and a smart business plan.

You can be confident about one thing as you start your business—the competition will be fierce. To gain the business street smarts to beat the competition you must know your industry and the number of businesses in your field that have succeeded and failed. Knowing why these businesses survived or died quick deaths will help you in your planning efforts. In addition to understanding where you fit in the entrepreneurial world, you will need to carefully consider how you want to get into business.

Methods of Getting Into Business

As a potential business owner, you have three primary choices for starting your business.

- Start a business from the ground up—from home or elsewhere;
- Buy an existing business; or
- Buy a franchise.

Each method has its pros and cons and it is up to you to decide which is the best alternative for your situation.

Starting a Small Business

Starting a new venture allows you to let your imagination and efforts take you to wherever they may lead. You may be able to start your business on a shoestring in your home or small office with little capital. If so, you can design all the business identification signage, logos, letterhead, and business name. If you are very successful, you may even be able to franchise your idea.

The main factor in starting the business is you.

The main factor in starting the business is you. As previously discussed, you will need to have the drive, energy, passion, and determination to make the business work—no matter how many hours, days, or weeks it takes. If the business succeeds, you will reap the financial rewards, pride of ownership, and sense of accomplishment that a new venture can bring. And, if the business fails to live up to your expectations, you can make your own changes.

The reality of starting a new venture—not buying an existing business nor buying into a franchise—is shouldering the responsibility for each and every detail of business operation. You will have to build the business from the ground up and attract customers based on your own efforts and reputation. You and, if applicable, your partner(s) are the individuals solely responsible for anticipating problems, defining marketing, finding the proper location, and achieving your business plan goals.

Buying an Existing Business

When you purchase a business, you buy many unknowns. For instance, what is the true reputation of the previous owner and did the business truly make a profit or do the books give a false impression of the business' true profitability? How current and usable is the inventory and equipment? Will you inherit employees that you don't want to retain? These and numerous other concerns face the would-be buyer. Research and investigation are critical to buying an existing business.

As the buyer of an existing business you will need to have your attorney or other qualified professional look at all accounting records for the last three to five years minimum. In addition, you need to arrange for a thorough inspection of the inventory and all contracts. Your goal in doing this research is to protect yourself from future liabilities. For instance, make sure your attorney checks for any judgment liens or other recorded security interests. Usually, the secretary of state will have this information. Further, if you will be purchasing real property, get a title search done to make sure the seller has good title and that there are no recorded claims or deeds against the property.

Today's business owners are faced with many environmental responsibilities for their businesses including proper handling of hazardous materials, maintaining proper water or air quality standards, proper waste disposal methods, or removal or monitoring of underground storage tanks.

Also, although not necessary, you may want to have a licensed professional conduct an environmental audit of the property. The last thing you want to deal with are federal or state liabilities for environmental hazards. (For more information on business environmental issues, see chapters 3 and 4.)

When purchasing a business, be aware of the current status of the bulk sale law in your state.

The method of amortizing the amount paid for a business changed as a result of federal legislation. As a buyer of an existing business, you may now amortize intangible items such as goodwill, customer lists, patents, copyrights, and permits and licenses. The old law only allowed amortization of tangible items. The new law requires amortization to occur over a 15-year period. Ask your tax accountant about the best tax treatment for your situation before buying a business.

Many states have repealed their bulk sale laws that required sellers and buyers of certain types of businesses to notify creditors of the impending sale of the business. When purchasing a business, be aware of the current status of the bulk sale law in your state. You can obtain information from your secretary of state's office or consult your attorney.

The IRS now requires the buyer and seller to file Form 8594, Asset Acquisition Statement. Whether you are the buyer or seller, the business' taxable situation will be affected. A copy of Form 8594 is available via the Internet at www.irs.ustreas.gov. If you prefer, contact an IRS field office near you. See Appendix B for address and phone number information.

PURCHASE AGREEMENT

Another important factor of buying an existing business is that both parties agree to a purchase price, terms of payment, and the items involved in the sale. These matters are all addressed in a purchase agreement. Consult your attorney for more information on drafting a purchase agreement.

Buying a Franchise

Approximately 850,000 franchised outlets exist nationwide and it is estimated that a new franchisee opens for business approximately every ten minutes. With figures like these, it's no wonder that people across the nation are buying into the more than 3,000 U.S. franchise operations. Even the U.S. Small Business Administration (SBA) has found that your chances of business success are higher with a franchise than with a typical startup. And, Department of Commerce figures show that 92 percent of all franchise companies formed during the last decade are still in business. But before you jump the gun and decide a franchise is your best bet, consider the advantages and disadvantages of franchising.

The biggest advantage is that the franchisor has done most of the work for you. For instance, the franchisor will have already developed the product(s) or service(s), a positive name recognition, eye-catching signage and interior and exterior store layout, training methods, and effective ways of operating the business. The franchisor should assist you in finding a location for the business as well. Since the franchisor wants you to succeed, the franchisor often provides help for developing your business. Much of the trial-and-error that all business must experience has been learned by the franchisor or by other franchisees and this knowledge is passed on to new franchisees. Overall, you may have a lower risk when you buy a franchise than when you start a business from scratch.

Overall, you may have a lower risk when you buy a franchise than when you start a business from scratch.

In looking at the downsides of franchising, the first concern is cost. Some franchises cost $500,000 in total capital investment and may even require ongoing payments of up to 20 percent of gross sales for rent, marketing, royalties, and advertising. Also, when you buy a franchise you give up quite a bit of freedom. Because the franchise has its own protocol, you will have very specific limits on what you can and cannot do.

The Federal Trade Commission (FTC) regulates the franchise industry. The FTC has a hotline that will give information on:

- Federal disclosure for franchises,
- Getting a copy of a disclosure statement for a specific franchise, and

- How to file a complaint against a particular franchisor.

An attorney is available to answer your questions regarding franchises. For more information, contact the Bureau of Consumer Protection of the Federal Trade Commission.

State governments also have shown their interest in franchising by publishing guidelines like those issued by the FTC. Several states have franchise investment laws that allow potential investors a chance to review pre-sale disclosure information—also known as an offering circular. But remember, all states are subject to the FTC regulations whether or not they have statutes that govern franchises. For more information, refer to Appendix B for the addresses and phone numbers for the FTC headquarters or a regional office that serves your state.

Although legal guidelines exist, this is not to say that the legislation has prevented bad business practices. If you are considering purchasing a franchise, you are encouraged to look at all FTC disclosure documents before signing any agreements. Also, review the franchisor's financial statements and Securities and Exchange Commission (SEC) quarterly and yearly filings to determine its financial strength. You can also contact other franchisees to determine if they are satisfied with the franchisor. In addition, know how to read and understand the prospectus offered by the franchisor.

Research is to small business what location is to real estate.

Research, Research, Research

Research is to small business what location is to real estate. With so many businesses, so many personalities, so many approaches, it is easy to get overwhelmed. Although numerous variables exist, the reality of starting a business is actually more tangible now than ever before. But where do you start? One of the most important things you can do for your startup is to research all matters related to your business. You can conduct preliminary research via numerous routes, including:

- Local, public and college libraries;
- Federal, state, and community business organizations and assistance programs; and
- The Internet.

After reading through this book, you will have a jump start on your research and be able to significantly reduce the time it will take.

Chapter Wrap-Up

This chapter has helped you consider many of the initial factors of starting your small business. Despite what the experts may tell you, there is no "right" way to start your business. You cannot follow ten easy steps to ensure success of your venture. What you can do, however, is know the various tasks that lie ahead and approach each task with a can-do attitude. Use the following worksheet as a primer for the many business decisions you will need to make. For your convenience, use the chapter reference column of the worksheet to learn more about the various tasks you must complete.

Despite what the experts may tell you, there is no "right" way to start your business.

Planning Primer for New Entrepreneurs

YOUR PRODUCT OR SERVICE	YES	NO	N/A	IN CHAPTER
Have you clearly defined your business?				1 and 7
What distinguishes your product or service from your competitors?				6 and 7
Do you plan to manufacture or purchase parts?				7
Do you know the turnaround time for ordering parts and are they guaranteed?				6
Is there a discount for purchasing a larger quantity?				6
Do you know how your product or service will reach its market?				6

YOUR PERSONAL NEEDS	YES	NO	N/A	IN CHAPTER
How long can you survive financially without drawing your assigned salary or wage?				1

YOUR PERSONAL NEEDS, CONTINUED	YES	NO	N/A	IN CHAPTER
Are your family members prepared to withstand the time constraints placed on you as a new business owner?				1
If yours will be a home-based business, how will your home office space accommodate both your customers, vendors, and family members?				12
Are you ready to work long hours and weekends?				1
If you will have partners or co-owners, have you clearly identified what each member will bring to the overall operation? (Think in terms of time, money, equipment, and commitment)				2
If yours is a partnership, do all partners have similar goals and can you work with them?				2
Are you a self starter and can you maintain a disciplined approach to making your business succeed?				1

YOUR BUSINESS' INDUSTRY	YES	NO	N/A	IN CHAPTER
Have you explored the risks associated with selling or manufacturing your product or service?				7
Do you know the seasonal or cyclical nature of your industry and how these changes can affect your ability to sell?				7
Have you researched the credit terms that your suppliers offer and can these terms accommodate your business' needs?				6
How much control do you want or are you willing to give up based on your choice of legal structure?				2

MARKETING ISSUES	YES	NO	N/A	IN CHAPTER
Are there sufficient willing buyers who will be attracted to your current price, quality, and convenience levels?				6
What is the demographic makeup of your customer base?				1 and 6

MARKETING ISSUES, CONTINUED	YES	NO	N/A	IN CHAPTER
Do you know your target consumers' buying habits?				6
What advertising mediums will you use to promote your business' image and/or message?				6 and 7
How will you reach your customers?				6 and 7

THE COMPETITION	YES	NO	N/A	IN CHAPTER
Do you know who your competitors are?				1, 6, and 7
How does your business measure against the competition (i.e., higher quality or lower price)?				1, 6, and 7
What sets your business apart from the competitors?				6 and 7
Will your product or service meet a need for an under-served market?				6 and 7
How do you plan to communicate your business' uniqueness?				6 and 7

YOUR FINANCES	YES	NO	N/A	IN CHAPTER
Where will your start-up funds come from?				7 and 8
Do you know of the numerous federal and state government loans available to your type of small business?				8
Are you aware of how many months (or years) it will take before you start to see a profit?				7, 8, and 9
Do you know the cost of sales (merchandise, freight, labor, etc.)?				6
Have you calculated the monthly fixed costs of your business, including rent, utilities, and insurance?				9
Do you know what your monthly net profits will be?				9

YOUR FINANCES, CONTINUED	YES	NO	N/A	IN CHAPTER
Will you use money from profits or other sources to fund expansion of your business?				7 and 9
Do you know where to get a loan for your start-up or expansion efforts?				9
Have you developed a pricing strategy for your product or service?				6
Do you know the costs associated with obtaining insurance and bonds to cover your business' liability issues?				11
Are you familiar with the basic proforma financial statements—balance sheet, income statement, and cash flow analysis?				7 and 9
Can you interpret your proforma statements?				9
Have you found a bank that will meet your business' needs?				9
Are you aware of how your business structure is taxed?				2 and 3

START-UP EXPENSES	YES	NO	N/A	IN CHAPTER
Do you know the down payment for leasing or purchasing office space? (Keep in mind, negotiating the lease or purchase price of property is usually an option.)				9 and 12
Have you calculated the expenses of equipment leases, inventory needs, fixtures, and office furniture and supplies?				9 and 12
Are you aware of all the necessary deposits you must make for things like sales tax, utilities, credit card acceptance, and leases?				3 and 12
Do you have enough funds to cover your start-up employee salaries?				10
Do you know the costs associated with paying estimated taxes, and obtaining permits and licenses to operate?				3 and 4

START-UP EXPENSES, CONTINUED	YES	NO	N/A	IN CHAPTER
Are you familiar with the financial requirements for withholding taxes, unemployment tax, and workers' compensation?				4
Have you projected your initial advertising budget?				6
Have you thought of allotting money toward paying a professional, like a lawyer or accountant?				9
Do you know the cost of setting up a FAX machine, getting on the Internet, and establishing an e-mail address or Web site?				12
How many phone lines will you require?				12
Will you need a separate post office box for incoming mail?				12
Do you know the fees for setting up your business' legal form (sole proprietorship, partnership, corporation, or LLC)? (Keep in mind, if these expenses become overwhelming, then only calculate the major priorities now and budget the other expenses later.)				2

EMPLOYMENT ISSUES	YES	NO	N/A	IN CHAPTER
Will you need to hire employees?				4 and 10
Have you considered using independent contractors or leasing employees instead of hiring permanent employees?				4 and 10
Are you familiar with the wages for your industry?				13
Do you know your state's minimum wage laws?				4
Does the area in which you wish to locate have a skilled labor pool from which you can hire and retain the best qualified employees?				13
Do you know the federal and state regulations that govern employee and employer rights (i.e., fair employment practices and antidiscrimination issues)?				4 and 10

EMPLOYMENT ISSUES, CONTINUED	YES	NO	N/A	IN CHAPTER
Will you offer a benefits package to your employees?				10
Have you written a clear set of company policy and procedures for your employees?				10
Do you have all employer posters required for display (minimum wage, equal opportunity, etc.)?				4 and 10

INSURANCE ISSUES	YES	NO	N/A	IN CHAPTER
Do you know what kind of property coverage your business will need (i.e., fire, burglary, robbery, business interruptions)?				11
Do you know what kind of casualty insurance your business requires (i.e., liability, automobile, employee theft)?				11

LOCATION	YES	NO	N/A	IN CHAPTER
Are you aware of any environmental issues relating to your business?				3 and 4
How will you address safety and health issues and do you know how to stay in compliance with both federal and state OSHA laws?				4
Does your product or service require specific location needs?				12
Have you checked the makeup of the population and the number and type of competitors in the area?				12
Can the area support a business like the one you propose?				12
Do traffic count, parking facilities, and other business establishments play an important part in location?				12
Do you know the four critical factors for locating your business?				12
Do you know the zoning restrictions and permit requirements for the area in which you will locate?				3

CHAPTER 2

Your Business' Structure

As a small business owner, one of the first major decisions you will make is to choose a legal form under which to operate your business. It is important, therefore, to understand the four basic legal forms: sole proprietorship, partnership, corporation, and limited liability company, then weigh the advantages and disadvantages of each.

Variations of these four entities are available to most business owners in most states. These variations, such as the S corporation and the limited liability partnership, are discussed in greater detail in this chapter. Further, the major advantages and disadvantages of each entity are covered to help you better evaluate which one may be right for your situation. Consult your attorney or accountant, or both, to find out which form makes the most sense for your business' financial condition.

To get started, first consider the criteria you must take into account when making your decision.

Five Factors

Five critical factors will influence which way you decide to go:

- *Legal liability.* Determine whether your business has potential liability and if you can afford that risk.
- *Tax implications.* Look at your business goals and individual situation to find out how you can best minimize your tax burden.
- *Cost of formation and recordkeeping.* If you choose a structure that offers more legal protection to you as an individual, you can bet on increased administrative time and costs to ensure that liability protection.
- *Flexibility.* You want to choose a form that maximizes the flexibility of the ownership structure—achieving both short-term and long-term goals.
- *Future needs.* Even during the start-up phase, you will need to look down the road to what will happen when you retire, die, or sell the business.

With these key factors fresh in your mind, you are ready to explore the pros and cons of each form.

A sole proprietorship is the simplest, most common form of business organization.

Sole Proprietorship

A sole proprietorship is the simplest, most common form of business organization. It is defined as a business that is owned by a single individual. It is the easiest and least costly means of getting into business. As the owner of a sole proprietorship, you are personally responsible for all business debts and liabilities. All your business profits will be considered as income to you and will be taxed at the personal income level. Refer to the discussion below on tax situations for Utah sole proprietors. Conversely, all personal assets and properties are at risk if a sole proprietorship incurs debts beyond its ability to pay.

Advantages of a Sole Proprietorship

- It is easy and inexpensive to establish.
- A sole proprietor has full control over all business decisions.
- There are minimal legal restrictions or requirements.
- A sole proprietor owns all profits and reaps all benefits of ownership.
- There is no requirement to pay unemployment taxes.
- There may be no requirement for the owners to purchase workers' compensation insurance for themselves.

Disadvantages of a Sole Proprietorship

- A sole proprietor is personally liable for all business debts.
- A sole proprietor may have difficulty obtaining long-term financing.

- The success of the business depends wholly on the efforts of the sole proprietor.
- Illness, injury, or death of the sole proprietor will directly threaten his or her business.
- There are no unemployment benefits if the business fails.

If you will operate your sole proprietorship under a name other than your own, you should register the business name (commonly known as "doing business as" or "d.b.a.") with the One-Stop Center in the Division of Corporations and Commercial Code of the Utah Department of Commerce. For more information, refer to the discussion on naming your business in Chapter 3.

If your business will conduct retail sales, you must also apply for a sales tax number from the Utah State Tax Commission. If your sole proprietorship will hire one or more employees, you must have a withholding account number also issued by the tax commission. Both your sales tax number and withholding account number may be requested by filing *Form TC-69, Utah State Business and Tax Registration*, with the Utah State Tax Commission. Utah sales tax and withholding are discussed in more detail in Chapter 3. In addition, you must contact your local government offices to determine if a city or county business license is required.

If you are the owner of a sole proprietorship in Utah, your business profits and losses will be subject to your personal income tax. You will be required to report these earnings or losses on your individual income tax return. Additional information on individual income tax in Utah is provided in Chapter 3.

For more information on sole proprietorships in Utah, contact the One Stop Center in the Utah Department of Commerce's Division of Corporations and Commercial Code. You can find this address in Appendix C.

General Partnership

A general partnership is the association of two or more persons who have agreed to operate a business. You can form a general partnership by a simple verbal agreement of the partners. However, it is in your best interest and the best interest of all parties that you have an attorney prepare, or at least review, a formal, written partnership agreement that addresses such issues as:

- The amount, type, and valuation of property each partner will contribute;

You can form a general partnership by a simple verbal agreement of the partners.

- The method for disbursement of profits and liabilities among the partners;
- A plan for sharing any gains, losses, deductions, and credits;
- A provision for changing the conditions of the partnership; and
- A provision for dealing with the loss or death of one of the partners.

The actions of a single partner are binding upon all partners.

In a general partnership, any partner may hire or fire employees, contract for services, commit to sales, or accomplish any activity required to operate the business independently from the other partners. The actions of a single partner are binding upon all partners.

Advantages of a General Partnership

- A partnership is easy to establish.
- There is more than one person to shoulder the workload and responsibilities.
- Financing is easier to obtain than for a sole proprietorship.
- The partners share all profits and reap all benefits of ownership.

Disadvantages of a General Partnership

- A partnership may be more expensive to initially set up.
- The partners are exposed to unlimited liability for business expenses.
- Each partner is bound by the actions of the other partner.
- Decision-making authority is divided.
- The loss of one partner may dissolve the business.
- The partnership may be difficult to end.

A general partnership does not pay state or federal taxes. The partnership is, however, required to report income and expenses of the partnership on federal and state information returns. Your Utah partnership will need to file *Form 1065, Partner's Share of Income, Credits, and Losses* for federal reporting. You will use *Form TC-65, Utah Partnership Return of Income,* to file your state informational return. Keep in mind, all partners doing business in Utah will need to report their share of the partnership's profit or loss on their personal individual income tax returns. For more information on individual income taxes, refer to Chapter 3.

In Utah, the registration requirements for a general partnership are the same as for a sole proprietorship; registering the business' name with the Utah Division of Corporations and Commercial Code, and registering with the Utah State Tax Commission for a sales tax number and a withholding account number. The addresses and phone numbers for these agencies are included in Appendix C. You must also determine the need for any city or county business licenses or permits by contacting the local government offices.

Limited Partnership

If a partnership sounds appealing to you but you fear the liability issues associated with a general partnership, you may want to consider a limited partnership. A limited partnership is similar to a general partnership and has most of the same advantages and disadvantages. However, be aware of a few significant differences between the roles of the limited and general partners. In a limited partnership, you must always have at least one general and one limited partner. If you are a limited partner you will invest assets into the business and your risk will be typically limited to the amount of capital you have invested. As a limited partner, you will not be otherwise involved in the management of the business and, therefore, will not share in liability for its debts or losses.

In a limited partnership, you must always have at least one general and one limited partner.

If you are an operating or general partner in a business, you are responsible for the liability and operation of the business. You assume responsibility for all management decisions and debts. As in a general partnership, as an operating partner your personal assets are not protected from the creditors of the business.

Advantages of a Limited Partnership

- A limited partnership is relatively easy to establish.
- There is more than one person to share in start-up expenses.
- It is easier for a partnership to get financing than it is for a sole proprietorship.
- The partners share all profits and reap all benefits of ownership.
- The limited partner's personal assets are not at risk from creditors.

Disadvantages of a Limited Partnership

- A partnership is more expensive to set up initially, due to the requirement for a written agreement.
- An operating (general) partner is exposed to unlimited liability for business expenses.
- The loss of one partner may dissolve the business.
- A partnership may be difficult to end.

As a limited partnership in Utah you are required to file a certificate of limited partnership with the Utah Department of Commerce's Division of Corporations and Commercial Code. This can be accomplished at its

One-Stop Center (see Appendix C). The certificate must include the following information:

- The name of the limited partnership (must contain the words "Limited Partnership," "Limited," "L.P.," or "Ltd.");
- The street address of the principal place of business;
- The name and street address of the partnership's registered agent;
- The name, street address, and signature of each general partner; and
- The duration of the partnership's existence.

When filing your certificate of limited partnership, you must submit the original and two copies, all with original signatures. There is a filing fee. Further, you are required by law to draft a formal, written agreement when setting up a limited partnership.

Corporation

A corporation is the most complex type of business organization. It is formed by law as a separate legal entity, fully distinct from its owners—also called stockholders or shareholders. As such, it exists independently from its owners and endures as a legal entity even at the death, retirement, or resignation of a stockholder. Thus, the corporation, not the individuals, handles the responsibilities of the organization. The corporation is taxed and can be held legally liable for its actions. Any person or group of people operating a business of any size may incorporate. Similarly, any group engaged in religious, civil, nonprofit, or charitable endeavors may incorporate and enjoy the legal and financial benefits of incorporation.

Any person or group of people operating a business of any size may incorporate.

You may find that incorporating offers your business a number of benefits. For example, your corporation may be able to more easily raise capital through the sale of stock. Also, as an owner of stock you do not have to be publicly listed, affording you and other stockholders a degree of anonymity. Further, the cost of fringe benefits such as life and health insurance, travel expenses, and retirement plans are tax-deductible.

Until recently, only corporations were allowed to deduct health insurance costs, which provided significant financial incentive to incorporate. However, as of 2003, a congressional amendment to the tax law allows all business forms to deduct health insurance costs.

Corporations can take on several different forms depending on the individual business situation. For the most part, if you decide to incorporate your business, you will need to know the differences between a:

- General (C) corporation—also referred to as a domestic corporation,
- S corporation,

- Foreign corporation,
- Professional corporation, and
- Not-for-profit corporation—also called a nonprofit corporation.

General (C) Corporation

A general business corporation is the most formalized type of business structure and is usually formed for profit-making organizations. A general corporation is the most common type of corporation. In a general corporation, its owners are stockholders, and ownership is based on shares of stock. There is no limitation to the number of stockholders. Since the corporation operates as a separate entity, each stockholder's personal assets are protected from attachment by creditors of the corporation. Thus, as a stockholder, your liability is limited to the capital that you have invested in the purchase of stock.

As a stockholder, your liability is limited to the capital you have invested in the purchase of stock.

Advantages of a General Corporation

- A corporation has a lifespan independent from its owners (stockholders).
- Fringe benefit costs are tax-deductible.
- Personal assets are protected from business liability.
- Ownership can be transferred through the sale of stock.
- It may be easy to raise operating capital through the sale of stock.
- Ownership of a corporation can change without affecting its day-to-day management.

Disadvantages of a General Corporation

- Incorporating involves considerable start-up expenses.
- Corporations are subject to more state and federal legislation.
- Profits are subject to dual taxation—as profits and again as dividends.
- Many legal formalities exist when filing and trying to maintain corporate status.
- Activities are limited to those defined in the corporate charter.

The basics of registering and operating your general corporation are presented later in this chapter under "Handling Corporate Formalities."

S Corporation

The S corporation is a form of the general corporation that has a special tax status with the IRS and many states. The most attractive benefit of an S corporation is the avoidance of double taxation. You have learned that if a dividend is declared, then shareholders must declare that dividend as income and it is taxed again—hence, the double taxation stigma. S corporations avoid this dual taxation because all losses and profits are "passed through" the corporation to the shareholders and are declared only once to the IRS as part of each shareholder's income.

> If the corporation makes a profit, each shareholder is required to pay taxes on his or her proportionate share of that profit.

As in other forms of incorporation, each shareholder's personal assets are protected from the business' debts. There is, however, a downside to the S corporation when it comes to tax time for the corporation's shareholders. If the corporation makes a profit, each shareholder is required to pay taxes on his or her proportionate share of that profit—regardless of whether the corporation distributes the profit to its shareholders or not. Even if the profit is not distributed to the shareholders, the IRS still considers it part of the individual shareholder's income and taxes it at the appropriate rate.

If there is a disagreement with the IRS about who should pay the tax, the IRS can obtain payment from the assets of individual shareholders thereby going around the protection from confiscation by the IRS if the tax is not paid. This can result in a big surprise for a shareholder who helps fund the business but doesn't get payments for the profits because the corporation is either not liquid enough to pay the share of profit to a shareholder or because the managers want to use the profits to build the business and keep the profit in the corporation. Even if the S corporation distributes its profits to shareholders, the additional income for a shareholder may result in a higher tax rate for the shareholder—depending on the amount of other income the shareholder has.

On the other hand, if the S corporation loses money, there may be a significant tax benefit to its shareholders. The loss is passed on to each shareholder, proportionate to his or her stock ownership. This loss can then be applied to the shareholder's overall income and potentially lower his or her tax liability. As in other forms of incorporation, each shareholder's personal assets are protected from the business' debts. Because of this duality of benefit versus liability when it comes to S corporations, you should check with your accountant or attorney to determine which corporation is the best form for you.

If you want to form as an S corporation, your general corporation must meet specific requirements before applying for or being granted S corporation status by the IRS. To qualify for federal S corporation status, your business must:

- Already exist as a corporation;
- Have no more than 75 shareholders;

- Count beneficiaries and shareholders of a small business trust toward the maximum 75 shareholders;
- Be headquartered in the United States;
- Issue only one class of stock;
- Not have nonresident aliens who are shareholders;
- Not be a financial institution that takes deposits or makes loans, an insurance company taxed under subchapter L, or a Domestic International Sales Corporation (DISC);
- Not take a tax credit for doing business in a U.S. possession; and
- Not have more than 25 percent of the corporation's gross receipts from passive sources, such as interest, dividends, rent, royalties or proceeds from the sale of securities. This provision has several conditions, so be sure to clearly understand how it may affect you if your company expects income from these sources.

If your corporation meets the above criteria, you may then apply for S corporation status if all shareholders consent to the election of S corporation status and your business files *IRS Form 2553, Election by a Small Business Corporation.* A copy of this form is located in Appendix A.

Keeping S Corporation Status

S corporation status is subject to many IRS regulations and qualifications. The special tax advantages of S corporation status will be lost if your corporation fails to maintain eligibility. Once S corporation status is terminated, it cannot be reactivated for five years. Your S corporation status can be terminated if your corporation:

- Exceeds 75 shareholders;
- Transfers S corporation stock to a corporation, partnership, ineligible trust, or nonresident alien;
- Creates a second class of stock;
- Acquires an operational subsidiary; or
- Loses corporate status.

S corporation status is subject to many IRS regulations and qualifications.

Utah recognizes the federal S corporation provision. To qualify, you must have an approved *Form 2553* from the IRS and submit your Articles of Incorporation in duplicate with the Division of the Corporations and Commercial Code in the Utah Department of Commerce. There is a filing fee. You may file your documents at the division's One-Stop Center (see Appendix C).

Take a big-picture perspective when considering S corporation status for your business. You will avoid double taxation, yet may not be able to participate in health and accident plans and other fringe benefits that are normally allowed to the general (C) corporation. For more information about S corporations, get a copy of *IRS Publication 589, Tax Information on S Corporations*, from your accountant, local IRS office, or the Internet at www.irs.gov.

When your corporation does business outside the state in which it was incorporated, it is considered a foreign corporation.

Foreign Corporation

When your corporation does business outside the state in which it was incorporated, it is considered a foreign corporation. For instance, suppose you originally incorporate in the state of Maryland but later find you want to do business in New Jersey. Your company, a domestic corporation in Maryland, will become a foreign corporation in New Jersey. If your business will operate as a foreign corporation, it will be subject to potential liabilities, penalties, and problems unless it is qualified to operate in that state. If your business fails to qualify, you may be subject to corporate fines, criminal charges, or a lack of legal recognition in a court of law.

To qualify as a foreign corporation in Utah, you must register with the Division of Corporations and Commercial Code in the Utah Department of Commerce by filing an application for a certificate of authority to do business in Utah. You must also have a certificate of good standing or certificate of existence from your corporation's home state. Contact the One-Stop Center in the Utah Division of Corporations and Commercial Code to obtain the necessary forms and filing procedures. The address and phone number are located in Appendix C.

Professional Corporation

Professional corporations are for individuals whose service requires a professional license. Examples of these professionals include doctors, lawyers, and accountants, but may include others depending on individual state law.

Licensed professionals who incorporate enjoy tax benefits for the costs associated with fringe benefits. However, the shareholders of a professional corporation are personally liable to their clients. Liability spreads to all shareholders even if only one was negligent or accused of wrongdoing.

Advantages of a Professional Corporation

- Personal assets are protected from business debts.

- There are certain tax breaks or deferments for the cost of fringe benefits.

Disadvantages of a Professional Corporation

- The corporation is limited to a single profession.
- Only licensed professionals may be shareholders.
- Shares may only be sold to a licensed member of the same profession.
- Shareholders are liable to their clients as a group.

Utah allows the formation of professional corporations. For more information, contact the Department of Commerce's Division of Corporations and Commercial Code.

Contact your lawyer or accountant to understand the tax law changes that will affect your business. Further, compare the pros and cons of the limited liability partnership (LLP)—akin to the limited liability company (LLC). LLCs and LLPs are discussed in greater detail later in this chapter.

Contact your lawyer or accountant to understand the tax law changes that will affect your business.

Not-for-Profit Corporation

Not-for-profit corporations, also called nonprofit organizations, are usually formed by religious, civil, or social groups. Profits cannot be distributed to members, officers, or directors of a corporation, but instead must be disbursed in support of the beneficial purposes outlined in its articles of incorporation.

A nonprofit corporation does not issue stock, and all activities are controlled by a self-perpetuating board of directors. If your business will operate as a nonprofit corporation, clearly spell out all business operations in your articles of incorporation.

A tax-exempt organization is closely related to a nonprofit organization. Most nonprofit organizations try to qualify as tax-exempt under Section 501(c)(3) of the Internal Revenue Code.

To qualify as a tax-exempt organization your business must be formed for:

- Religious, charitable, scientific, literary, or educational purposes,
- The testing of public safety,
- Fostering amateur sports competition, or
- The prevention of cruelty to animals or children.

A nonprofit organization can benefit from tax-exempt status because all contributions are tax-exempt.

Advantages of a Nonprofit Corporation

- A nonprofit organization can benefit from tax-exempt status because all contributions are tax-exempt.
- There is some flexibility in operations of the business.

Disadvantages of a Nonprofit Corporation

- All income must go to the not-for-profit purpose.
- Members, officers, or directors cannot benefit from dissolution of the corporation.
- A nonprofit corporation cannot merge with another corporation unless it is also classified as nonprofit.

For more information on tax-exempt organizations, contact your local IRS office or Web site for a copy of *Publication 557, Tax-Exempt Status for Your Organization.*

Handling Corporate Formalities

You have heard about the major benefit of incorporation—personal asset protection. Now consider some of the responsibilities of corporations to maintain their corporate status. So that the IRS will not find good cause to pierce your corporate veil, your corporation must:

- Draft, approve, and file articles of incorporation with the Division of Corporations and Commercial Code in the Utah Department of Commerce. This filing may be made at the division's One-Stop Center (see Appendix C). There is a filing fee;
- Domestic corporations file an annual report with the Utah Division of Corporations and Commercial Code during the month of the anniversary of the business' formation. A foreign corporation must file by the anniversary month in which authority was granted to transact business in Utah;
- Pay state and federal corporate taxes;
- Keep bylaws and minutes;
- Issue official stock certificates; and
- Maintain an official corporate seal.

Although time consuming, incorporating your business is a simple process. In fact, the trend for many small business owners is do-it-yourself incorporation. Although you may want to consult with your accountant regarding the tax consequences of switching from doing business as a sole proprietor to doing business as a corporation.

Limited Liability Company (LLC)

A limited liability company (LLC) is a relatively new and highly touted business entity. Limited liability companies have been adopted into legislation in all 50 states and the District of Columbia.

The LLC is a hybrid business form that draws advantageous characteristics from both corporations and partnerships. It is similar to an S corporation without its restrictions. Like a partnership, an LLC's existence rests with its owners—in an LLC, owners are referred to as members. The loss of a member through death, retirement, or resignation can result in the dissolution of the business. However, like a corporation, a limited liability company offers some protection for personal assets from business creditors. Due to its dual qualities—corporate protection and partnership tax treatment—many feel the LLC could replace general partnerships, limited partnerships, and even S corporations as the future entity of choice.

The LLC is a hybrid business form that draws advantages from both corporations and partnerships.

An interesting LLC characteristic is the lack of limitation on the number and nature of its members. However, most states will require at least two members to form an LLC. Members may be foreign persons or nonresidents, or even partnerships, corporations, trusts, estates, or other limited liability companies. An LLC is a good choice for real estate ventures that involve corporations, trusts, or foreign investors, or for new business ventures that involve existing corporations. Also, an LLC is an excellent estate planning vehicle for investment between you and your family corporation, trust, or partnership.

Advantages of an LLC

- Profits and losses pass through the company to its owners for tax purposes.
- Personal assets are protected from business liability.
- There is no limitation on the number or nature of owners.
- An LLC is simpler to operate than a corporation.
- LLCs are not subject to corporate formalities.
- Owners may participate in management of the business.
- Some tax advantages result from business losses or high profits.

Disadvantages of an LLC

- An LLC may be recognized differently in different states.
- Limits of liability have not been extensively tested in litigation.
- Legal assistance is needed to properly set up and structure an LLC.

- Professionals, such as lawyers, accountants, and doctors, are prohibited from registering as an LLC.

Simplicity and great flexibility are the hallmarks of the LLC.

Simplicity and great flexibility are the hallmarks of the LLC. To start an LLC in Utah, you must file the original and one copy of your Articles of Organization with the Division of Corporations and Commercial Code of the Utah Department of Commerce. You can file your documents at the division's One-Stop Center (see Appendix C). There is a filing fee. There are no specific forms for your Articles of Organization but, the following information must be included:

- The name of the LLC which must include the words "Limited Liability Company," "Limited Company," "L.C.," or "L.L.C.;"
- The period of existence of the LLC—not to exceed 99 years from the date of filing;
- The purpose for which the LLC was formed;
- The street address of the registered office in Utah;
- The name, address, and signature of the registered agent;
- A statement indicating whether the LLC will be managed by a manager or managers, and the names and addresses of such managers; and
- If the LLC will be managed by its members, the names and addresses of all members must be included in the articles.

Also, as an owner—or member—of an LLC in Utah, you will need to draft an operating agreement. Similar to a corporation's bylaws, this agreement will define the rights, powers, and duties of members and managers. For example, you would want to spell out how investments in the entity—or contributions—can be made.

Because an LLC is a relatively new entity, little legal precedent for it exists. Even though the IRS has ruled the LLC will qualify as a partnership for tax purposes, the Congress has yet to pass any tax legislation to that effect. A 1997 decision by the IRS allows sole proprietorships to change to LLC status without any negative tax ramifications. This "check-the-box" legislation allows LLCs to be treated as corporations or partnerships for tax purposes. All existing LLCs must do is file *Form 8832* with the IRS and check which box applies to them. If no box is checked, the IRS will automatically treat the LLC as a partnership for tax purposes. Discuss the issues around LLC selection with your accountant or lawyer to determine what is best for your situation.

Limited Liability Partnership (LLP)

Yet another new entity, the limited liability partnership (LLP), is now available to small business owners in all 50 states. In an LLP, partners are afforded the same limited liability protection as professional corporations. A limited liability partnership is a general partnership that provides professional services and is registered as a limited liability partnership under the laws of Utah or any other jurisdiction.

In a LLP, partners are afforded the same limited liability protection as professional corporations.

Advantages of an LLP

- As a partner in an LLP you can enjoy the tax advantage of flow-through tax treatment.
- An LLP is not subject to the numerous limitations regarding ownership, capital structure, and division of profits.
- It is simple and familiar for an existing partnership to elect to become an LLP.

Disadvantages of an LLP

- A sole owner cannot set up an LLP because, as a partnership, an LLP must have at least two partners to exist.
- It is a relatively new legal form, thus, little legal precedent has been set.

Utah allows the formation of limited liability partnerships. You must register with the Division of Corporations and Commercial Code's One-Stop Center. There is a filing fee.

Legal Form Checklist

- ❑ If you will operate as a general partnership, draft a partnership agreement that outlines business issues.
- ❑ If you will operate as a limited partnership, write a limited partnership agreement (required by law) and file a certificate of limited partnership with the Utah Department of Commerce's One-Stop Center in the Division of Corporations and Commercial Code.
- ❑ If your business will be a corporation, file your Articles of Incorporation with the Utah Department of Commerce's One-Stop Center in the Division of Corporations and Commercial Code and pay a fee.

- ❑ If you will do business as a foreign corporation, make sure you file an application for a certificate of authority to do business in Utah, and a certificate of existence from your corporation's home state with the One-Stop Center, and pay a fee.
- ❑ If you will file as a limited liability company (LLC), then draft your business' operating agreement, register with the One-Stop Center, and pay a fee.
- ❑ If you will file as a limited liability partnership (LLP), register your business with the One-Stop Center and pay a fee.

Choosing the legal form for your business is the first of many decisions you will make as you start your Utah business.

Chapter Wrap-Up

Choosing the legal form for your business is the first of many decisions you will make as you start your Utah business. As you begin to make sense of the various legal forms, determine which of the five important factors—legal liability, tax implications, formation costs and recordkeeping requirements, ownership flexibility, and future goals—are the most critical for your business' needs.

Are you most concerned with protecting your personal assets from your business' creditors? Then you may want to avoid forming a sole proprietorship and set up a corporation or limited liability company (LLC). What about the tax situation for your business? You may be interested in forming a corporation, but unless you form as an S corporation or LLC you will suffer the dreaded double taxation. You may have an excellent opportunity to start a partnership with an associate whom you respect. Do you know the ups and downs of a general versus limited partnership and how these legal forms affect your ownership flexibility and future needs? And, finally, although the LLC and S corporation remain the most talked about legal forms, make sure you understand the potentially overwhelming recordkeeping rules and formation costs associated with starting your business as either of these two entities.

Keep this chapter handy as you weigh the pros and cons of each legal form. Make sure your decision involves a consultation with your attorney or accountant, or both.Also, contact the Utah Department of Commerce's One-Stop Center in the Division of Corporations and Commercial Code for any published material that will give you advice on structuring your business in Utah.

CHAPTER 3

Business Start-Up Details

Your decision regarding the legal form for your business is the first of many decisions you will make as you begin your enterprise. Now it's time to tackle the maze of business start-up details that face the approximately ten million people in the United States who are actively pursuing starting their own businesses.

You are responsible for a number of start-up activities that center around licensing and registrations and may include:

- Naming your business, possibly under a fictitious business name;
- Applying for a trade name, trademark, or servicemark;
- Contacting the business assistance or business information centers in the state in which you will do business;
- Obtaining the necessary state and local licenses and permits to get your business running; and
- Learning which taxes your business will be responsible to pay.

This chapter will guide you through the bureaucratic snarls that entangle many start-ups. In short, this information will give you the confidence you need to approach the various state and federal agencies and the know-how to effectively deal with the mounds of paperwork you may encounter. In addition, once you have completed these start-up tasks, your business will become more of a reality—giving you a sense of being an official business owner.

Once you have survived this phase of start-up, and you know that you will have employees, then look to the following chapter to learn about your duties as an employer.

Naming Your Business

The name you choose for your business is another important step you will take as a business owner. Many entrepreneurs underestimate the significance of naming their businesses. In choosing a name, you may want to consider the following tips.

- Select a name that is easy to understand, spell, pronounce, and remember.
- Create a name that can be easily located in a telephone directory.
- Ensure that it portrays the image you want for your business. For example, if quick turnaround and quality service are part of your marketing strategy, then choose identifiers that will convey these aspects.
- Stay away from individual letters or acronyms that may confuse the potential customer trying to locate your business in the telephone directory.
- Steer clear of names that are similar or identical to those used by another business.
- Avoid unusual spellings that may cause your customer difficulty in finding your business name or listing.

Many entrepreneurs underestimate the significance of naming their businesses.

If you need assistance with selecting a name for your business, consult a public relations, advertising, or marketing consultant.

Trade Name

Any business entity can operate under an assumed business name. If you will operate your business under your actual name, you need not file an assumed business name statement—also called d.b.a. or doing business as. In fact, most sole proprietors operate under their own actual names. However, if you operate your business under any other name, you are required to contact the One-Stop Center in the Utah Department of Commerce's Division of Corporations and

Commercial Code for complete requirements. You can find the address in Appendix C.

Many businesses operate under a trade name, often referred to as a fictitious business name or an assumed business name. For example, The Book Nook may be the name of a local bookstore, but this name does not reveal anything about the ownership of the business. It may be owned by a sole proprietor, a partner, a corporation, or a limited liability company. (If it is a corporation, it may contain the word, "Inc." in its name.) To operate the store as The Book Nook, the corporation, Books, Inc. will have to file with county recorder in the store's county of residence, or file an assumed business name statement with the Utah Division of Corporations and Commercial Code, so the public can determine the true ownership of the store. Anyone wanting to serve legal papers to the business would need to determine the true owners, and in this case, the address and officers of Books, Inc.

Many businesses operate under a trade name, often referred to as a fictitious business name or an assumed business name.

Trademarks or ServiceMarks

You can protect your business name by registering it as a trademark, trade name, or servicemark. Trade name or trademark protection is usually good for a specified period of time, usually five to ten years. Once that time period has elapsed, you will be responsible for reregistering your business.

Trademarks and servicemarks may be registered in Utah for a term of 10 years. There is an initial fee and a renewal fee. For more information, contact the Trademark Coordinator in the Division of Corporations and Commercial Code in Utah's Department of Commerce. The address and phone number for this office is included in Appendix C.

If you will do business in other states, it may be to your benefit to obtain a federal trademark registration. Your trademark will distinguish your product or service from those of others that offer similar products or services. To find out more about federal trademark registration, obtain the free booklet *Basic Facts about Trademarks.* To order this booklet, use the address and phone number in Appendix B.

Name Reservation for Corporations and LLCs

If you will operate your business as an LLC or a corporation, you will need to reserve your company name. Most states charge a minimal fee to reserve a name for a specific period of time, usually 60 to 180 days. Utah business entities must pay a name reservation fee per name

Many states have formed centralized business assistance offices to help business owners who are starting, expanding, or relocating to their state.

for 120 days. For more information, contact the Utah Department of Commerce's Division of Corporations and Commercial Code. The address and phone number for the division's One-Stop Center is included in Appendix C.

One-Stop Center

Many states have formed centralized business assistance offices to help business owners who are starting, expanding, or relocating to their state. Referred to as a one-stop center or business assistance center, this office works in coordination with the numerous other state agencies that will regulate your business.

Utah has a one-stop center where you can register your business and obtain all the information you will need to keep your business legally operating in Utah. Utah's One-Stop Center is operated by the Division of Corporations and Commercial Code in the Utah Department of Commerce.

The one stop center will most likely contact other agencies, like the tax or revenue department, to make them aware of your business. Once these agencies are aware of your business' existence, they will usually contact you regarding any filing requirement. However, be aware of their reporting requirements because you may not be excused from reporting even though you were not sent reporting forms. A method to contact the center is provided in Appendix C.

State Licenses

Many businesses and professions require special licenses to operate their specific types of businesses. A license is always needed for professionals such as doctors, lawyers, and dentists. A license is usually necessary for occupations such as cosmetologists, morticians, and contractors. A license may be granted by a state, county, or city agency. Some of the more frequently licensed occupations in Utah are:

- Caterer
- Electrician
- Florist
- Meat packer
- Plumber
- Veterinarian

This is not an inclusive list, but if you are in a profession that is licensed, you likely already know that the requirement exists. No single department has responsibility for all licensing, and fees may vary. If you are uncertain of the status of licensing requirements for your Utah business, the best place to start is the One-Stop Center in the Utah Division of Corporations and Commercial Code. It can help you determine which licensing agency you will need to contact. Refer to Appendix C for the center's address and phone number.

Keep in mind, the licensing agency may require some form of annual licensing renewal.

It is unlikely that your small business will need a federal license to operate. Licenses from the federal government generally are required for businesses that deal with securities, firearms, and use of the airwaves for transmission of information, such as television and radio. If you deal with firearms or ammunition, the consumption or sale of alcoholic beverages or tobacco, or transportation by taxi or bus service, be sure to know the licensing requirements.

Local County and City Permits

If you plan to operate a retail or manufacturing business you will probably be required to get permits either for construction or to open your particular type of business. There are often requirements or restrictions regarding signage, parking, or the type of business allowed in a particular area. Check with the local city and county governments regarding any special zoning ordinances.

Most cities and counties in Utah require some type of business license. Contact your local government offices for information about registration procedures, forms, and fees.

Environmental Permits

Permits often are required to conduct a business that may be regulated by a local or state government. Some federal agencies such the Environmental Protection Agency (EPA) have state equivalents. In Utah, the state equivalent of the federal EPA is the Utah Department of Environmental Quality (UDEQ).

Do not make the assumption that since you are a new or small business you will have little or no contact with these agencies. Due to the requirements of the Clean Air Act of 1991, local, federal, and state laws and regulations affect even one-person operations. You may find that new regulations are put into effect after you start your business, so you must be aware of changes in the laws for which these agencies are

Permits often are required to conduct a business that may be regulated by a local or state government.

responsible. If your business will use any solvent or substance that could become airborne or get into the water in the form or seepage or runoff, you will have reason to contact these agencies. Even if you don't operate a business that may release controlled substances, you may sell equipment that has a harmful effect on the environment. So it is best to know what the rules are when you represent your product or service. Also, if you are buying an existing business, make sure you thoroughly investigate any potential environmental liabilities. It is not uncommon for the buyer of an existing business to be held liable for environmental problems caused by the business' previous owners. You are encouraged to contact a licensed environmental professional to perform an environmental assessment of the business. This assessment will show you any liabilities before it is too late.

If you are buying an existing business, make sure you thoroughly investigate any potential environmental liabilities.

The Utah DEQ's process for obtaining environmental permits is not overwhelming. Processing time usually takes from 21 to 180 days, and can be accelerated if you submit complete and accurate information in the beginning.

The UDEQ operates a Pre-Design Program to assist new or expanding businesses. Its representatives can meet with you to introduce the permit process and teach you pollution prevention techniques. All you need to do is write to the DEQ's Office of Planning and Public Affairs. You should allow at least two weeks notice to ensure appropriate staff is available to serve you. Special assistance is also available through the DEQ's Small Business Ombudsman.

For contact information for many of the Utah DEQ's services, refer to Appendix C.

Registering to Pay Taxes

Once you have officially obtained the necessary licenses and permits for your business, you will be responsible for notifying the IRS. In many cases, you can simply contact a central tax agency, which in turn will get you started with the appropriate forms and filing requirements. Once your business is listed in their database, you may receive periodic inquiries about your business or forms that you must complete to comply with state or federal laws, or both. The main taxes you will need to be aware of include:

- Estimated federal and state individual income taxes,
- Estimated federal and state corporate income taxes,

- A sales and use tax, and
- Property taxes.

Often, there may be a single form or tax application that will get you registered with several agencies regarding several different taxes. Utah's *Form TC-69, Utah State Business and Tax Registration*, is used to register your business' name with the Utah Department of Commerce or to register with the Utah State Tax Commission for withholding, sales, and use taxes. Separate forms are required to register for unemployment insurance and worker's compensation insurance. These forms are described in Chapter 4.

Often, there may be a single form or tax application that will get you registered with several agencies regarding several different taxes.

Get an Employer Identification Number (EIN)

You must obtain an employer identification number (EIN), even if you do not have employees, unless you form a sole proprietorship and have no employees. The first registration you should make is to file *Form SS-4, Application for Employer Identification Number,* with the federal government. You will receive an employer identification number that you will need in many cases to complete other registrations. It is somewhat similar to your personal Social Security number, only it relates to your business.

You can obtain *Form SS-4* from your local IRS office or your accountant. A copy of this form is included in Appendix A. The form is in the appendix for information only. Obtain an official form from the IRS. Once you have the form, you can apply for an EIN either by mail or by telephone. If you want an EIN immediately, call the Tele-TIN phone number for the service center for Utah. The Tele-TIN phone and address are located in Appendix B. If you are not in a hurry, you can apply for your EIN through the mail. You will need to complete *Form SS-4* at least four to five weeks before you will need your EIN. After you receive your EIN, you will need to register with the IRS' Philadelphia office. See Chapter 4 for more information on filing employee taxes.

Estimated Income Tax

As a small business owner in Utah, you will need to estimate the amount of money your business has made and pay taxes on these estimates. Regardless of the form of business you have chosen, you will be responsible for paying estimated income taxes several times throughout the year—usually on a quarterly basis. And, if you have underpaid, you will be required to pay underpayment penalties at the end of the year.

Make sure you calculate these amounts or any underpayment penalties in your monthly cash flow projections. Your accountant may be able to advise you on how best to plan for paying estimated income taxes.

When you are a sole proprietor, a partner, or a shareholder in an S corporation, you are considered self-employed.

Individual Federal Income Tax

When you are a sole proprietor, a partner, or a shareholder in an S corporation, you are considered self-employed. Since there is no employer to deduct federal income tax from your wages, you must make quarterly advance payments against your estimated federal income tax. You must report this business income even if it wasn't actually distributed to you. File your payments along with *IRS Form 1040-ES*. You will then file *Form 1040* at the end of the year along with Schedule C—which itemizes your business expenses for the year. Check with your accountant to make sure you know how to estimate, file, and pay correctly.

Individual State Income Tax

Utah does not require individuals to file estimated tax returns nor make prepayments. It does, however, provide *Form TC-546, Income Tax Prepayment*, for taxpayers who prefer to file and pay on a quarterly basis. Payment may be made on the same schedule as for federal estimated taxes.

As a business owner, it is your responsibility to remain informed of these requirements. Contact your local small business administration (SBA) office, small business development center (SBDC), or the Utah State Tax Commission for more information. The addresses and phone numbers of these resources are listed in Appendix B and Appendix C.

In addition to estimated tax payments you must pay a self-employment tax, which is your contribution to Social Security and Medicare. This tax is paid quarterly and is included in your estimated tax payment. Since you are self-employed, you are responsible for the full amount of the contribution, rather than the 50 percent you would pay as an employee. One-half of the self-employment tax is deductible as a business expense on federal *Form 1040*. See Chapter 4 for more information on FICA, SSI, and Medicare.

Corporate Income Tax

Your corporation will be required to make quarterly federal payments based on its estimated tax using *Form 1120-W, Federal Estimated Tax Payment*. Corporate taxes are typically due on April 15, June 15, September 15, and December 15, unless your corporation operates on a different fiscal year. In this case, your taxes will be due on the 15th day of the 4th month following the end of the fiscal year.

If your Utah corporation's annual tax liability is expected to exceed $3,000, you must also file and pay quarterly estimated state income tax. Use *Form TC-559, Corporation Coupon Booklet*, to file your reports and remit your taxes on the same schedule as your federal quarterly estimated tax returns.

Sales and Use Tax

Utah imposes a sales tax on merchandise rented or sold within the state. If you operate a retail business or provide certain services, you will be required to collect and pay this sales tax to the Utah State Tax Commission. Also, you will be required to obtain a sales tax license from the Utah State Tax Commission, which will register your firm as a retail business that is authorized to collect sales tax.

Utah imposes a sales tax on merchandise sold within the state.

Use tax is a tax on goods or taxable services purchased outside the state for use, storage, or other consumption in Utah. Use tax only applies if sales tax is not applicable.

In most cases you will not be required to pay sales taxes to wholesalers and distributors so long as you provide them with resale certificates on the goods you purchase. In like manner, as a wholesaler, distributor, or manufacturer, you will not be required to collect sales tax on the goods you sell provided the buyer is a retailer purchasing those goods for resale and provides you with resale certificates at the time of sale. For example, if you sell exclusively to other resellers or if your primary business is mail order, you may only be required to collect the tax for items sold and delivered within the state. However, this area of the law is being challenged, so you will find it wise to stay informed about how these changes affect you.

You will be assessed additional taxes on certain types of goods provided for resale. The federal government and most states assess pass-through taxes on certain goods such as gasoline, tobacco, and alcohol. As a retailer, you will pay taxes on these goods at the time of purchase and pass the tax through to the consumer. In the case of these taxes, you do not have to pay them separately to the state. The manufacturer, wholesaler, or distributor does this for you. However, you will still be required to maintain thorough records on all sales.

You are required to keep detailed records of the your gross receipts regardless of whether those receipts are taxable or not. These receipts will justify the taxes you pay and the deductions you take on gross sales

You are responsible for getting forms, filing them, and paying the tax.

throughout the year. You will be required to file a sales tax return on the following schedule:

- File annually if your annual sales and use tax is $999 or less;
- File quarterly if your annual sales and use tax is $1,000 to $49,000;
- File monthly if your annual sales and use tax is $50,000 to $95,999;
- File monthly and EFT (electronic funds transfer) if your annual sales and use tax is more than $96,000.

Forms used for filing sales and use tax returns include:

- *Form TC-71, Sales and Use Tax Return,* (single place of business);
- *Form TC-71S, Sales and Use Tax Return,* (monthly filer, single location);
- *Form TC-71M, Sales and Use Tax Return,* (multiple locations with schedules attached);
- *Form TC-71-V, Sales and Use Tax Return,* (monthly filer; EFT);
- *Schedule A,* (sales and use tax collected from multiple locations);
- *Schedules B and D,* (nonfixed place of business); or
- *Schedule C,* (tax collected for goods or services shipped outside Utah).

Many Utah cities or counties may also impose some form of business tax. Contact your local government office to determine if your business is subject to any local taxes.

Be careful to report on a timely basis. Utah should send copies of reporting forms in advance of the due date. A late or incorrect form can result in heavy penalties or fines. Keep in mind, if you don't receive your forms, don't assume that you have no tax liability. You are responsible for getting the forms, filing them, and paying the tax.

Property Tax

Property taxes are assessed to pay the operating expenses of your locality, pay for bonds, and provide for special projects at the county and community level. Taxes are usually paid on an annual basis to the county treasurer. In most cases the county tax assessor will automatically bill you as the owner of record, so you will not need to contact this office when purchasing property for your business.

In Utah, property taxes are billed annually by November 1st and must be paid by November 30th.

Start-Up Details Checklist

- ❑ Contact the Utah Department of Commerce's One-Stop Center in the Division of Corporations and Commercial Code to determine whether you need to register your business name as an assumed business name.
- ❑ Register any trademark, trade name, or servicemark you feel is necessary with the Trademark Coordinator in the Utah Department of Commerce.
- ❑ Contact the Utah Department of Commerce's One-Stop Center in the Division of Corporations and Commercial Code to find out if it can help you register your business or can send you a start-up kit.
- ❑ Contact the one-stop center to find out whether your business or profession is subject to any special state licensing requirements.
- ❑ Find out whether your business will be required to obtain a city sales or local business/occupation license.
- ❑ Make sure your operations are consistent with current zoning and environmental regulations.
- ❑ Get a local certification of occupancy, if applicable.
- ❑ Obtain a federal employer identification number (EIN) by completing *Form SS-4.*
- ❑ Contact the IRS and the Utah State Tax Commission for information on how and when to pay your federal and state estimated taxes.
- ❑ If you will operate as a corporation, determine your corporate income tax obligations.
- ❑ Register with the Utah State Tax Commission to pay the state sales and use tax and determine how and when you will pay the tax to the state.
- ❑ Obtain a sales tax license and display it at your place of business.
- ❑ Find out your property tax (city and county) obligations and make sure you project these figures into your monthly cash flow statements.

Obtain a sales tax license and display it at your place of business.

Chapter Wrap-Up

You will need to be aware of the city and county rules and regulations that govern your small business.

As you will soon find out, the details of running a small business can be overwhelming. Your best line of defense is to educate yourself about the many requirements placed on your new Utah business.

This chapter has introduced you to most of the start-up details that today's small businesses face. Some of these details are related to federal laws that affect businesses in all 50 states and Washington, DC. However, many of these details will vary according to Utah state laws—and, in some cases, are superseded by state laws. In addition, you will need to be aware of the city and county rules and regulations that govern your small business. From choosing a name for your business to applying for a trademark or trade name; from getting state permits and licenses to registering to pay taxes, as a small business owner you will be responsible for making sure your business is "official."

To help you stay educated and informed of the latest rules and regulations that affect your Utah business, stay in close communication with the Utah Department of Commerce's One-Stop Center in the Division of Corporations and Commercial Code. This office may be able to put you on its mailing list for updates regarding issues that relate to not only starting, but operating a small business in Utah. Also, if you have Internet access, visit the Web sites of your state and its economic development or trade and commerce agencies for the most current information. Refer to Chapter 5 for more information on the role of your state's department of commerce.

CHAPTER 4

Your Duties as an Employer

Minimum wage. Affirmative action. ADA. Immigration. FUTA. FICA. OSHA. No, you won't have to completely learn a new language; but you will need to add more than a few dozen acronyms, buzzwords, and phrases to your vocabulary. Welcome to the world of employment.

Your duties as an entrepreneur will seem like a walk in the park compared to your responsibilities as an employer. In fact, your ability to conquer the multi-faceted job of employer can cause your business to sink or stay afloat in both lean and profitable times. Your best course of action is to thoroughly understand and apply the numerous requirements of being an employer in Utah. You will be responsible for complying with federal and state laws that govern fair employment, anti-discrimination, withholding taxes, workers' compensation, and safety in the workplace. Some of the responsibilities that lie ahead include:

- The minimum amount you will pay your employees, the amount you will pay if they work in excess of a certain timeframe, and if you will employ minors;
- How you will report these wages and, in so doing, which taxes you will withhold;

- The anti-discriminatory manner in which to hire, promote, and retain your employees;
- Your obligations to grant various types of employee leave requests and how to accommodate individuals with disabilities;
- How to properly hire and use independent contractors for your business; and
- The safety and health programs that must be implemented to comply with the regulations.

Much of what you need to understand about being an employer is contained in this chapter. And, to help you further, there is a checklist at the end of the chapter to help you remember your duties.

Fair Employment Practices

One of the first things you must do as an employer in Utah—and that means before you hire employees—is to understand both the federal and state laws that govern fair employment practices. Much of these fair practices centers around the laws that cover payment of wages and working conditions, including number of hours worked.

Drastic changes to employment standards came about in 1938 as a result of the Great Depression.

A good place to start is to understand the beginning of what is today called fair employment practices. Drastic changes to employment standards came about in 1938 as a result of the Great Depression. Also known as the Fair Labor Standards Act (FLSA), this federal law requires overtime for hours worked in excess of 40 hours in a week and sets minimum wages. In addition, the law includes child labor and recordkeeping provisions.

In August 1996, the Fair Labor Standards Act was amended to provide a two-step increase in the minimum wage and a subminimum rate for youth during their first 90 days of employment. The amendments also:

- Change certain provisions of the FLSA with respect to the tip credit that can be claimed by employers of "tipped employees";
- Provide an exemption for certain computer professionals; and
- Redefine home-to-work travel time in employer-provided vehicles.

Every employer of employees subject to the Fair Labor Standards Act's wage-hour provisions must post, and keep posted, a notice explaining the act in a conspicuous place in all of their establishments to permit employees to easily read it. The content of the notice is prescribed by the wage and hour division of the U.S. Department of Labor. An approved copy of the minimum wage poster is available for informational purposes or for employers to use as posters via the Internet. For more information, contact www.dol.gov.

Minimum Wage

The federal government has a minimum wage law. Pursuant to the Minimum Wage Increase Act of 1996, on September 1, 1997, the federal minimum wage increased from $4.75 per hour to $5.15 per hour.

Utah's minimum wage law requires all qualified employers to pay adults at least $5.15 per hour. Minors under 18 years of age must be paid at least $4.25 per hour for the first 90 days of employment and $5.15 per hour, thereafter. Tipped adults and minors must be paid at least $2.13 per hour. There are some exemptions from state minimum wage coverage. For more information, contact the Employment Standards Bureau in the Utah Labor Commission. The address and phone number for this office is included in Appendix C.

Generally, the state minimum wage law relates to employees who work in companies that are exempt from the federal minimum wage law, or those that primarily involve intrastate commerce. To find out if your business can be categorized as involving interstate or intrastate commerce, contact the Labor Standards and Safety Division to be certain which minimum wage amount applies to your business.

Be aware that in addition to minimum wage, there are federal and state laws that govern overtime pay

Overtime Pay

Be aware that in addition to minimum wage, there are federal and state laws that govern overtime pay. If you pay your employees hourly, you are probably required to pay overtime. However, executive, administrative, and professional employees who are paid on a salaried basis are not covered by the FLSA. To determine if your employees fall within one of these categories, consider the following:

- *Executive* means your employee spends a majority of time in management activities, exercises some discretion and independent judgment, and supervises at least two full-time employees.
- *Administrative* means your employee exercises some discretion and independent judgment in performing nonclerical office work directly related to management policies or business operations.
- *Professional* means your employee exercises discretion and independent judgment in a position requiring knowledge of an advanced type in a field of science or learning, or the employee

works in a position requiring invention, imagination, or talent in a recognized field of artistic endeavor.

You should compute pay on a weekly basis to determine if overtime pay is payable to an employee.

Generally, you should compute pay on a weekly basis to determine if overtime pay is payable to an employee. An employee may work more than eight hours in a day without earning overtime pay. However, if an employee works in excess of 40 hours in a week, the additional hours must be paid at one and one-half times that employee's normal rate. Even if you reduce an employee's hours in the previous or following week so as to average 40 hours over two or more weeks, you must pay overtime pay for the week when more than 40 hours of work was conducted.

There are different requirements for exempt and nonexempt employees. You do not have to pay overtime for exempt employees, but you should be aware of the definition of an exempt employee. The above requirements apply to nonexempt employees. Retain payroll records in the event someone claims that overtime pay was not paid.

Utah has an overtime pay law in addition to the federal law. The state law requires you to pay your employees at a rate of one and one-half times their regular rate for all hours worked in excess of 40 hours.

Equal Pay

A part of the Fair Labor Standards Act, the Equal Pay Act requires equal pay to men and women doing substantially the same work with similar skill levels, responsibilities, and effort under similar working conditions. It applies to all local, state, and federal agencies and to any business engaged in interstate commerce. It is regulated by the wage and hour division of the U.S. Department of Labor. If you don't comply with equal pay statutes, you may receive a claim based on wage or sex discrimination. If you are found liable, you may be forced to pay back wages or fines up to $10,000 and may possibly face imprisonment.

Employment of Minors

Both Utah and the federal government regulate the employment of children. These laws usually define the type of work done, the maximum number of hours and days worked, and other conditions that may affect a minor's ability to complete his or her education.

In general, federal law allows anyone 18 years or older to perform any job, whether hazardous or not, for unlimited hours. Youths 16 or 17 years may perform any nonhazardous job for unlimited hours; and 14 or 15 year olds may work outside school hours in various nonmanufacturing, nonmining, nonhazardous job, but they cannot work more than 3 hours on a school day, 18 hours per week in a school week, more than 8 hours per day on a nonschool day or more than 40 hours per week when school is not in session.

If you plan to employ anyone under the age of 18, be sure to contact the Employment Standards Bureau in the Utah Labor Commission for the rules and exceptions that apply to your Utah business. The type of work a minor will perform is a major determinant in whether or not you can employ that individual. There are some exemptions for work such as delivering newspapers.

In Utah, no youth under the age of 16 shall be allowed to work more than four hours in a school day nor before 5:00 A.M. or after 9:30 P.M. unless the following day is not a school day.

Minors 14 and 15 years of age may work in nonhazardous occupations such as fast food restaurants, retail stores, janitorial services, or lawn care. There are 17 hazardous occupations that minors under the age of 18 years are not permitted to perform. For example:

- Working in establishments that manufacture or store explosives;
- Working with power-driven woodworking machines, circular saws, band saws, and guillotine shears;
- Operation of power-driven metal forming, punching, and shearing machines;
- Working in establishments that manufacture brick, tile, and clay products;
- Meat processing operations; or
- Roofing operations.

This is only a partial list of prohibited occupations for minors. For complete details, contact the Employment Standards Bureau in the Utah Labor Commission. Refer to Appendix C for the address and phone number for the Utah Employment Standards Bureau.

Reporting Wages

You are required to provide each employee who worked for your business during the previous year a completed *IRS Form W-2, Annual Wage and Tax Statement*. The W-2 is the form the employee files with his or her state and federal tax reports to show the amount earned at your business. It also shows the state and federal withholdings. More on withholding taxes is located at the end of this chapter.

All W-2 forms and a summary form (W-3) must be sent to the IRS no later than February 28 of each year. When you apply for your employer

All W-2 forms and a summary form (W-3) must be sent to the IRS no later than February 28 of each year.

identification number (EIN) on *Form SS-4, Application for Employer Identification Number,* you will receive the appropriate documents and instructions on how to properly report yearly wages.

See Chapter 3 for details on applying for an EIN and Appendix A for a copy of the form. Strict regulations for sending *W-2s* to your employees exist, so be sure to read and understand the information provided by the IRS.

Anti-Discrimination Laws

The last century brought much change to the ways employers can treat their employees and prospective employees. Legislation that prevents discriminatory practices now pervades the day-to-day operations of U.S. businesses—touching the practices of both big and small businesses. It is critical that you know the various anti-discrimination laws that affect your business, which may include one or more of the following:

- The Civil Rights Act of 1964,
- The Civil Rights Act of 1991,
- Affirmative Action,
- Rehabilitation Act,
- Age Discrimination in Employment Act,
- The Americans with Disabilities Act,
- The Immigration and Reform Act of 1986,
- The Family and Medical Leave Act of 1993,
- Uniformed Services Employment and Re-employment Rights Act of 1994, and
- The National Labor Relations Act of 1935.

Don't let the lengthy and official titles scare you. Compliance with these laws is simple to understand and even simpler to accomplish.

The CRA protects individuals attempting to exercise equal employment opportunity rights from discriminatory practices.

The Civil Rights Act of 1964

The Civil Rights Act of 1964 (CRA) is the principal federal legislation governing employment discrimination. The CRA protects individuals attempting to exercise equal employment opportunity rights from discriminatory practices. Title VII of the CRA prohibits employers from discriminating against employees and job applicants based on race, religion, sex, color, or national origin. In addition, it prohibits discrimination in recruiting, hiring, job advertising, testing, pre-hire investigations, pay and compensation, benefits plans, promotion, seniority, and retirement.

The CRA is regulated by the Equal Employment Opportunity Commission (EEOC). The act applies to:

- Public and private employers with 15 or more employees,
- Public and private employment agencies, and
- Hiring halls or labor unions with 15 or more members.

Employers that fail to comply with the CRA face severe penalties including court-decreed affirmative action programs and court-ordered back pay to the victim.

Employers that fail to comply with the CRA face severe penalties including court-decreed affirmative action programs.

Sexual harassment is prohibited under Title VII of the Civil Rights Act of 1964. Unwelcome sexual advances, requests for sexual favors, or verbal or physical conduct of a sexual nature are all forms of sexual harassment. Specifically, these behaviors cannot be presented as a condition of employment or as the basis for employment decisions, nor can they create an environment that is hostile, intimidating, or offensive.

The Civil Rights Act of 1991

The Civil Rights Act of 1991 extends punitive actions and jury trials to victims of employment discrimination based on the employee's sex, religion, disability, and race. Under previous legislation (the CRA of 1964), employees could only seek back pay. The new act is regulated by the EEOC and applies to all businesses with 15 or more employees. Punitive damage awards are limited to $50,000 for businesses with 100 or fewer employees; $100,000 for businesses with 101 to 500 employees; and $300,000 for businesses with more than 500 employees.

Affirmative Action

The concept of affirmative action was born when, in 1965, President Lyndon B. Johnson signed an executive order that placed strict requirements on companies that provided goods or services to the federal government. This legislation made all employers practice affirmative action by actively recruiting and promoting qualified veterans, minorities, women, and individuals with disabilities. The law requires these companies to achieve and maintain an equitable distribution of each group within its workplaces.

Affirmative action is regulated by the Office of Federal Contract Compliance Programs (OFCCP) and the Civil Service Commission. It

Companies with more than $50,000 per year in federal contracts must additionally file a written affirmative action plan with the OFCCP.

applies to companies with federal contracts of $10,000 or more per year as well as all federal agencies and the U.S. Postal Service. Companies with more than $50,000 per year in federal contracts must additionally file a written affirmative action plan with the OFCCP. Failure to comply with these requirements could result in cancellation of the company's federal contract(s).

Rehabilitation Act

Similar to the President Johnson's executive order requiring affirmative action, this act requires firms providing goods and services to the federal government to hire and promote qualified individuals with disabilities. This act is regulated by the OFCCP and the Civil Service Commission and applies to companies with more than $2,500 per year in federal contracts. Failure to comply with these requirements could result in cancellation of your company's federal contract(s).

Age Discrimination in Employment Act

This act prohibits employers from age discrimination when hiring, retaining, and promoting employees who are 40 years of age or older. It encourages the hiring of older persons based on ability rather than age and it provides a basis for resolving age-related employment problems. The Age Discrimination in Employment Act is regulated by the EEOC and applies to all:

- Government employers,
- Private employers of 20 or more persons, or
- Employment agencies or unions with 25 or more members.

Employers who don't comply may face court-ordered affirmative action programs, court-ordered back pay, fines of up to $10,000, and possible imprisonment.

Americans with Disabilities Act (ADA)

The Americans with Disabilities Act (ADA) prohibits discrimination against qualified employees and job applicants with disabilities regarding job application procedures, hiring, firing, advancement, compensation, job training, discharge, retirement, and other benefits or terms of employment. The ADA is enforced by the Equal Employment Opportunity Commission and applies to all employers with 15 or more employees during 20 weeks of any calendar year. Penalties for noncompliance can include administrative enforcement, back pay, and injunctive relief. The ADA is a very complex act and can be costly if you don't understand it. Unfortunately, not even attorneys can provide definitive information about the act. It was written to help disabled workers find employment, but has been broadened to cover many physical and mental problems of potential employees. Some restrictions are:

- Employers must make reasonable accommodation for modifying a position to employ a disabled person. The term "reasonable accommodation" has not been well defined and is the source of much confusion and potential employer liability.
- Employers may not ask job applicants about the existence, nature, or severity of a disability.
- The act does not apply to employees or potential employees with temporary disabilities.
- The act protects persons with AIDS and HIV from discrimination.
- It provides limited protection for recovering drug addicts and alcoholics.

There are also tax benefits for making changes in your company to accommodate the disabled. To find out how to receive tax breaks for accommodating employees with disabilities, contact the IRS. To learn more about your responsibilities relative to the ADA, contact the Equal Employment Opportunity Commission. See Appendix B for contact information for these two agencies.

Immigration Policy

The Immigration Reform and Control Act of 1986 (IRCA) is legislation designed to prevent illegal immigrants from easily finding employment in the United States. The law protects your right to hire legal immigrants and prohibits the hiring of illegal immigrants. You are subject to fines up to $20,000 for each illegal alien that you hire.

IRCA protects your right to hire legal immigrants and prohibits the hiring of illegal immigrants.

The Bureau of Citizenship and Immigration Services (BCIS), which is under the U.S. Department of Homeland Security, is responsible for administering the post-9/11 rules and regulations affecting noncitizens who work in this country and their employers.

To comply with the law you must request identification from everyone you hire and have them complete a *Form I-9, Employment Eligibility Verification*. *Form I-9* was developed to help you verify an employee's right to work in the United States. A copy of this form is in Appendix A.

Although you may not refuse to hire anyone because you think the person may be an illegal alien, you must obtain identification that is specified on *Form I-9*. Overall, as an employer you must:

- Have new employees fill out Part I of *Form I-9* within three days of being hired;

- Have new employees present documents that prove eligibility to work in the United States;
- Complete Part II of *Form I-9;*
- Retain *Form I-9* on file for each employee for at least three years, or for at least one year after the employee is terminated, whichever is longer;
- Present original *Form I-9*s upon request to an officer of the Bureau of Immigration and Customs Services, the Department of Labor (DOL), or the Justice Department's Office of Special Counsel for Unfair Immigration-Related Employment Practices. You will get at least three days notice before being required to do so; and
- Employers can use *Form I-766, Employment Authorization Document,* to verify employability. This form is used by noncitizens who are approved by the BCIS to work in the United States.

Detailed instructions are printed on *Form I-9.* For further information refer to the booklet, *Handbook for Employers,* which is available from the Office of Business Liaison (OBL) of the BCIS. Use Appendix B to find contact information for the OBL. You will find the field office nearest you on their Web site. Both *Form I-9* and *Handbook for Employers* are being revised in 2003, so check the OBL Web site for changes that will affect you.

The FMLA permits employees to take up to 12 weeks of unpaid leave each year for the birth of a son or daughter.

Family Leave

The U.S. Department of Labor's Employment Standards Administration, Wage and Hour Division, administers and enforces the Family and Medical Leave Act (FMLA) for all private, state, and local government employees, and some federal employees. The FMLA became effective on August 5, 1993, for most employers.

The act permits employees to take up to 12 weeks of unpaid leave each year:

- For the birth of a son or daughter, and to care for the newborn child;
- For the placement with the employee of a child for adoption or foster care, and to care for the newly placed child;
- To care for an immediate family member (spouse, child, or parent, but not a parent "in-law") with a serious health condition; or
- When the employee is unable to work because of a serious health condition.

As an employer you must guarantee that your employee can return to the same job or a comparable job and you must continue health care coverage, if provided, during the leave period. This law is regulated by the EEOC and applies to employers with 50 or more employees within a 75-mile radius. The law does not apply to employees with less than one year on the job or to employees who have not worked at least 1,250 hours or at least 25 hours per week in the past year. Workers who are on family leave are not eligible for unemployment benefits or other government compensation.

The Family and Medical Leave Act can be another source of problems for the unwary employer. Be sure you understand all the provisions of the act before you disallow a request by an employee who wants to take advantage of the provisions of the act.

Utah does not have a family leave act independent of the federal law. Utah employers must comply with federal requirements.

All covered employers are required to display and keep displayed a poster prepared by the U.S. Department of Labor that summarizes the major provisions of The Family and Medical Leave Act (FMLA) and tells employees how to file a complaint. The poster must be displayed in a conspicuous place where employees and applicants for employment can see it. A poster must be displayed at all locations even if there are no eligible employees. For more information and a downloadable copy of this poster log on to www.dol.gov.

Military Leave

The Uniformed Services Employment and Re-employment Rights Act of 1994 requires that military leave must be granted for up to five years. Thus, as an employer you must rehire an employee if that person was inducted into or voluntarily enlisted in the armed forces of the United States. The law also protects reservists who are called to active duty.

The law also grants insurance benefits if your company provides company insurance. Further, it applies to voluntary as well as involuntary military service—in peacetime as well as wartime. However, it does not apply to a state activation of the National Guard for disaster relief or riots. The protection for such duty must be provided by the laws of the state involved.

If you have questions regarding employer, Guard, or reservist rights and responsibilities concerning military leave, you can obtain additional information from a volunteer organization called the Employer Support of the Guard and Reserve. This organization also provides assistance to employers on a local basis if problems develop between a guardsman or reservist and the employer. See Appendix B for contact information.

An employer must rehire an employee if that person was inducted into or voluntarily enlisted in the armed forces of the United States.

Union Organization

The National Labor Relations Act of 1935, also known as the Wagner Act, established a national policy that encourages collective bargaining and guarantees certain employee rights. This legislation was amended by the Labor Management Relations (Taft-Hartley) Act of 1947 and the Labor Management Reporting and Disclosure (Landrum-Griffin) Act of 1959. Together these laws establish a balance between management and union power to protect public interest and provide regulations for internal union affairs.

These laws apply to all private employers and unions and are governed by the National Labor Relations Board (NLRB). The NLRB has the power to investigate, dismiss charges, hold hearings, issue cease and desist orders, or pursue cases via the Circuit Court of Appeals or the U.S. Supreme Court.

Many states have right-to-work laws that prohibit employers from denying employment to individuals who have refused to join a union.

Right-to-Work

Many states have right-to-work laws that prohibit employers from denying employment to individuals who have refused to join a union. These laws also make it illegal for an employer to force mandatory payment of union dues by nonunion workers so as to keep their jobs. If your business will not need a unionized workforce, you may want to seek to do business in a state that has a right-to-work law.

Utah has a right-to-work law. That makes Utah appealing to businesses that prefer to have a non-unionized workforce.

Independent Contractors

Many small business owners use independent contractors to complete certain tasks necessary for their businesses rather than go through the process of hiring additional employees. There are several advantages to contracting an independent worker. First, instead of paying the significant overhead costs for an employee—including taxes, benefits, and insurance—you pay a contractor only for the end result. Second, hiring a contractor involves a much smaller administrative workload. You need only file *IRS Form MISC-1099* as opposed to handling the numerous forms and deductions required for a regular employee.

When using an independent contractor, it is crucial that you don't treat that individual as an employee. Be cautious that the contractor meets the FLSA's definition of contract labor.

The Supreme Court has said that there is no definition that solves all problems relating to the employer-employee relationship under the

Fair Labor Standards Act (FLSA). The Court has also said that determination of the relation cannot be based on isolated factors or upon a single characteristic, but depends upon the circumstances of the whole activity. The goal of the analysis is to determine the underlying economic reality of the situation and whether the individual is economically dependent on the supposed employer. In general, an employee, as distinguished from an independent contractor who is engaged in a business of his own, is one who "follows the usual path of an employee" and is dependent on the business she serves. The following are factors the Supreme Court has considered significant, although no single one is regarded as controlling:

> The Supreme Court has said that there is no definition that solves all problems relating to the employer-employee relationship under the Fair Labor Standards Act (FLSA).

- The extent to which the worker's services are an integral part of the employer's business (e.g., Does the worker play an integral role in the business by performing the primary type of work that the employer performs for his customers or clients? Does the worker perform a discrete job that is one part of the business' overall process of production? Does the worker supervise any of the company's employees?);
- The permanency of the relationship (e.g., How long has the worker worked for the same company?);
- The amount of the worker's investment in facilities and equipment (e.g., Is the worker reimbursed for any purchases or materials, supplies, etc.? Does the worker use his or her own tools or equipment?);
- The nature and degree of control by the principal (e.g., Who decides on what hours to be worked? Who is responsible for quality control? Does the worker work for any other company? Who sets the pay rate);
- The worker's opportunities for profit and loss (e.g., Did the worker make any investments such as insurance or bonding? Can the worker earn a profit by performing the job more efficiently or exercising managerial skill or suffer a loss of capital investment?); and
- The level of skill required in performing the job and the amount of initiative, judgment, or foresight in open market competition with others required for the success of the claimed independent enterprise (e.g., Does the worker perform routine tasks requiring little training? Does the worker advertise independently via yellow pages, business cards, etc.? Does the worker have a separate business site?).

The penalties for incorrectly labeling a worker as a contractor can be expensive. You are liable for the employer taxes that you failed to withhold as well as a portion of the employees' taxes that were not paid. You must file *MISC-1099* for each contractor that you paid in excess of $600 during the year. Failure to file could double your percentage of the employee taxes you may owe should the IRS determine that your contractor was actually an employee. In like manner, contractors will report the income on *Schedule C* or *Schedule F* along with their personal income tax returns.

A written agreement with any independent contractor you will use will help to define your relationship with the contractor for the IRS.

A written agreement with any independent contractor you will use will help to define your relationship with the contractor for the IRS. The agreement should define the work being accomplished and clearly state that the contractor is responsible for paying self-employment taxes. Further, the agreement can do the following:

- Determine start and stop dates but not working hours;
- Make payment dependent on results, not the amount of time spent to get them; and
- Make the working relationship clear and base it strictly on a given result.

You can get an opinion from the IRS as to whether a relationship is a contract or employee by submitting *Form SS-8* to the IRS. You can get a copy of the form from the IRS Web site or by contacting the IRS. See Appendix B for contact information.

Withholding Taxes

When your business has employees, you must withhold federal income tax from their wages. In addition, you must contribute to Social Security, Medicare, and unemployment funds. Requirements for submitting withheld funds are somewhat complex, so be sure to clearly understand what is expected for your business. Contact the IRS for information relating to the remittance of withholding taxes.

Federal Unemployment Taxes (FUTA)

Unemployment benefits are paid from state unemployment taxes and unemployment insurance. The cost of administering the unemployment program is paid from Federal Unemployment Tax Act (FUTA) funds. The federal unemployment tax is your company's contribution to the unemployment insurance fund. You are required to pay 6.2 percent on the first $7,000 of each employee's annual pay. The actual rate you pay is normally 0.8 percent because you receive a 5.4 percent credit for the state unemployment taxes you pay.

You will be required to pay FUTA if you employ one or more persons (not farm or household workers) for at least one day in each of 20 calendar weeks (not necessarily consecutive) and if you pay wages of $1,500 or more during the year. You may be required to pay federal unemployment tax even if you are exempt from paying state taxes. If your FUTA liability is more than $100 in any quarter, you are required to make a federal tax deposit for the amount owing.

FUTA tax is reported annually on *Form 940, Employer's Annual Federal Unemployment Tax Return,* which is due by January 31 of the next calendar year. If you have made timely deposits, however, you have until February 10 to file. In addition, if at the end of any calendar quarter you owe more than $100 FUTA tax for the year, you must make a deposit by the end of the next month.

Some employers can qualify to file a simplified FUTA return. To be eligible to file *Form 940-EZ,* you must:

- Pay unemployment tax to only one state;
- Pay state unemployment taxes by the due date on *Form 940-EZ;* and
- Have wages that are subject to FUTA and are also taxable for state unemployment tax purposes.

To find out more about this simplified filing, obtain a copy of one of the following publications:

- *Publication #334, Tax Guide for Small Business*
- *Publication #15, Circular E, Employer's Tax Guide*
- *Publication #509, Tax Calendar and Checklist*

The locations and phone numbers of regional IRS offices are listed in Appendix B.

State Unemployment Taxes

As an employer in Utah, you are responsible for paying unemployment tax at the state level if you pay $140 in wages in a calendar quarter. Under this program, wages include payments made in cash or any other medium such as merchandise, meals, lodging, or exchange of services. Although the tax is on your employees' covered wages, you are not allowed to deduct this tax from their wages. The burden of paying the state unemployment tax lies on your shoulders as the employer.

The burden of paying the state unemployment tax lies on your shoulders as the employer.

If you operate as a sole proprietor or partner, you won't be required to pay unemployment tax because you will not be considered an actual employee of your business. Also, in Utah, your sole proprietorship is exempt from paying state unemployment tax on your spouse or children under 18 if they are employees of your business. However, if you fire them or lay them off they will not be eligible to collect unemployment benefits.

To register to pay unemployment tax in Utah, you must file *Form 1, Status Report*, with the Utah Department of Workforce Services within 10 days of starting your business. This report is required even though your business may have no employees.

Employers who are subject to the Utah unemployment tax must file a quarterly report using *Form 3, Employer's Contribution Report*. This report will be mailed to you near the end of each calendar quarter. It contains all the information necessary for you to report gross wages paid and remit the tax for which your business is liable. Your report must be filed by the last day of the month following the close of the quarter. Be sure to file and pay on time to avoid penalties.

> The unemployment tax rate for your business is related to the overall experience your company has had with benefits claims over a certain number of years.

Tax Experience Rating

The unemployment tax rate for your business is related to the overall experience your company has had with benefits claims over a certain number of years; hence, the name tax experience rating. For example, if you have had many employees who have claimed benefits, your business will probably have a higher experience rating. On the flip side, if you have had few employees claiming benefits in the past, you will have a lower experience rating.

As a new employer, Utah will assign your business a standard rate. Your experience with unemployment claims and benefits from the point you start your business or purchase an existing business will dictate whether your rate will increase or decrease. If the seller of the business has an excellent rating, talk to the Utah Department of Workforce Services' Employer Accounts Division (see Appendix C) to learn how you can take over that rate.

As a precautionary measure, if you are buying an existing business make sure the seller is current and has filed all necessary unemployment taxes and reports. If you don't, you may be held responsible for unpaid taxes. You are encouraged to get an unemployment tax release from the Utah Department of Workforce Services. Discuss this important aspect of the sale with your attorney. If you do find unemployment taxes owing, make sure this amount is negotiated in the sale price of the business.

Social Security and Medicare (FICA)

Passed into law by Congress in 1935 as the Federal Insurance Contribution Act (FICA), all employers are required to pay Social Security taxes to the government to provide for old age, survivor, and disability benefits as well as hospital insurance (Medicare). Payments are made in equal amounts by an employee and his or her employer, with collection responsibilities falling on the employer. The rate in 2003 is 7.65 percent for the employer and each employee, which includes 6.2 percent for Social Security and 1.45 percent for Medicare. You need to pay the Social Security rate of 6.2 percent for the first $87,000 of wages. This amount normally increases annually, so check for the maximum amount you have to pay for Social Security. There is no limit for the Medicare tax. Refer to *IRS Publication 15, Circular E* for updates and more information.

New Hire Reporting

In compliance with the federal Personal Responsibility and Work Opportunity Reconciliation Act of 1996, all employers must report each newly hired employee to the Utah New Hire Registry. This legislation was enacted to expedite child support collections.

You have 20 calendar days from the hiring date to report the name, address, Social Security number, and hire date of each new hire, as well as the name, address, and federal employer identification number (EIN) of your business. Employees who are rehired after a layoff or other break in service of more than 26 consecutive weeks are considered as new hires. Your report may be a copy of the federal *Form W-4, Employee's Withholding Allowance Certificate* or an equivalent form developed by the employer.

There is a penalty for not filing the required information, which will be raised substantially if there is conspiracy between the employer and employee.

For more information about new hire reporting requirements, contact the Utah New Hire Registry. You will find the address and phone number in Appendix C.

Employees who are rehired after a layoff or other break in service of more than 26 consecutive weeks are considered as new hires.

Federal Income Tax Withholding

You must withhold federal income tax from the wages of any employee who meets threshold wage levels. This requirement applies to all employees who do not claim an exemption from withholding. The amount withheld is recomputed each pay period. Federal income tax is based on gross wages before deductions for FICA, retirement funds, or insurance. Most employers base income tax withholding on percentage or wage brackets. Refer to *IRS Publication 15, Employer's Tax Guide* for detailed descriptions of these withholding methods.

State Income Tax Withholding

You must also withhold a portion of an employee's wages for the state income tax. Again, this requirement applies to all employees who do not claim an exemption from withholding. You are required to have a withholding tax account which is obtained from the Utah State Tax Commission when you file *Form TC-69, Utah State Business and Tax Registration.*

Withholding tax returns must be filed quarterly using *Form TC-96Q, Quarterly Income Withholding Return.* However, if your withholding amount is more than $1,000 per month, you are required to submit your reports monthly using *Form TC-96M, Monthly Income Withholding Return.* You should receive a set of return forms by the beginning of each calendar year. You will significantly improve the processing of your returns by using these forms. Contact the Utah State Tax Commission if you do not receive your forms. Be sure to file on time; late filing can result in penalties.

Electronic Funds Transfer (EFT) is also available for making tax payments for your withholding tax account. This is a voluntary method of payment and it does not eliminate the need to file your return through the mail. Prior approval by the tax commission to use EFT is required.

Workers' Compensation

Before 1911, if an employee was injured on the job that employee had to take legal action against the employer to collect compensation. This led to a high risk of lawsuits against employers. But, in 1911, Wisconsin passed the first workers' compensation laws—paving the way for complex yet beneficial state-by-state workers' compensation laws. Although the general trend is to expand coverage to protect as many workers as possible, each state's mandated coverage is based on the perceived risks of their employees. For instance, manufacturing-based states have more comprehensive coverage whereas agricultural-based states are not as comprehensive. Because of these variations, workers' compensation laws don't cover all occupations in all states.

If you have one or more employees in your Utah business, you are required to obtain workers' compensation insurance.

If you have one or more employees in your Utah business, you are required to obtain workers' compensation insurance.

This type of insurance pays the benefits for covered employees for job-related illnesses, injuries, and deaths. Benefits include medical expenses, death benefits, lost wages, and vocational rehabilitation. If you fail to carry workers' compensation coverage, you will be vulnerable to paying all of the benefits and possible fines. Workers' compensation is offered in most states in one of three ways.

1. A wholly state owned insurance company—or monopoly state fund—is the only insurance available;
2. A wholly state owned insurance company—or state fund—competes with other insurance companies to provide coverage; or
3. No state owned insurance company offers coverage, only private insurance companies.

Utah is one of 13 states that has a state fund that competes with other insurance companies. Thus, you have the option to use either type of insurer. You can purchase insurance through the Workers' Compensation Fund of Utah (WCFU) or through a private insurance carrier.

As an employer in Utah, your business is not responsible for workers' compensation coverage for some agricultural laborers, casual or domestic workers, or real estate brokers.

Also, if you are the owner of a sole proprietorship or a partner in a partnership, you are not required by law to obtain coverage for yourself. Keep in mind, you cannot substitute workers' compensation insurance with other types of insurance like general liability and health and accident insurance.

For more information on the workers' compensation requirements for Utah, contact the Division of Industrial Accidents in the Utah Labor Commission (see Appendix C). Chapter 11 provides more in-depth information about workers' compensation as well as information on how you can reduce your costs.

> Any business engaging in interstate commerce that has one or more employees is responsible for complying with OSHA standards.

Safety and Health Regulations

As part of the U.S. Department of Labor, the Occupational Safety and Health Administration (OSHA) creates regulations and enforcement practices to render the nation's workplaces safe and healthy for employees. Basically, any business engaging in interstate commerce that has one or more employees is responsible for complying with OSHA standards. A few types of businesses are exempt from OSHA compliance and include:

- Self-employed persons;
- Farms on which only immediate members of the farm employer's family are employed; and

- Working conditions regulated by other federal agencies under other federal statutes.

Since many of the OSHA standards are specific to certain types of industry, equipment, substances, environments, or conditions, it is important to have a clear understanding of OSHA regulations that apply to your business. The administration has established and is continually upgrading legally enforceable standards that fall into four major industry categories—general industry, maritime, construction, and agriculture. To help you better understand the federal OSHA standards that may apply to your business, consider hiring a professional safety consultant or refer to a comprehensive reference on workplace safety programs.

Your local OSHA division of the U.S. Department of Labor can provide you with two helpful publications, including:

1. *All About OSHA, OSHA 2056;* and
2. *Employer Rights and Responsibilities Following an OSHA Inspection, OSHA 3000.*

Check Appendix B to find out how you can contact the OSHA office nearest you.

One requirement that you should be aware of is the need to keep a record of industrial injuries and illnesses. All employers with 11 or more employees are required to maintain specified records of all occupational injuries and illnesses as they occur on *Log and Summary of Occupational Injuries and Illnesses, OSHA 200.* This recordkeeping is not required for employers in retail trade, finance, insurance, real estate, and service industries. Further, employers must complete a detailed report for each occupational death, injury, or illness on *Supplementary Record of Injuries and Illnesses, OSHA 101.* You can request the booklet, *Recordkeeping Requirements for the Occupational Injuries and Illnesses,* from the U.S. Department of Labor. Although you will not be required to send the reports to the government, they should be available should OSHA inspect your business.

Some states have their own occupational health and safety programs.

Some states have their own occupational health and safety programs. Similar to federal OSHA standards, your Utah business must comply with state OSHA regulations. Utah's Occupational Safety and Health Act does not cover mine operations, railroads, or federal employers. In these instances, federal laws will be enforced. You may request free job safety and health consultation services from the Utah OSH Division. This service is confidential and will not result in an inspection.

To learn more about state OSHA rules, contact the Utah Labor Commission's UOSH Division (see Appendix C).

Environmental Regulations

Environmental protection is one of the fastest growing areas of legislation relating to small business today. If your business handles hazardous materials, uses natural resources, or expels anything to air, water or land, you could be subject to dozens of federal, state, and local laws that will regulate how you do business. You should become familiar with the laws that may affect your business regarding clean air and water.

Just as important, conserving, recycling, reducing waste, and being environmentally friendly can save you hundreds to thousands of dollars each year. These "green" policies will establish your reputation with customers as a socially responsible, environmentally sound businessperson.

Conserving, recycling, reducing waste, and being environmentally friendly can save you hundreds to thousands of dollars each year.

The Environmental Protection Agency (EPA) is the federal agency that enforces environmental laws and regulations. Like OSHA, Utah has a state agency that represents the EPA in your state.

The Utah Department of Environmental Quality (UDEQ) manages growth in Utah so that it does not sacrifice public health or the environmental quality of the state's mountain ranges, red rock canyons, and desert terrain. It has simplified its permit processing and offers compliance assistance to new and expanding businesses.

Contact the UDEQ and request information about its services and publications. The address and phone number for this agency is included in Appendix C.

Further, your state ombudsman may help you stay informed about potential problems you may encounter because of the federal or state legislation regarding the environment. See Appendix C for contact information.

Employer Duties Checklist

- ❑ Register with the Utah State Tax Commission and the IRS to withhold state and federal income taxes from the compensation paid to your employees and learn the requirements for submitting quarterly reports.
- ❑ Contact the Employer Accounts Division of the Utah Department of Workforce Services to register to pay state taxes and submit quarterly reports for the unemployment coverage for your employees.
- ❑ File with the IRS to pay federal unemployment taxes and submit quarterly reports.
- ❑ Determine your obligations to carry workers' compensation insurance coverage.

- ❑ Review state and federal labor laws to determine the personnel-related policies your business will follow.
- ❑ Check with the Utah Department of Environmental Quality to identify the environmental regulations your business must follow regarding all air, water, and solid waste standards.

Chapter Wrap-Up

To get a jump-start on your duties as an employer means to understand what lies ahead before you post your first job opening. As an employer in Utah, you will be subject to numerous state and federal laws that govern employment. Although it probably wasn't part of your original job description, you must function as a personnel manager until your business grows to a size that warrants hiring such an individual. There are a multitude of state and federal agencies that can assist you with personnel management information.

Fair employment means that you will comply with both federal and state laws regarding things like minimum wage, overtime pay, equal pay, employing minors, and wage reporting.

Your main concerns will center around what is dubbed as fair employment practices. Fair employment means that you will comply with both federal and state laws regarding things like minimum wage, overtime pay, equal pay, employing minors, and wage reporting. In addition to these practices, you will be required to have a basic knowledge of what are known as anti-discrimination laws. The various acts described in this chapter—dealing with affirmative action, ADA, immigration, and family leave, to name a few—just scratch the surface. However, as you get to know these common federal laws, you will gain a bigger picture perspective that will help you better understand the sometimes elusive phrase "personnel management."

Further, as an employer in Utah, you must withhold payments for Social Security and Medicare (also known as FICA) and federal income taxes from the wages you pay to all covered employees. To protect your business and your employees, you must also comply with state workers' compensation requirements.

Of course, as a new business you may not need to hire anyone for a while. However, if you do need employees to get your business running, it is essential that you understand what it means to be an employer in Utah. Use this chapter as a quick reference for future employment issues. Also, refer to Chapter 10 for a more detailed discussion of human resources management.

CHAPTER 5

Sources of Business Assistance

As you've learned so far, starting a business is hard work. You can make your life easier by getting to know the resources available to you and, more importantly, by learning how to use them effectively in your start-up endeavors. In fact, at the heart of your venture are knowledge and know-how—and these amount to power. If you want the power to successfully start your business, you will seek help from qualified business experts. For today's burgeoning entrepreneur, this help is closer than you think.

Numerous federal, state, and private agencies and organizations are available to assist you. This chapter introduces you to the most important and most helpful organizations. Take the time to familiarize yourself with each resource—you will double your investment in time once you know how and where to get the answers you need to start and grow your business.

Federal Resources

Surprisingly enough, your biggest source of help comes from the federal government. Your government watches out for small businesses and wants to see them grow and prosper in the 21st century.

For every federal regulation and legal requirement that the federal government places on America's small businesses, there exists at least one federal agency that will go the extra mile to help those same business owners get their businesses started on the right track. Thus, your first points of contact should be one or more of the following agencies:

- The U.S. Small Business Administration (SBA), which includes the Service Corps of Retired Executives (SCORE), business information centers (BICs), and small business incubators;
- The U.S. Department of Commerce, which includes numerous bureaus and administrations like the Census Bureau and the Economic Development Administration;
- The Internal Revenue Service (IRS); and
- The Equal Employment Opportunity Commission (EEOC).

You will find that many of these agencies offer state-specific business assistance and have their own state-level offices to better serve your business' needs. See Appendix B for further information.

U.S. Small Business Administration (SBA)

Many of the SBA programs and services are free-of-charge.

Formed in 1953, the U.S. Small Business Administration (SBA) provides assistance to entrepreneurs who are starting and expanding their own businesses. Many of the SBA programs and services are free-of-charge and include:

- Financial assistance through numerous loan and loan guarantee programs;
- Assistance with government procurement of small business products and services;
- Minority business assistance programs;
- Counseling on a variety of topics from marketing your products and services to managing your business, to developing a business plan; and
- Educating entrepreneurs about international trade, technology, and research.

The SBA is easy to reach and is praised by numerous business owners as being one of the easiest government agencies to deal with. There is an SBA field office in Utah to serve your needs; see Appendix B for address and phone number. Also, you can quickly access a store house of information by using one of the SBA's telephone hotline or computer online services. On its Web site there is detailed information on its services and other business services. For more information, log on to www.sba.gov.

A computerized telephone message system is available from SBA Answer Desk and can be accessed 24 hours a day, seven days a week. This toll-free number, listed in Appendix B, will put you in touch with operators who will answer your start-up questions and give you guidance on how to get additional assistance. Operators are available Monday through Friday, from 9:00 A.M. to 5:00 P.M. (eastern standard time).

Another way to get help from the SBA is by using the SBA Online Library—a Web site that provides the most current and accurate information on starting and running a business in Utah. The address for the SBA Online Library is in Appendix B.

Another way to get help from the SBA is by using the SBA Online Library.

In addition to offering a myriad of services for the new or expanding business owner, the U.S. SBA provides business counseling and training through other service programs as described below.

SERVICE CORPS OF RETIRED EXECUTIVES (SCORE)

Sponsored by the SBA, the Service Corps of Retired Executives (SCORE) has 12,400 volunteers in nearly 400 offices throughout the nation. These retired businesspeople offer expert advice based on their many years of firsthand experience in virtually every phase of starting and operating a business. To set up a free appointment with a SCORE counselor nearest you, call your SBA field office or contact your nearest small business development center (SBDC). SBDCs are covered in more detail later in this chapter.

BUSINESS INFORMATION CENTERS (BIC)

Business Information Centers (BICs) are joint ventures between the U.S. SBA and private partners. They provide the latest in high-tech hardware, software, and telecommunications to help start-up and expanding businesses. BICs also offer a wide array of counseling services and training opportunities.

Whether you are considering starting a new business or need assistance in expanding or improving an existing business, BICs can help. BICs provide the tools and advice necessary to evaluate and improve your marketing and sales techniques, price your products, or investigate the possibilities of exporting. The research tools and invaluable advice can help your new business get off the ground or help your existing business grow.

BICs combine the latest in state-of-the-art personal computers, graphic work stations, CD-ROM technology, and interactive videos through on-site counseling and helpful training courses. Using a BIC's resources can result in a well-crafted, comprehensive business plan, which can be used to guide you through the first steps of business ownership or through product or service expansion.

Utah has a business information center (BIC) that provides free assistance and advice, on-site counseling, and self-help information. To find the address and phone number of the BIC in Utah, refer to Appendix B.

Business incubation is a dynamic process of business enterprise development.

SMALL BUSINESS INCUBATORS

Although relatively new, small business incubators have become a breeding ground for a number of start-up businesses throughout the United States. Business incubation is a dynamic process of business enterprise development. Incubators nurture young firms, helping them to survive and grow during the start-up period when they are most vulnerable. These incubators sometimes offer a lower than market rate rent and shared housing with a number of other new enterprises in one facility. These businesses can then share conference rooms, secretarial help, accounting expertise, research personnel, and on-site financial management counseling. Then, once a business is ready stand on its own and wants to relocate, the incubator program will assist the business in finding a new location.

To qualify for participation in a small business incubator program, your business will have to go through a selection process. As part of this process, qualified individuals will review your business plan to determine if your business will fit into their program. To find out if there is an SBA-sponsored incubator program in Utah, contact your local SBA office.

The National Business Incubation Association (NBIA) provides members with the resources needed to develop and manage successful business incubators. Whether you are exploring the concept of a business incubator for your community or already have an established incubation program, NBIA services are designed to keep you apprised of industry best practices and save you time and money.

With approximately 800 members worldwide, NBIA is the largest membership organization of incubator developers and managers.

Servicing technology, industrial, mixed-use, economic empowerment, and industry-specific incubators since 1985, the association provides members with critical tools and promotes awareness of incubators' value for economic development. The NBIA's overall objectives include:

- Providing information, research, and networking resources to help members develop and manage successful incubation programs;
- Sponsoring annual conferences and training programs;
- Building awareness of business incubation as a valuable business development tool; and
- Informing and educating leaders, potential supporters, and stakeholders of the significant benefits of incubation.

To find out about private sector incubators, contact NBIA. Refer to Appendix B for address and phone information for this helpful organization.

MINORITY ENTERPRISE DEVELOPMENT (MED)

The SBA offers two main programs through its Minority Enterprise Development (MED) that seek to foster business ownership for those who are socially and economically disadvantaged.

1. *8(a) Small Disadvantaged Business Development.* Qualified minority small business owners can take advantage of the 8(a) program, which offers business development assistance through federal procurement opportunities.
2. *7(j) Management and Technical Assistance.* The 7(j) program provides management and technical training in four main areas: accounting, marketing, proposal/bid preparation, and industry-specific technical assistance.

The U.S. Department of Commerce has developed a number of programs that assist small business owners.

U.S. Department of Commerce

The U.S. Department of Commerce has developed a number of programs that assist small business owners. These programs are headed up by several different bureaus and administrations:

- *Bureau of Economic Analysis,* which reports on the state of the U.S. economy and provides technical information that helps calculate the gross national product figures.
- *Census Bureau,* which produces statistical information in the forms of catalogs, guides, and directories that cover things such as U.S.

population and housing, agriculture, state and local expenditures, transportation, and industries.

- *Economic Development Administration,* which helps generate new jobs, protect existing jobs, and stimulates commercial and industrial growth in economically distressed areas.
- *International Trade Administration,* which helps American exporters find assistance in locating, gaining access to, and developing foreign markets.
- *Minority and Business Development Agency,* which helps minority business owners in their attempts to overcome the social and economic disadvantages that may have limited past participation in business.
- *Patent and Trademark Office,* which will help protect new products and unusual trade names.

Although the department doesn't have the one-on-one relationship with small business owners that the SBA does, it does provide information that can help your business profit. To learn more about the U.S. Department of Commerce, contact it via phone or mail at the address listed in Appendix B.

One of the primary roles of the U.S. Chamber of Commerce is to help the public understand the danger that results from excessive government intervention in the economy.

U.S. Chamber of Commerce

The U.S. Chamber of Commerce was established in 1912 at the suggestion of President William Howard Taft to provide a strong link between business and government. Since then it has played a vital role in helping businesses, especially small businesses, succeed and prosper. In addition, the chamber represents businesses on critical legislative and regulatory issues.

One of the primary roles of the U.S. Chamber of Commerce is to help the public understand the danger that results from excessive government intervention in the economy. Costly and far-reaching federal programs and mandates on businesses raise the costs of doing business and weaken the U.S. competitive position in the global marketplace. To serve the needs of this small business sector, the U.S. Chamber of Commerce has developed programs that are both affordable and effective. As a small business member of the U.S. Chamber of Commerce, you can:

- Obtain access to a wide-range of affordable and leading-edge training tools and products developed exclusively for small and growing businesses through the chamber's Small Business Institute;

- Receive *Nation's Business,* the organization's own magazine that serves as a vital resource to the owners and top management of small businesses by providing practical, how-to information about growing and running a business;
- Access information on small business legislative issues and SBA loans through the chamber's Small Business Center;
- Attend leading technology expositions, conferences, and seminars for small business offered by the chamber's Small Business Institute; and
- Gain your competitive edge in the morning with "First Business," a daily, live, half-hour business-news television program that focuses on the interests of small businesspeople.

To learn more about the U.S. Chamber of Commerce, you can go to its Web site or contact it via phone or mail. The addresses are listed in Appendix B.

Your local chamber of commerce will give you information about general business conditions, available space and rentals, and local business organizations and associations.

LOCAL CHAMBERS OF COMMERCE

If you want to learn more about the region or community where you plan to locate your business, then turn to your local chamber of commerce for assistance. Your local chamber of commerce will give you information about general business conditions, available space and rentals, and local business organizations and associations. Usually chambers of commerce are a good place for referrals. To locate the chamber nearest you, look in the white pages of your telephone directory.

Internal Revenue Service (IRS)

The Internal Revenue Service (IRS) has developed several programs to help you stay informed and one step ahead of the taxes for which you are responsible as a small business owner. Through its Tele-Tax program, the IRS offers quick and easy access to tax help and forms on about 150 tax topics. In fact, you can order forms, instructions, and publications toll-free by phone between 7:30 A.M. and 5:30 P.M., Monday through Friday. See Appendix B for the contact number of the Tele-Tax program.

If you prefer, use your personal computer and modem to get the forms and information you need. The IRS's Internet Web site not only contains forms, instructions, and publications, but educational materials, IRS press releases and fact sheets, and answers to frequently asked questions. For more information on IRS assistance for your business, refer to Appendix B.

Equal Employment Opportunity Commission (EEOC)

If you will employ individuals in your business you will need to understand the laws that cover civil rights, age discrimination, and equal pay.

As described in Chapter 4, a multitude of duties awaits employers in Utah. If you employ individuals in your business you will need to understand the laws that cover civil rights, age discrimination, and equal pay. These laws were created and are enforced by the Equal Employment Opportunity Commission (EEOC).

Created by Congress, the EEOC enforces Title VII of the Civil Rights Act of 1964. In addition, since 1979 the EEOC has also enforced the Age Discrimination in Employment Act of 1967, the Equal Pay Act of 1963, and Section 501 of the Rehabilitation Act of 1973. In 1992, the EEOC began enforcing the Americans with Disabilities Act, commonly known as ADA.

Every employer in the United States, including all employment agencies, labor organizations, and joint labor-management committees must post and keep posted in a conspicuous place upon their premises, a notice that describes the applicable provisions of Title VII and the ADA. Such notice must be posted in a prominent and accessible place where notices to employees, applicants, and members are customarily maintained. Failure to comply may result in fines to your business. To obtain a poster or to learn how the laws mentioned above affect your business, consider obtaining a copy of *Laws Enforced by the U.S. Equal Employment Opportunity Commission*. To order this free publication and poster, use the toll-free phone number listed in Appendix B.

State Resources

In order to attract new business and keep existing business, most states have adopted a "small business-friendly" philosophy. In line with this philosophy, you will find numerous state agency programs and services—most of them free-of-charge—simply for the asking. Take a moment to get to know what Utah agencies are available to you and how you can best utilize their services.

Utah Department of Commerce

In many states, businesses must register with the office of the secretary of state. This is not the case in Utah. All business entities must register with the Utah Department of Commerce's Division of Corporations and Commercial Code. To simplify the registration process, the Division of Corporations and Commercial Code operates a One-Stop Center where a business owner can register his or her business, file an assumed name report, apply for a sales and use tax number, a tax withholding account, or get information regarding occupational and professional licensing requirements. The One-Stop Center also has a trademark coordinator for registering a trademark or servicemark. All of these services are available at one convenient location, co-located with its parent organization, the Utah Department of Commerce's Division of Corporations and Commercial Code.

Utah State Tax Commission

The Utah State Tax Commission is responsible for collecting the various taxes that apply to individuals and business entities residing and operating in Utah. The commission has four types of applications for business tax registration and your Utah business is most likely subject to one or more of these taxes. The commission processes all returns for personal and corporate income tax, sales and use taxes, withholding tax, and any other tax that is levied on your type of business.

> Your business must register with the Utah Department of Workforce Services to pay its unemployment insurance taxes.

Utah Department of Workforce Services

The Utah Department of Workforce Services oversees the state unemployment insurance program, provides job placement services for employers, and operates the Utah New Hire Registry. Your business must register with this agency to pay its unemployment insurance taxes and file monthly, quarterly, or annual reports. Your business must also submit new hire reports to the New Hire Registry to ensure the collection of child support payments mandated by federal and state laws.

Utah Labor Commission

The Utah Labor Commission oversees several bureaus and divisions. At some time, you will probably need to contact its Employment Standards Bureau for information about minimum wage, equal pay, child labor laws, anti-discrimination, or other state labor laws. Utah has its own federally approved occupational safety and health act administered by the Utah Labor Commission's Occupational Safety and Health Division. This agency can assist you with compliance and reporting requirements. Workers' compensation insurance is administered by the Commission's Division of Industrial Accidents. This division can direct you to the state's insurance program or private insurers that offer workers' compensation insurance, which is a state-mandated program.

All of the agencies within the Utah Labor Commission can provide you with informational pamphlets any posters that must be displayed in your employees' workplaces.

Utah Department of Environmental Quality

The Utah Department of Environmental Quality has several divisions that deal with pollution prevention, protection of air and water resources, radiation control, and the disposal of solid and hazardous waste. The department issues various environmental permits required prior to building refurbishment or the construction of new business facilities. The department offers its Pre-Design Program to educate business owners and assist them with compliance issues.

Small Business Development Centers (SBDC)

The small business development center (SBDC) network is a cooperative effort of the U.S. SBA, the state academic community, the private sector, and state and local governments. Over 900 SBDCs are located in colleges and universities throughout the nation. Similar to a SCORE counselor, your local SBDC can offer advice on a variety of start-up issues. Frequently, your local SBDC will sponsor business-oriented seminars. In 2001, SBDCs provided counseling to 610,000 clients at more than 1,000 service locations. Over eight million entrepreneurs have received service from SBDCs since 1980. To find the nearest SBDC, contact the lead center listed in Appendix C.

The Utah SBDC lead center is located in the Salt Lake Community College in Salt Lake City and there are several other SBDCs located throughout the state. The lead center can direct you to the SBDC nearest to your business location. The address and phone number for the lead center is included in Appendix C.

In addition to the various state and federal resources, you will find a wealth of business information from private organizations and agencies.

Private Sources of Help

In addition to the various state and federal resources, you will find a wealth of business information from private organizations and agencies. Keep in mind, the private resources listed here represent some of the most popular and well-established organizations and by no means represent all the private resources available in Utah. To learn about other private sources of help, do an Internet search or contact your local library for assistance.

State Business Publications

Utah has a business journals that will help you stay current on business activities and issues in Utah. See Appendix C for the phone number and address for the publishers.

National Federation of Independent Businesses (NFIB)

The National Federation of Independent Businesses (NFIB) is the oldest and largest small business advocacy group in the nation. This nonprofit organization is the only business organization with the strength of a combined federal and state lobbying program. Representing approximately 600,000 small and independent business owners, NFIB has offices in every state capital and in Washington, DC.

You can become a member of NFIB. As a member you will receive:

- A bimonthly publication called *My Business,* which features articles geared toward the interests of small business owners;
- Copies of state and federal mandate ballots that show you how NFIB's legislative lobbying agenda is established; and
- An annual publication, *How Congress Voted,* gives details of the Congressional voting record and how these votes affected and will affect you as a small business owner.

To learn more about NFIB, see Appendix C.

National Association for the Self-Employed (NASE)

Another helpful membership organization is the National Association for the Self-Employed (NASE). Since 1981, NASE has established one of the largest business associations of its kind. Attributing its success to the "strength in numbers" theory, NASE has more than 320,000 members.

NASE offers it members a chance to get involved with small business advocacy issues through its Legislative Action Network (LAN). Further, members will have access to medical and dental plan savings, travel savings, and discounts on special business training, eye care and legal services. To contact NASE, use the address and phone number in Appendix C.

NAWBO currently has over 75 chapters.

The National Association of Women Business Owners (NAWBO)

The National Association of Women Business Owners (NAWBO), headquartered in the Washington, DC metropolitan area, is the only dues-based national organization representing the interests of all women entrepreneurs in all types of businesses. The organization currently has over 75 chapters. Membership is open to sole proprietors, partners, and corporate owners with day-to-day management responsibility. Active members who live in a chapter area automatically join both chapter and national. Those who do not live in a chapter area join as at-large members. Contact information is provided in Appendix C.

CHAPTER 6

Successfully Marketing Your Product or Service

Most new business owners understand that they will have to partake in some degree of marketing and promotion to make their businesses' products or services visible to the world. But all too often, these same business owners forego developing a solid marketing and public relations strategy so they can deal with the more immediate aspects of starting a business, such as obtaining financing or filing the right paperwork with state and federal offices.

Regardless of the type of business you plan to open—whether it be a retail shop or a home-based consulting business—you will need to know how to attract and retain customers to ensure your business remains profitable. By choosing to look at your market before you open your business, you will be able to do the following:

- Understand the specific habits and characteristics of your business' clientele;
- Safely evaluate your pricing based on your production demands versus your market demands;
- Be better prepared for the cycles of your business' field or industry; and

- Know what your business' best methods of communication are.

All of this information will give you the keen insight to be more responsive to your business' needs and financial stability.

This chapter will help you gather information about your business and formulate it into a meaningful marketing and public relations plan. One of the first steps to building a sturdy framework to your plan is to understand some basic principles behind marketing and public relations. If you are familiar with this field of business already, you know that there are innumerable books, articles, and seminars on marketing and public relations. Unfortunately, not all of them follow the same definitions or standards. So, to maintain some sense of clarity, this chapter treats marketing and public relations as two separate vehicles of communication.

> A favorable review of your business in a local newspaper or sponsoring a student in a 4-H program both qualify as good public relations.

Public Relations or Marketing First?

Public relations is the practice of developing and maintaining a positive connection between your business, the community, and those who either are or will soon become loyal, satisfied customers. A favorable review of your business in a local newspaper or sponsoring a student in a 4-H program both qualify as good public relations. The options that are available for you to position your business in a favorable light are limitless. Marketing on the other hand, defines and perpetuates demand and is directly related to the goal of "making a sale" or creating revenue for your business. Advertising your products or services on television or even deciding to have a sidewalk sale are functions of marketing.

Many business owners decide to jump into the world of marketing and advertising before dealing with how the public perceives them. Obviously, if you can first establish an awareness that you will soon be open for business and ready to meet your customers' demands, then your marketing efforts to make sales will be more effective and show better returns. In other words, by first establishing healthy public relations, you will clear the way to make sound decisions about marketing and generate money back to your business.

Don't be misled by the lure of marketing and advertising professionals. You would be amazed at how quickly salespeople will catch wind of your new business. Not far from the snake oil peddlers of decades past, they will want to sell you on a variety of schemes to bring in immediate revenue. Whether it is selling advertising space in phone books, designing a Web site for your company, or selling you a blimp emblazoned with your company name to hover about your city's skyline, you are in no position to determine what will actually work unless you understand how the general public will perceive these promotional attempts—assuming the public will even notice.

Until you can identify who your best customers are and who can help you further your business' exposure, you are at the mercy of salespeople and general advice-givers. Since it is unlikely that your startup will be able to afford a marketing and public relations staff, much of this responsibility will be on your shoulders.

Define Your Key Audiences

Your public relations and marketing efforts will be much easier if you start off by identifying the groups of people that will (or could) affect the livelihood of your business. Your key audiences might include:

- The general public,
- Your customers,
- Your employees,
- Your investors,
- Government and civic leaders, and
- The media.

Keep in mind, this is a general list of potential audiences and you should take time to think about any additional groups of people that may influence the success of your specific type of business. For example, keeping unionized truckers on your side may be a top priority if you plan to start a big-rig transportation brokerage, but certainly not if you intend to run a typing service for college students. You will definitely want to add those specific groups to the more obvious key audiences in your public relations strategy.

Regardless of the type of business you own, it is important that the general public supports your company.

The General Public

Regardless of the type of business you own, it is important that the general public supports (or at least tolerates) your company. If the general public does not support your business, the likelihood is strong that even your best customers or clients will be swayed to support another business. You may want to focus primarily on your money-spending customers; however, the general public should always be on your mind too. Developing a favorable standing with the general public is sometimes referred to as community relations. The idea is to establish your company as a "good neighbor," not a money-hungry entity with little regard to the environment or community.

To illustrate the importance of community relations, consider the following scenario. Suppose you want to open a skateboard shop that targets teenagers. You take a lot of time to cater to the likes of your young customers, and as a result they view your store as a hangout. On the other hand, the general public is far from being fascinated by the sport and may view your shop as an eyesore—"full of kids out front with nothing better to do." This does not bother you because you have established a loyal following among your customers and are reaping the financial rewards. That is, until one day a skateboarder accidentally knocks down an elderly woman in front of your shop. Suddenly you are faced with a crisis as the media takes hold of the negative publicity this brings to your store as an indirect cause of the accident, not to mention the impending lawsuit filed by the woman. Because you have not maintained a positive image among the general public, you must spend a great deal of effort to reclaim your business from rumors, angry parents who no longer want their children to support your store, and negative media reports.

Developing a favorable standing with the general public is sometimes referred to as community relations.

If on the other hand, your business had promoted a "responsible use campaign" before the accident—without alienating the kids that support it—you would have been in a better position to recover from the crisis. You could have accomplished this by offering free "responsible use" workshops or by bringing a well-known personality in the skateboarding world to demonstrate safer places to skate. By writing press releases, you might lure the local newspaper or television stations to cover the event.

Although the time and money spent on such a campaign may not show any financial return—as the same amount applied to advertising a sale might—being aware of your business' overall perception and its place in the community can help you prevent or at least recover from situations that could dramatically affect future sales.

Your Customers

Naturally, you will want your business to be the first choice of your potential clientele. This means you will have to conduct some research as to who specifically will be your best type of customer. Determine the common characteristics—age, ethnic group, gender, income level, education level, interests, and buying habits of the public who want your goods or services. This will be a crucial element to any of your future marketing needs. Specific methods for defining your best customers are discussed in greater detail in the marketing section of this chapter.

As soon as you have a good idea of who your customers are, you should always put your best foot forward when you choose to communicate to them. Your customers keep your business going. You want to create a comfortable experience for your customers to buy and use your products or services. Begin thinking about what will appeal to your customers on a subconscious level and what steps you can take to meet their interests. Will they identify and be drawn toward the design of your company logo or letterhead? Will the fixtures, furniture, and colors in your office or store appeal to your customers? All of these small details affect the big picture of your business and their importance should not be overlooked.

Your customers keep your business going.

Your Employees

If you will have employees, train them on the importance of portraying your company image in a favorable fashion. That includes how your business' customers or clients are greeted when they call on the phone, walk in the door, or how they are received when they have a problem with a product or service. Inform employees about your company's goals and objectives and motivate them to make the business work. If you include your employees in your efforts and get them excited and proud of their roles, you are more likely to see the positive effects trickle over to your customers. Being concerned about staying in a favorable standing with your employees can improve morale, lessen employee turnover, cut down on rumors and gossip, as well as offer crucial information about company policies. For more information on establishing a healthy relationship with your employees, refer to Chapter 10.

Your Investors

Although your business is not publicly held and you will not have to worry about how shareholders and security analysts view your business, you may want to make an effort to establish a healthy relationship and company image with your banker or other financial consultants. Of course you will focus the message that is relevant to your investors from a different standpoint than you would project to another key audience, like your customers. In other words, you will want to take steps to ensure that your business appears financially sound to your investors.

Taking time to educate yourself and project your willingness to work and communicate with your investors are preliminary steps to reaching lasting healthy relations with your investors. This time spent may be just as, if not more important than the efforts you make with other key audiences, especially when you need funding. See Chapter 8 for more details on working with your bank.

Government and Civic Leaders

Developing a good relationship with local, state, federal, and even international officials can be crucial. Simply put, since these officials have a direct hand in creating legislation that could affect your business, make certain they know about your business and industry.

By maintaining a productive and active voice with the various levels of government, you are more likely to improve or maintain the working standards, taxes, and other government interventions that your business faces. If your business has a voice and a strong image, you are more likely to be respected and heard.

> Developing a good relationship with local, state, federal, and even international officials can be crucial.

The Media

Last, but certainly not the least important to your public relations efforts, is the role of the media. Work with the media to build your image. The media can include everything from your local newspaper, an international cable news network like CNN, and even the Internet. By sending a press release about your company to editors and journalists, the chances are you can influence positive coverage of your business in news stories. If journalists can rely on you or your business for advice or pertinent information for their news stories, then the chances are they are more likely to listen to you when you have something to say about your business.

THE MEDIA CAN BE MORE THAN AN AUDIENCE

The media cannot only serve as an audience, but as a definable conduit to communicate to several of your key audiences. Because the media—television, radio, newpapers, magazines, and Internet—can reach so many different quantities and types of people, you can use this to your advantage and pinpoint press releases to better serve your business' different key audiences. For example, you may discover through interviews that your customers primarily watch the evening news on television for information about the community. With this insight, you know that you should direct news releases to the television news programs with a focus on your customers' interests and needs. But you can also position that same news story for a different medium with elements that would interest your financial backers, if for example, you know they prefer to read the local business journal. By continually learning about your key audiences' habits and characteristics, you will also be better able to assume which is the best medium for the key audience you want to reach.

Keep in mind, a third-party endorsement from the media can often be more effective than a high-priced advertisement. In fact, the Wirthlin Group for Allen Communications, a New York-based public relations firm, found that 28 percent of its 1,023 respondents said a news article would impact their buying decisions, as compared to 8 percent who said they would be influenced more by an advertisement. The respondents also said that they felt magazines and newspapers were more reliable for information than television or the Internet.

Carefully establish a relationship with any useful media contacts.

TAKE TIME TO BUILD RELATIONSHIPS WITH THE MEDIA

Carefully establish a relationship with any useful media contacts. Make it as easy as possible for them to know you're available to provide insight into a particular issue and available for their needs. They want resources to rely upon—experts in a variety of fields—and if they can determine that you are an acceptable resource, the chances of promoting your company are greater too. Don't expect to submit a press release then watch the story unfold on the six o'clock news. Avoid a press release that is just a strong sales pitch. Instead, try to gauge what the media is likely to want to report—what would make a newsworthy story. If you can provide the lead to a good story within the realm of your business, then you may very well have an "in." If not, it's probably better to wait until you do, rather than alienate essential media contacts.

USE THE INTERNET AS A MEDIA TOOL

Although subject to a lot of current media attention, the Internet is proving to be an invaluable medium for all types of business communication. Beyond developing a Web site for your business, you can monitor discussion groups about your business and industry that might generate ideas for press releases and potential news stories. Use email to communicate with journalists and send press releases, if it is an acceptable form of submission for them. You can even use the Internet as your medium of choice to reach specific segments of your key audiences to communicate your message and to further your business' image, rather than blatant marketing or sales pitches.

Build a Public Relations Strategy

Now that you have information about your key audiences, you are ready for a more formal plan of attack—a public relations strategy.

Your first step is to look at the overall picture—or your business' place in the world. Paint a portrait of your business in the marketplace by finding articles about similar businesses, statistics or information about your customers and the community in which your business will serve, or any other indicators that will help you overcome potential image problems and stay in good standing with all your key audiences. You can find this information in the library, in magazines and trade journals, on the Internet, and even by surveying the public about its attitudes and opinions.

Consider what messages you need to communicate to what key audiences to position your business in a favorable light.

Analyze Your Information

When you feel you have gathered enough information to start with, write down what you believe to be an accurate representation of your new business in relation to its competitors and the issues that face you and your competition. Consider what messages you need to communicate to what key audiences to position your business in a favorable light. Consider the limitations that your business has to face in order to communicate those messages to the key audiences. In addition, determine if there are government regulations that could affect your company or contribute to your problem.

Identify Potential Problems

You may discover that there are potential image problems that could affect your business' operations immediately or down the road. Although you cannot predict the future, if you suspect an issue lingers ahead, it may be wise to publicly address the issue before it balloons into general consciousness or, even worse, a crisis. Be as specific as possible in determining these problems and their source, as well as what might happen if you chose to ignore them.

For example, if you have decided to start a timber harvesting operation in the Pacific Northwest, you could face some fairly tough battles trying to keep your business' image favorable in both the eyes of people who consider your business destructive to the forest ecosystem and to the industry that relies on timber for income. By siding with one or the other, you could face repercussions such as environmentalist demonstrations or a loss of support from your vendors and other business allies. Ideally, you may want to take steps to remain acceptable with both parties to a certain degree, assuming that you don't want to take on the risk of boycotts or other actions. You may also discover that you can only bend so far to meet the demands of either extreme side to the issue in order to keep your business profitable. Of course, there may be simply nothing you can do in some cases, other than monitor the noise-makers and hope they do not become the majority of your key audiences. The process of identifying and monitoring problems should be ongoing from the point you decide to open your business to the day when you sell or close it.

Once you have identified any problems, try to come up with ways to resolve them.

Set Goals to Prevent and Resolve Problems

Now you are ready to set goals and identify the methods to position your business in an agreeable manner. Once you have identified any problems, try to come up with ways to resolve them. Find solutions to your questions, based on research, surveys, and instinct. You might ask yourself some questions to find an answer. Will holding a grand opening meet your goals of more exposure for your business? Would coming up with a relevant news story for the media meet your goal? Could your goal be achieved if you find more time to identify and meet the needs to some of your identified audiences' needs? Would creating a newsletter or a Web site help?

Always keep in mind which members of your key audiences will be most affected by the problem and your solution. Your message should cater to their specific interests and needs. Using different types of media—such as a business journal that your vendors and distributors read or a national news program viewed by your general customers—will help you target your message.

Imagine your business develops a better way to reduce production costs and, in return, receive more profit. Information such as this, might be very newsworthy for a business journal that is read by your financial supporters. However, the information is not useful to your customers, since you are not passing a lower price for the goods on to them. From your research, you may have discovered that your customers are concerned about the environment, so instead of restating the news to them about your cut in costs, you can slant the focus of the story to show the added benefit for your customers of having less packaging to throw away.

Once you have identified your business' potential image problems, define your target audience and determine how to best shape the information to suit your audience's needs. Then, you must develop your strategy. You have four options:

1. *Ignore the problem.* You may not have time to deal with the issue now or may think it is simply too early to effectively address it.
2. *React only if you absolutely have to.* You may decide that it is best for the business if you don't address the problem unless one or more of your key audiences becomes concerned about it.
3. *Prevent the problem.* It may be best to be proactive before the problem becomes uncontrollable or too time consuming.
4. *Involve others.* You can sometimes involve groups (the media, government officials, or even media consultants) to solve or head off an image problem for your business.

Don't be concerned if you choose to ignore the problem; it may be in your best interest considering your other business demands. Weigh your decisions according to your workload, other demands, and the importance of keeping up with your business' image. There will always be a tradeoff, and it is okay to decide that dealing with an image problem may be the least of your worries at any given point. In a larger context, do not write off the power of solid public relations throughout your business' lifespan.

If you choose to actively pursue a goal, you will want to outline exactly what you are going to do to reach your goal. You might determine that it is best to have an action event, such as holding a special event, an exhibit, or some other sort of community involvement project. The involvement of the news media will be crucial to publicize these sorts of events and to get your message across.

If you choose to actively pursue a goal, you will want to outline exactly what you are going to do to reach your goal.

Of course, you may decide that it would be better to pursue communications tactics instead. This might include distributing a newsletter, brochure, press release, or direct mail advertisement. It might include coming up with a business logo, developing a Web site, or renting that blimp mentioned earlier with your company name across it.

Make a Timeline

Taking time to create a schedule will help you reach your planned goal. Suppose you are going to hold a grand opening for your business. You must determine when your business will be ready to hold the event, how long it will take to get a "Grand Opening" banner made, when a string quartet can come to perform for your guests, and whether the day and time will be convenient for your key audiences. By planning ahead and doing some research, you can ensure a much more successful launch than if you went without any insight or planning.

Along with creating a timeline, you will also want to examine the cost and time it will take to meet your goals.

Allot Money and Resources

Along with creating a timeline, you will also want to examine the cost and time it will take to meet your goals. It is wise to create a detailed line-item budget, especially for the larger events you may be planning. Be sure to look for hidden costs, as well.

Evaluate Your Efforts

At some point, you will want to determine if your efforts were successful. You determine success based on your original goals, initial strategy, and the methods you used to achieve those objectives. You can survey your customers or potential customers to find out if their perception of your business has changed. You may simply notice that a news story featuring information about your business' activities has brought in more curious customers. Whatever the case, you will want to weigh the effort it took to meet your objectives and what you have learned from the event. You may discover that your goals were not realistic or find a very effective way to build a healthy image with your business. This process can provide some real, qualitative insight into your business and its market.

How to Market Your Positive Image

Suppose you want to increase the public's awareness that your business is going to be open soon. After careful consideration, you decide that having a grand opening is the best method of meeting your objectives. You have flyers printed, alert the media, and even book the string quartet mentioned earlier to add some atmosphere. Your intent is to introduce yourself to the community and provide it with an enjoyable evening. And, after carefully orchestrating something close to the social event of the season, you can't help but feel your business is off to a great start.

Yet, in the weeks that follow, you may notice that interest in your business is waning. More importantly, you aren't earning enough money to keep your cash flow at a healthy level. What may have appeared to be the grandest of grand openings may leave you frantically searching for any means to attract customers.

It is important to establish your business with a positive image, but you will still need a certain amount of sales to keep your business alive and profitable. It is now time to transition your company's positive image into healthy sales. In short, you are ready to work on marketing your product or service.

Marketing is the pursuit of keeping your business financially stable through promotion. This can include running an advertisement in a magazine or taking the time to identify your best potential customers, then using available resources to communicate to their interests and needs through the type of business you operate.

Marketing is the pursuit of keeping your business financially stable through promotion.

By taking steps prior to opening your business, you will be better equipped to meet the needs of your best customers and help ensure that they continue to support your business throughout the months and years that follow.

Define Your Ideal Customers

Go back to the key audiences you identified earlier in this chapter. Out of these groups, which do you see as your cash-spending customers? Base your assumption on indicators, such as:

- What you already know about the industry and its consumers;
- What your competitors have done and continue to do to market to specific groups of people; and
- What business journals, association newsletters, industry magazines, and other resources are saying about your ideal customers.

Your business' marketing efforts—which take time and money—should be calculated and precise. You want to hit the right segment of people who are likely to support your business and hopefully support it loyally.

Of course to achieve this, you may want to pinpoint your general customers even further. To find your best customers, learn as much as you can about them. One excellent way to do this is through interviews or surveys. You can choose to do them on the street, near a competitor's store, or even over the telephone. By developing useful questions about your potential customers' likes and dislikes, you develop a better understanding of what exactly makes your customers tick. By getting to know their habits, knowing what types of entertainment they like, and understanding their motives for seeking out your business, you will be much more capable of making decisions about how to communicate to your best customers.

Defining your ideal customers through market research may even turn up a few surprises. For example, if you are planning to open an automotive parts store, you might assume that your primary customers are middle-aged men, who are either mechanics or like to do things for themselves. However, through your surveys of the general public, you discover that many women would be interested in supporting a retail store that offers automotive parts. By examining your competition, you realize that this segment of the general market is virtually ignored. You decide that it is worth allocating some money toward trying to develop women as a primary customer segment in your store. By taking steps to appeal to this group's interests and needs, you are building additional sales and gaining a one-up on your competition.

Defining your ideal customers through market research may even turn up a few surprises.

Use Your Competition's Strategy to Your Benefit

Although it may seem strange at first, you can learn a lot from your competitors. Observing how they run and promote their businesses and who visits their stores can provide insight as to who might migrate to your business.

Examine your competitors' prices. Document the pros and cons of their products or services. Find out as much as you can about their operating costs. Visit their Web site and determine what type of customer they are trying to reach. Find out who their distributors and suppliers are, if any. Determine whether their location is convenient and to their benefit. You have the luxury of evaluating their work and deciding whether or not they are doing something as well as it can be done. If not, you can implement a better way of performing these functions in your business.

Distinguish Yourself from Your Competitors

After you have finished obtaining as much publicly available information as you can from your competition, compile it and analyze it.

Compare your results with what you intend to do as a new business. Compare everything from your customers to what costs will affect daily operations. From this information, you can build ways to give you an advantage over your competition. Maybe you can operate at a lower cost and reduced prices. Maybe your business is in a better location. Whatever the differences, your business will need to develop some unique selling points to lure customers. These can be as subtle or blatant as you want, from providing a more comfortable atmosphere in your business to heavy promotions for your rock-bottom prices resembling those for monster-truck rallys.

Blaze Your Own Creative Marketing Trail

Unfortunately, as a new business you are not likely to have a great sum of money for any major marketing efforts. Certainly don't try to keep up with your competition if they are large and can sink millions into highly targeted advertising campaigns—you will only drain what resources you do have and put your business in financial jeopardy. Yet, don't be discouraged by having Goliath corporate competitors. Your creativity, research, and public image can give you an advantage to sway your customers "to support the community" rather than some corporate giant.

You will need to find inexpensive, yet quality ways to produce your message.

Determine the Factors that Will Affect Sales

Of course, before you can really partake in a creative marketing idea to bring in customers, you need to examine some essential factors that could influence your overall marketing and sales. You will need to find inexpensive, yet quality ways to produce your message. You may have to find a reputable printer or television production crew to produce your marketing message. However, before you commit to creating and producing a marketing idea, you need to be firm on what your internal cost demands are, the revenue you can commit to marketing, and how much you can invest to maintain a quick return on your money.

Beware of the Impacts of Pricing

Your operating costs may play a larger role in your marketing decisions than you may think. You may discover that your potential customers seek a business with lower prices. So it may seem best to reduce your prices. Without prior examination, you may be doing more business, but not able to keep your production or operating costs in check.

Pricing your product or service will have an extraordinary impact on the success of your business. If you price your product or service too low, you will experience low profits and may even experience significant losses. Price your product or service too high and your customer base will migrate to your competitors or never form at all.

ANALYZE COSTS

Fortunately, most of the mystery associated with pricing can be easily dispelled with a simple analysis of your costs. Once you know the cost of goods and cost of sales, you have most of the information you need to determine the correct pricing for your product.

For example, suppose you plan to start a tie-dye T-shirt business. Each shirt you make requires $2.50 of raw material and costs $1.50 to dye and treat properly, including all of the overhead manufacturing expenses. After discovering it is more lucrative to run a mail-order business, you determine that the average shipping cost of a shirt is another $0.50. Your distributor near Haight-Ashbury in San Francisco warehouses your shirts by the thousands and ships them to clothing stores throughout the nation on demand. The distributor's average handling cost is $1.25 per shirt. The clothing stores determine the final price for the shirts based on a standard markup that takes into account many of the sales costs. So the total for your tie-dye shirts works out like this:

Raw material	$2.50		
Manufacturing	$1.50		
Shipping	$0.50		
Cost of Goods		$4.50	
Distribution		$1.25	
Your profit		$0.50	
Cost to Store			$6.25
Markup—100%			$6.25 (50% of selling price)
Final Selling Price			$12.50

Once you know the cost of goods and cost of sales, you have most of the information you need to determine the correct pricing for your product.

The final price the customer pays is $12.50. If the price is slightly lower than or equal to your competitors' prices, you're in business. If, however, the final price is higher than your competitors' pricing, there is something wrong with your process and you will need to rethink your production.

Production Considerations

When you set prices for your goods or services, consider what costs will be after you get into full production or to a production level that you consider adequate to support your business. Do not price your product or service solely with low overhead costs built in if you may have to rent other space or obtain equipment and hire employees to deliver your product or service. As production increases, you will obtain some efficiencies of sale. If you could purchase ten items at a unit price to make up a product, purchasing 500 will probably substantially decrease your unit cost.

However, the need for cash will also increase as production increases and you risk the chance of not being able to deliver to meet demand. You may not get paid for a finished product until several months after you have produced it and shipped it to your customer. You may also find that your vendors cannot meet the increased demand on the time-frame you expect. You should have alternative sources of all materials when possible.

Get your suppliers to guarantee prices and supplies of material.

Get your suppliers to guarantee prices and supplies of material. Discuss potential orders with suppliers in plenty of time for them to obtain the material they need to deliver to you. In today's global market, you can expect that foreign-made items will constitute some of your manufactured goods. Unless the materials can be easily air shipped, you may have a significant delay in getting items from manufacturers who depend on raw material or finished goods from other countries. You may also find that price and quality vary considerably from one shipment to another, so you will probably want guarantees relating to different deliveries and the ability to return defective or substandard quality materials.

USE SALES TO DRIVE PRODUCTION GOALS

Production goals are directly driven by sales. It does no good to make 10,000 tie-dye T-shirts if nobody buys them. Conversely, if you are unable to provide T-shirts on demand, your customers may choose to take their business elsewhere. Your goal then, is to manufacture T-shirts at full capacity and sell 100 percent of your inventory as it is made. Of course, the reality of actually doing this is very difficult, but certainly not impossible.

Determine Other Factors that Will Affect Sales

Other factors may also influence your best methods to market your business. You may want to consider the economy of the community you serve, looking at its population and where your business is located in comparison to competitors or other businesses that your customers may support. If you are catering to only a small population or to a small percentage who desire or can afford your product, you may want to be very careful about what money you spend to communicate to that select group.

Your business' location can play a big role in your sales too. If you are located near a competitor, you may find that you can draw upon its customers who may be comparison shopping. You may also discover that if you are not near any other business that your customers may support, that they have to find more reason than impulse to come to your business. See Chapter 12 about other considerations for choosing your business' site.

Devise a Workable Sales and Marketing Plan

By taking into account the information you have gathered about your customers, competition, and your operating costs, you should be able to determine how much money you can devote to reaching your customers. Document your objectives and goals in a similar fashion to any public relations strategy you had done earlier.

The process of coming up with an idea to increase sales is never a sure-fire thing, despite what salespeople's gimmicks may tell you. Realize that you will be taking a risk—although necessary to build your sales and profits—anytime you partake in a marketing effort. Fortunately, with some early planning and some research as to who your best customers are and what they are seeking in a business, you can feel a little more assured that your decisions will show positive results. Marketing and gathering information about your market is an ongoing process. You may start out small and gradually build enough additional revenue to market your business with more expensive methods, such as television advertising or large promotional events.

The process of coming up with an idea to increase sales is never a sure-fire thing.

Chapter Wrap-Up

How you choose to promote your business will largely depend on your costs and your time; but, keep in mind that there are several interconnected factors. Your marketing will be based largely on your production costs, the economy, your location, and the size of your market. Your company's image is just as important to your banker or financial lender as it is to your customers and other key audiences. Although the desire may be strong to delay your marketing and public relations until after you have opened your doors for business, the ability to be more responsive to the demands and costs of your business will come much quicker if you begin considering your market now.

CHAPTER 7

Your Smart Business Plan

Before undertaking any endeavor, you must have a plan. This is true whether you are embarking on a skiing trip or launching a new business. Even if you haven't yet written a business plan, you probably have at least a general idea about your business goals, your customers, and your product. But have you considered such things as business expansion, second or third year profits, or financing?

Writing a business plan will force you to consider the management of your business for the next three to five years. A top-notch business plan will take a lot of work. You must think through your entire business at least once.

Drafting a business plan causes you to think about yourself, your product or service, your market, your customers, and your finances at least once before you get into business. A smart business plan will convey prospects and growth potential. As a savvy entrepreneur you can use your business plan to give you greater control of your business.

Frequently, new business owners do not write a business plan until forced to do so by a bank or financial institution as a part of a loan application package. By taking this approach, they miss out on some of the most important benefits associated with having a business plan. If you write a business plan, benefits you gain include:

- A clear picture of the financial condition of your business projected over the next five years;
- Critical marketing information related to your business;
- Specific business goals and milestones for the foreseeable future;
- Key information for business goal-related decision making; and
- Ready documentation available, if needed, for business financing.

You have a story to tell—that is not enough. The way you present the story is crucial to your success. This chapter will help you present your story in the best possible light to attract the investors and give you the control you need.

Get Help Before You Begin

Most business plans follow a specific format that has been largely standardized throughout the business community.

A business plan is not difficult to create. Most plans follow a specific format that has been largely standardized throughout the business community. This specific format is not to be used as a boiler plate for your plan; rather, use it as a guideline to incorporate your business' unique characteristics. The basic elements are the same for all plans. Feel free to modify or expand on the basic elements of the business plan to better describe your business.

In preparing your business plan, you may refer to any number of resource materials on the market, including *Entrepreneur* magazine's *Business Plans Made Easy.* Written for both business start-ups and established businesses, this guide demonstrates how a business plan can vary depending on what type of business your start-up may be.

In addition, there are software packages on the market that will lead you through the process of preparing your business plan. One such software product is *Winning Business Plans in Color.* This application is an add-on to Microsoft's Office and integrates documents from Office applications into a single business plan document that is very effective.

Essential Components of a Smart Plan

Several examples included in Winning Business Plans in Color are used throughout this chapter and in the sample business plan at the end to illustrate the essential components of a successful business plan, which include:

- Section I: Executive Summary
- Section II: Company Background
- Section III: Owner/Management Background
- Section IV: Market Analysis
- Section V: Product/Service Offering
- Section VI: Marketing Plan
- Section VII: Financial Plan and Analysis

Be sure you read through these essential components and the sample business plan before you start your own plan. You may include other aspects of your business that you feel are important to understanding the business, but may not be in the outline above. Modify your plan to depict your business or business idea and clarify in the reader's mind why you think the business idea is viable. Feel free to add or delete parts of the business plan described in this chapter. However, be careful not to delete important parts of the plan that will limit the understanding of your business. You can also provide too much information that may not be read or digested by the reader. The outline provided here is modified to better accommodate the needs of the business.

Modify your plan to depict your business or business idea and clarify in the reader's mind why you think the business idea is viable.

Section I: Executive Summary

The executive summary is considered by many experts to be the most important part of a business plan. It functions as the front door to your plan and presents your entire business in condensed form. Many lending officials read the executive summary first. If it doesn't make a good impression, the rest of the business plan is often ignored. The end result: your loan proposal doesn't receive the level of attention it might deserve.

Because writing the executive summary requires you to have an extremely clear picture of your business, many business planners advise writing this section of the business plan last. In this way, you benefit from the information and knowledge gleaned by writing the rest of the plan, and all aspects of your business are fresh in your mind. Even when a business plan is prepared for internal use only, the executive summary plays an important role. It provides you with a snapshot of your entire business concept—all your goals, marketing plans, and financial predictions. The overview should include:

- Type of business;
- Company business summary;
- Financial objectives, including the highlights of your operating performance;

- Management overview; and
- Product/service and competition.

If you will be using your business plan to obtain financing, include two additional sections—funds requested and use of proceeds.

If you feel intimidated about writing a plan you can obtain outside help from a consultant or a small business development center. You should actively participate in the development of the plan and clearly understand all the financial calculations and what is said in the text sections. If a lender asks a question about the plan and you indicate that you don't have an answer because the consultant wrote the plan, or that section of the plan, the lender will not be impressed with what you know about your business or prospective business.

CONTENT

Because the executive summary is such an important part of your business plan, its content and tone must clearly convey to the reader the unique structure, capabilities, and expertise of your business and its management. Show your business as:

- Well planned,
- Competently managed,
- Positioned where a clear market exists based on market research,
- Competitive against similar businesses, and
- Financially sound and likely to remain so.

A well-written executive summary will tell the story of your business.

By convention, these points are generally made in the order listed, following the content of the business plan. Literally then, the executive summary summarizes the remaining sections of the business plan. If it is well written, it will motivate the reader to examine the remaining sections in detail.

STYLE

Writing the executive summary requires a little skill. As a narrative discussion of your business, it must have all of the compelling elements of the opening pages of a novel, yet be firmly based in reality. A well-written executive summary will tell the story of your business, and it will entice, excite, and motivate the reader. At the same time, it will avoid exaggeration and outright fantasy. Rather than an example of creative writing, an executive summary is business writing at its best.

When writing an executive summary, use language that presents a positive, confident business attitude. Write in an active voice, presenting your points in a clear and logical manner. If you don't feel confident writing the summary yourself, hire a professional writer or prevail upon a friend or family member with strong writing skills to write it for you.

Ideally, the executive summary is short, one to three pages in length. "White space is my friend" is a common mantra for professional business writers. What this means is that you should avoid having huge blocks of text dominating your page. Break up text with space between paragraphs and by using bold headings and bulleted points in much the same way that this book is designed.

Ideally, the executive summary is short, one to three pages in length.

Refer to the executive summary portion of the sample business plan at the end of this chapter. This summary is very well written and uses a compelling, easy-to-read page layout.

Section II: Company Background

This section of your business plan discusses the basic structure of your business as well as your business goals. It provides your readers with a detailed description of your business, preparing them for later discussion of your product line and marketing strategy. The company background section includes the following basic information:

- Your mission statement or purpose of your business;
- A brief history of your business or business concept;
- A discussion of your personal business goals, including anticipated growth and financial objectives;
- The legal form of your business and its ownership structure;
- A discussion of your business location and facilities;
- A discussion of the financial status of your company, including how you will finance the operation; and
- Other information that has a bearing on your company.

YOUR MISSION STATEMENT

The mission statement briefly describes the character, purpose, and goals of your business. In short, the statement tells about your business and business philosophy. Part declaration, part philosophy, part rallying cry, a well-thought-out mission statement provides the focus for all major business decisions. An example of a well-written mission statement might be:

> Fortune Branch Market is a mom-and-pop convenience store specializing in friendly, neighborly service to an isolated, rural customer base. We concentrate on serving our customers' needs

and work to maintain a diverse inventory, which includes special order items requested by individual customers. Our goal is to maintain moderate annual growth through good, old-fashioned service, a friendly smile, and word-of-mouth advertising.

If you prefer, you can use this section to point out to your readers that you have clearly identified your market and the opportunity for steady sales and future growth.

BUSINESS HISTORY

Next describe the history of your business, including when it was founded, milestones achieved, such as a break-even date, and the completion of specific goals. State which phase of development your company is in—whether it be in the start-up or expansion phases.

If you are developing a new product, this is the place to discuss the extent of its development, which might include:

- The completion of product testing;
- The acquisition of patents, copyrights, or trademarks; or
- The acceptance of initial orders.

For a start-up business, an important thing to include in this section is a discussion of the basis for the business concept. The business could be an original idea aimed at an all-new market niche or it could be based on an existing, successful business concept where you will employ a unique approach or advantage. It could also be a proven business concept being introduced into an untapped or underserviced market.

> If there are industry-standard sales figures for your business, use them to back up your assertions regarding projected sales and growth.

BUSINESS GOALS

In this section of the business plan, describe your business' future, including sales, growth, and expansion plans. To bolster this information, include charts, tables, and figures that show your sales, profit, and income projections. If there are industry-standard sales figures for your business, use them to back up your assertions regarding projected sales and growth. Use this section to describe how you will take advantage of your unique niche or concept.

LEGAL FORM OF BUSINESS

Describe the legal form of your business. Is it a sole proprietorship, partnership, corporation, or limited liability company? Explain why you chose the form for your business. Identify the state where your business is registered and any other state in which you are operating.

Identify the owners, managers, or corporate officers. If your business is a corporation, identify major shareholders and discuss the number of shares that are outstanding.

LOCATION AND FACILITIES

You can describe the location of your business and explain why the location is particularly suitable for your business. Include demographic and psychographic factors that contribute to the location's suitability. For example, list the number of potential customers within a ten-minute drive based on income, education, interests, or other factors that you identified in your assessment of why your business will be successful. List any branch offices or multiple locations. Identify the geographical area serviced by your business.

If your company requires specialized facilities for its operation, include a description of the facilities. Some examples may include machinery, equipment, computer software, display counters, cash registers, alarm systems, a loading dock, storage facilities, or even a railhead for loading and shipping by train.

FINANCIAL STATUS

Briefly discuss the financial state of your business, including funding sources to date, profitability, outstanding loans, owner equity (the amount of ownership you have in the business), the number of employees, and the character of the workforce (experience, education, or other important characteristics). If you are currently seeking additional funding, briefly describe how much money is being sought and why, as well as how much of the required funding will be provided through owner equity and personal investment. Save detailed discussion of your financial condition and loan requirements for the financial section of your business plan.

Include copies of prospective catalogs or other printed material that will advertise your business.

OTHER INFORMATION

You may have agreements to distribute or manufacture products that will give your company a competitive edge. Or you may have applied for patents or have copyrights that are important in the development of the business. Also include leases, options, or letters of intent that materially affect your business. Include copies of prospective catalogs or other printed material that will advertise your business. Include a brief description of any of these documents in your executive summary and include complete copies at the end of your plan.

Section III: Owner/Management Background

The purpose of this section of the business plan is to describe the abilities, experience, and qualifications of the people who will run the business. The greater the wealth of experience being brought to bear on the success of the business, the higher the level of confidence potential investors will feel when considering your business' investment potential.

The Management Team

While your business concept, service, or product is the core of your venture, it is the people who work for you that personify that business concept. For this reason, it is appropriate to provide an overview of the key people who will be representing your business to your customers. Describe the attributes of each key person, emphasizing their experience, background, and education as they pertain to your business.

Identify any professionals and consultants whose specialized expertise you will utilize or require. Examples of these professionals include technical consultants, accountants, equipment specialists, and attorneys. In those cases where you have planned to add specialists or additional management to your team, identify those skills you will be seeking and when you plan to bring them on board.

Identify any professionals and consultants whose specialized expertise you will utilize or require.

Management Retention

When your business relies on the expertise of key employees, it is a good business practice to provide those key players with appropriate incentives to remain with your company. Potential investors will be interested in the steps you have taken to retain your most valuable employees. The following incentives provide tangible evidence of your efforts:

- *Salary*. Salary is the amount of money paid to your employees on an annual basis, regardless of performance. If you pay a higher salary than your competitors, indicate how much higher and reflect this in percentage form.
- *Bonuses, commissions, and profit sharing*. A bonus is extra cash, generally paid at the end of the quarter or year, in recognition of superior performance at the company or at the individual level. A commission is cash payment in addition to salary, based on a percentage of total sales made. Profit sharing is a cash distribution to all employees based on the annual profitability of the company.

- *Stock.* Corporations can issue shares of stock to employees as a performance incentive, in effect making the employees part owners and giving them a stake in the financial success of the business. Alternately, employees can be given stock options that will allow them the opportunity to purchase stock in the future at today's prices.

The market analysis section of your business plan is your opportunity to demonstrate a thorough understanding of your customer base.

Section IV: Market Analysis

The market analysis section of your business plan is your opportunity to demonstrate a thorough understanding of your customer base. Developing a thorough knowledge of your market will require some research, but the effort expended here pays big dividends and it will show that you have done your homework. This homework will entail a comprehensive analysis of your industry, target market, customer profile, major competitors, and a description of your product.

SUMMARY

Begin with an overview of the market. Keep in mind, the person reading your plan is probably in a hurry and is likely to be scanning rapidly through your document, so give the good news first, and then back it up with the facts. Give the reader an interest in the subject and a desire to learn the details presented in the next sections of your business plan.

Your goal in this section is to identify the most beneficial aspects of the market and present them in a positive, concise, and convincing manner. These sample paragraphs illustrate how.

> Industry statistics indicate that this form of retail business requires a minimum population base of 10,000 people to achieve break-even sales. ABC Mousetraps serves a much larger population base of 25,000 people.
>
> There has been a growing concern for controlling mice infestations more humanely than by the using poisons or the old spring trap method. ABC Mousetrap's new trap design is a direct response to this issue.

INDUSTRY ANALYSIS

Industrial growth or decline is an important consideration in determining the health of your business. Use this section to discuss trends in your industry as they apply to your market sector. Your particular industry may be enjoying an annual growth rate of 10 percent nationwide, while experiencing a growth rate of only 6 percent in your market sector.

There may be underlying factors that affect the growth of your industry. Identify these factors and explain them here. For instance, a decline in the economy on either a national or a local level may have a significant impact on your business. Other factors may include seasonal influences, technological advances, government regulation, or environmental or ecological concerns. Include these factors and state them in a format similar to the following:

> A department of agriculture study predicts that mice populations in urban areas will increase approximately 12 percent per year during the next ten years.
>
> The mousetrap industry is seasonal by nature, with peak sales occurring in early to late fall. ABC Mousetraps has efficiently responded to this industry-wide condition through the implementation of innovative production methods and the extensive use of temporary labor resources.

There may be underlying factors that affect the growth of your industry.

TARGET MARKET

Identify your target market in this section. Describe the type of people you expect your customers to be and why. Include those specific aspects of your product or service that will appeal to those customers and the marketing approach you will use to direct sales to them. You will use demographic statistics to help you determine the characteristics of your market sector. This information is available at your local library, small business development centers (SBDCs), and through some Internet resources.

Some of the characteristics of your target market that might be significant include income bracket, educational level, gender, lifestyle, and family makeup. You must describe the characteristics of your target market in a way that demonstrates that you can reach potential customers in sufficient numbers to sustain your business. An example target market statement may read as follows:

> The market that ABC Mousetraps will serve is the middle class, suburban, and rural consumer who desires to control mouse infestation humanely, at a competitively low cost. Additionally, rural customers who stock feed or grain for livestock will benefit

from a control method that excludes poison and the expense of conventional extermination methods.

CUSTOMER PROFILE

Based on the target market analysis in the previous section, you will then develop a customer profile based on age, income, family status, geographic location, occupation, attitude, and motive for buying. Include any other factors that may be relevant to your product or service. Review the sample business plan at the end of this chapter for more information.

> If you are just starting out in business, more than likely your market is already being served by your competitors.

MAJOR COMPETITORS AND PARTICIPANTS

If you are just starting out in business, more than likely your market is already being served by your competitors. Use this section of your business plan to identify those competitors. This will demonstrate that you have a full understanding of your market sector and the role your business will assume in it. Also, your research will help identify those parts of the market that are not being adequately serviced, and allow you to target your money, time, and advertising efforts accordingly.

PROJECTED MARKET GROWTH

How will your business grow during the next year or during the next five years? Use this section to make some reasonable estimates regarding your projected market share for your product or service. Compare these figures against industry standards and adjust them according to the peculiarities of your market sector.

Section V: Product/Service Offering

Describe your product or service in this section of your business plan. Use detailed, descriptive phrases that clearly identify what it is that you sell as well as any unique characteristics about your product that set you apart from the competition.

PRODUCT SUMMARY

Describe your product or service in general terms, summarizing the detailed description that follows in much the same way that you first summarized your market analysis. Identify those other aspects of your business that enhance your product, such as personalized customer service, environmental considerations, or assistance after the sale. For example:

ABC Mousetraps manufactures and markets a unique mousetrap that does not kill the entrapped rodent. The trap is constructed of recycled paper. Once the trapped mouse is released to the wild or otherwise disposed of, the trap is fully disposable as normal paper waste. ABC Mousetraps also offers free trap placement advice and an industry-unique mouse disposal service that allows the customer to return the trap and rodent to the store for humane disposal at no additional cost—all without having to directly handle the rodent.

DETAILED DESCRIPTION

When your business has more than one product line, describe each one in detail in this section of the business plan. Your purpose here is to give the person reading your business plan a thorough understanding of what you sell as well as any services you provide before or after the sale. Identify how your product or service compares and contrasts with that of your competitors.

> Create a listing of the characteristics that you believe will identify your company.

COMPETITIVE COMPARISONS

Most businesses have some sort of competition. Even if you have a new product or service, there are usually alternatives to the product or service you provide. Prospective customers will consider the alternatives and determine if yours has advantages either in price, convenience, design, and other characteristics that distinguish your product or service.

To help communicate your uniqueness amongst the competitors, list the strengths and weaknesses of your product or service against all those you can identify. Create a listing of the characteristics that you believe will identify your company and do the same for other companies that are likely to be your direct or indirect competitors. For example, if you plan to open a paintball field, your direct competitors may be the other paintball fields in your area—probably within a 30- or 40-mile drive from your location. You will also need to consider the alternative recreation opportunities that will attract the age or income group you think is interested in playing.

PRODUCT OR SERVICE UNIQUENESS

As you develop your list of competitive comparisons, you will probably identify characteristics that are unique about your business. If you own a restaurant, you may emphasize your speed of service, food quality, ambiance, price, taste, or friendliness of the staff.

Again, itemize these characteristics that make your product or service desirable to a specific group of people. You may want to interview customers or prospective customers to see if they agree with your assessment of the unique characteristics of your business. If you believe that you have a unique approach to a product or problem, but others don't recognize the value of it, there is little value to the perceived difference. In the long run, your customers' perceptions of what they believe is unique will hold the most weight.

Itemize the characteristics that make your product or service desirable to a specific group of people.

RESEARCH AND DEVELOPMENT

Many businesses start with nothing but an investment in research and development (R&D). This investment usually leads to changes in the way something is manufactured or delivered. The value of R&D is difficult to measure until it is tested in the marketplace. However, R&D can give an important lead in obtaining business over other companies that have not invested in R&D.

PATENTS AND TRADEMARKS

Patents are processes for manufacture of an item that are protected by the U.S. government. In many cases the protection extends to other countries. The protection is for a limited time but there is normally enough time under patent protection to make a product commercially viable and for the patent holder to get a return on the investment required to take out a patent. Usually patents are obtained through the help of a patent attorney and can be very expensive to obtain. Once obtained, they can be an extremely valuable part of a business, due to the ability of the business to create a product under the patent, or license the patent for a royalty and allow other businesses to create the product.

Therefore, ownership of patents may be an extremely important part of a business plan. However, just mentioning the patent's existence is not enough. You must describe how the patent can generate income for the business and add to its overall success.

Trademarks are identifiers of a product or service that is unique to a company and is protected by the U.S. government from anyone else using the same identification. Trademarks are not as expensive to obtain as patents but often require the help of an attorney to obtain.

Make sure you identify any trademarks owned by your business in your business plan. Trademarks can have a significant value to a business if they carry a positive image by the public. A trademark that has not been advertised or is not well known is of little value until it has proven its value in the marketplace.

Section VI: Marketing Plan

A marketing plan is different than a market analysis. With a marketing plan, you will map out a strategy for reaching your customers and bringing them to you. The purpose of marketing is to get your message out to your potential customers.

Trademarks can have a significant value to a business if they carry a positive image by the public.

THE MESSAGE

The first step in marketing is identifying your message. In addition to the product or service itself, determine what you are selling. It may be convenience, value, quality, safety, fun, youth, or even sex appeal. Whatever your message is, the advertising media you use must push your message and identify your business with the message. This part of your business plan describes your message and how advertising will be used to associate your business with your message. Overall, your message must be geared toward creating and retaining customers.

PRODUCT PRICING STRATEGY

Describe your pricing strategy and how it will allow you to compete with other businesses in your industry. Determine whether you will set your prices to be greater than, less than, or the same as your competitors. Each pricing strategy has inherent advantages, and the one that you use will depend directly on your message. It would make little sense, for instance, to emphasize value in your advertising while pricing your product higher than the competition.

PRODUCT POSITIONING

Positioning refers to the process of ideally presenting your product to the segment of the market you are specifically targeting as your customer base. For instance, camping gear is positioned to attract younger, recreational consumers while garden tractors are positioned to attract older, primarily male consumers. Positioning will influence which advertising mediums you use to market your product or service. Briefly describe your product positioning strategy in this section of the business plan.

PROMOTIONAL STRATEGY

Promotion is the art of associating your company with your product in ways and under circumstances that wouldn't ordinarily occur. To promote your business, you can do one or more of the following:

- Sponsor local amateur sporting teams
- Contribute funds for public facilities
- Provide scholarship funds to graduating seniors
- Participate in charity events
- Pay for publishing church bulletins or newsletters

All of these activities provide you with the opportunity to promote and advertise your business as well as contribute to goodwill.

The financial plan is the meat of your business plan.

Section VII: Financial Plan and Analysis

The financial plan is the meat of your business plan. If you are preparing your business plan for the purpose of obtaining funding, this section will tell a lender whether the amount is reasonable and if you are capable of handling the additional debt. Most investors expect to see the information in this section presented in a specific format. Essential elements include:

- Start-up capital requirements
- Financial highlights
- A three- to five-year projected income statement
- A three- to five-year projected balance sheet
- Future cash budgets or cash flow statements
- A break-even analysis

INITIAL CAPITAL REQUIREMENTS

This section is sometimes called sources and uses of funds. You first mentioned the amount of required capital in your Executive Summary (Section I) of your business plan. This is the section where you amplify and explain that amount.

Break down and identify the costs associated with the start-up or improvements to your business, detailing where you expect the money to come from and how you expect to spend it once you receive it. Potential lenders will expect to see this information in a table format. If you have the capability to produce a graph of your information, it is acceptable to do so. Refer to Chapter 8 for details on how to obtain financing.

As a new business you won't be able to provide previous financial history. However, you can project your expenses and income based on some reasonable expectation. You should be able to defend your assumptions about sales as well as certain expenses. Too often, profits look very promising but fail to materialize because expenses, such as taxes, repairs, insurance, and other miscellaneous expenses, are not included in the projections. It is not uncommon for a new business to show a loss for the first year of operation. What lenders want to know is how much loss you may project and how you will recover from the loss with profits in future years.

FINANCIAL HIGHLIGHTS

This section highlights key financial information calculated for the next five years. This provides information at a glance as to the projected liquidity, leverage, efficiency, and profitability of your business for the planning period. Ideally, your debt-to-equity ratio should decrease over time while your gross margin should remain at or above the averages for your industry. For more information on how to prepare this section, consult your accountant.

The income statement shows how profitable your business is after all expenses are paid.

THREE- TO FIVE-YEAR INCOME STATEMENT

The income statement is frequently referred to as the profit and loss (P&L) statement and shows how profitable your business is after all expenses are paid. Income statements are read from top to bottom, and entries are listed in the following order: income from sales, cost of sales, and gross profit. These are followed by a listing of general and administrative expenses. Subtracting total expenses from the gross profit reveals net profit before taxes. Finally, taxes are subtracted to leave net profit as the bottom line.

Your accountant may help you prepare this financial form. If your business is too small to warrant an accountant, a computer program such as Quickbooks will generate this report for you provided the information you enter into the program is accurate. Alternately, many popular spreadsheet programs such as Lotus 1-2-3 or Microsoft Excel provide the basic tools necessary to produce these forms.

THREE- TO FIVE-YEAR BALANCE SHEET

The balance sheet provides a snapshot of your business' financial position for each planning period. More than an income statement, the balance sheet includes such things as the value of equipment, facilities, and property. For this reason, it provides the potential investor with better information about the financial condition of your company than can be derived merely from your income statements.

The balance sheet compares all assets and liabilities. Excess value is the company's net worth. Net worth is distributed as equity or retained as earnings for the company to use. In either case, the net worth is listed as a liability. Once done, liabilities and assets should balance out, hence the name balance sheet.

The balance sheet compares all assets and liabilities. Excess value is the company's net worth.

Balance sheets may be difficult to prepare without professional assistance. Buildings, facilities, and equipment depreciate in value over a set period. Property improvements result in appreciation of property, and inventory values vary with time and acquisition costs.

CASH FLOW OR CASH BUDGET STATEMENTS

Cash flow statements, sometimes referred to as cash budgets, tell the story about your business' ability to conduct business on a daily basis. Most businesses are subject to seasonal or market fluctuations. It is important to be sufficiently liquid to survive lean times. This is also true of businesses that maintain large inventories or that operate with a large credit base.

The cash flow statement is similar to your checking account ledger. You work to maintain a positive balance in your account at all times. If you run out of cash, you no longer have the resources necessary to conduct business, even if your income statement shows a continuous net profit. Many businesses have closed because of success. By trying to produce more product than cash flow permits, a business may run out of cash and be unable to deliver products on time, thus losing contracts or not collecting receivables when expected.

Most lenders will be very interested in your cash flow statements and will check them against your policies for accounts receivable, aging, inventory turn and other indicators of your business health.

BREAK-EVEN ANALYSIS

The break-even analysis tells you how much income in gross sales you must have to meet all expenses. Expenses include total fixed expenses plus the cost of goods. To arrive at a break-even figure, you divide total fixed expenses such as rent, utilities, and insurance by your gross profit margin. Profit margin may fluctuate from product line to product line, so you will have to adjust your figures accordingly. The main reason for including a break-even analysis in your business plan is to show that you have sufficient income to continue operations.

Chapter Wrap-Up

Your smart business plan will give you the edge your business needs to prosper in today's competitive environment. The key to your business plan is preparation and research. Make sure you allot sufficient time to research the various aspects of your business plan. Use the basic outline in this chapter to stay organized. While you focus on the critical aspects of your business, consider the following:

- *Clearly identify your business concept.* What product or service will you sell and what type of business is it?
- *Know your industry.* Become familiar with the ups and downs of your industry. Is it seasonal or are there cyclical economic influences that will affect your operation? How big is your industry and at what maturity level is it currently?
- *Understand your target market.* Know the demographics and psychographics of your customer base. Find out what appeals to your customers and work those things into your sales and marketing strategy.
- *Familiarize yourself with your competitors.* Take a close look at what you're up against. What are your competitors doing that you aren't? What things will you do better than your competitors?
- *Know what distinguishes your product or service.* Investors will want to know what makes your business concept unique. Is it a new product or service? Did you improve on an existing idea? Are you serving a new market or filling a need in a market that has yet to be reached?

The key to your business plan is preparation and research.

As you document the answers to these questions, you will begin to see the blueprint of your business. You can use this blueprint to approach investors and lenders and to build a successful business.

101 Wet Stone Hill Road
Wakefield, RI 02756
Telephone (401) 422-8888
evergreen@inter.net
Contact: Nolan Wentworth

SAMPLE BUSINESS PLAN

Evergreen Lawn Care

Professional Lawn Care

Proprietary Information: DO NOT DISTRIBUTE

TABLE OF CONTENTS

Evergreen Lawn Care
Business Plan

EXECUTIVE SUMMARY

Evergreen Lawn Care is a start-up company that will provide fertilizing and weed and insect control. The sole proprietor of the company is Mr. Nolan Wentworth who is contributing his own capital, significant lawn care experience, knowledge, and business skill. Mr. Wentworth is an area expert on lawn care with a very good reputation. His expertise and reputation give Evergreen a competitive service advantage. In addition to Mr. Wentworth's contributed capital, Evergreen will need another $75,000 for start-up capital. The business will operate in the South County, Rhode Island.

Evergreen's marketing plan was designed to initially attempt to convert a large portion of the more than 2,000 customers that Mr. Wentworth helped to service when he was employed by GreenThumb, an area lawn care company. Additional marketing and advertising strategies are designed to target the business executive/professional who doesn't have the time nor expertise to maintain a beautiful lawn but understand the value a nicely landscaped lawn adds to property values. Evergreen's particular niche and positioning will be to appeal to the environmentally conscious homeowners who are concerned about their kids, the long lasting health of their lawn and making a small contribution to mother earth.

Currently, the lawn care business in South County is dominated by one company—Mr. Wentworth's former employer, GreenThumb. Some landscapers and grass cutting companies also offer fertilizing services, but these providers hold an insignificant portion of the market. From all indicators, the South County lawn care market has experienced little competition; therefore, Evergreen has an excellent opportunity to create a large customer base if it can persuade people that it can offer greater expertise and value added services over the current supplier, GreenThumb.

While Evergreen will directly compete with GreenThumb, it is offering a service that is differentiated from that of GreenThumb's. Here are some of the ways that Evergreen's service will be different:

- *The 14-point lawn care evaluation.* Evergreen will offer every prospective customer a free lawn evaluation that can be used to develop a custom designed six step lawn care program. GreenThumb does not offer a comparable analysis.

- *Evergreen's organic alternative.* Evergreen will offer customers an organic alternative that is safer for the environment than the fertilizer used by GreenThumb. The facts will easily show how Evergreen's services will cost far less in the long run, while customers will appreciate the added safety the services afford their children and pets.
- *Evergreen's experience and expertise.* Evergreen is the only area company to have Nolan Wentworth: a lawn care professional who is highly respected in the South County region.

Type of Business

Evergreen Lawn Care is a service business specializing in fertilizing and weed and insect control.

Company/Business Summary

This is a start-up business that will be organized as a sole proprietorship; a business to be owned and operated by Nolan Wentworth. The firm will provide services for the care and maintenance of lawns, trees, and shrubs. The company will concentrate services on preventing plant life disease and promoting plant growth by utilizing natural alternatives.

Financial Objectives

The financial plan and analysis section of this business plan details the projected operating results, financial position, cash budgets, and break-even point. Below is a chart that summarizes the financial objectives for the five year planning period beginning in 2000.

OPERATING PERFORMANCE HIGHLIGHTS (all numbers in $000)

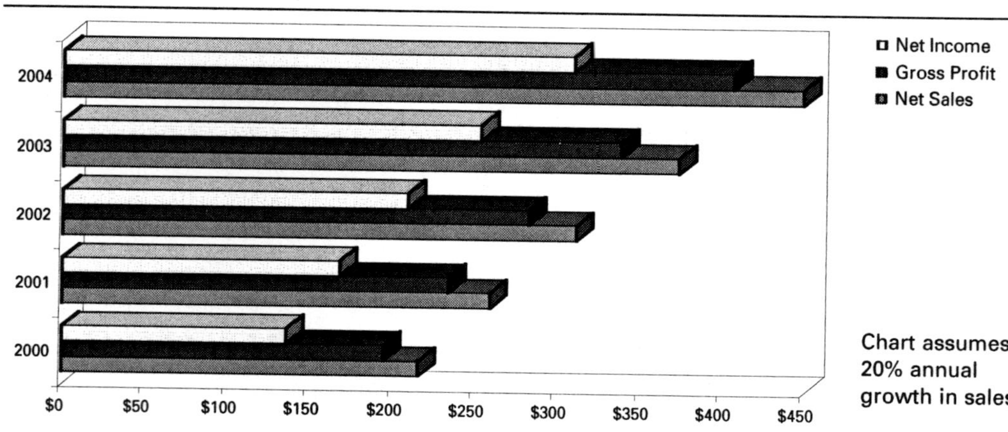

Chart assumes 20% annual growth in sales

OPERATING PERFORMANCE HIGHLIGHTS

	2000	2001	2002	2003	2004
Net Sales	$216	$259	$311	$373	$448
Gross Profit	$195	$234	$282	$338	$406
Net Income	$136	$168	$209	$253	$309

Management Overview

Nolan Wentworth is a graduate of the University of Rhode Island's Turf Sciences program. Mr. Wentworth also worked for five years as a greenskeeper at a large public golf course in Massachusetts and worked for another five years as a landscape architect for a nursery in Rhode Island. For the last two years, Mr. Wentworth worked for GreenThumb as a lawn specialist, a position that required him to become company certified. Mr. Wentworth worked under the direction of an agronomist for over 6 months while he was with GreenThumb.

Product/Service and Competition

Evergreen Lawn Care will offer a six application lawn care program. These applications will be custom designed for the particular grass type and location. Evergreen will be offering the homeowner safe, all-natural fertilizers and weed controllers.

Funds Requested

Evergreen is requesting a five year $75,000 loan to finance the start-up. Collateral of about $65,000 is available to secure the loan.

Use of Proceeds

The $75,000 loan proceeds will be used to purchase a truck and equipment that will cost approximately $65,000. The remaining loan proceeds will be used to purchase supplies (fertilizer and other related chemicals).

COMPANY BACKGROUND

Identification of Market Opportunity

Evergreen Lawn Care plans on providing fertilizing and weed and insect control services to the South County of Rhode Island. According to the statistics provided by the Small Business

Development Center of Rhode Island, the lawn care business is a $750,000 market in South County. There are no Rhode Island statistics on the rate of growth in revenues for the lawn care industry, but according to *Lawn and Turf Magazine*, a trade association publication, the national growth rate for lawn care services has been 20 percent for the last five years and is forecasted to grow at that rate into the near future.

South County Rhode Island is an excellent market opportunity for this service with only one competitor, GreenThumb, a national company that has granted a franchise in South County.

The Professional Landscapers of America estimate that the homeowner's return at resale can be between $800 and $1,200 over the cost of lawn care improvements. However, there is no debate that the value of a home is enhanced through the use of lawn care services. The use of lawn care services tends to be common in areas where home values are relatively high and where home sales are vigorous.

While Mr. Wentworth was with GreenThumb, he observed several things that convinced him that his Evergreen start-up has excellent chances for success:

- There is an overwhelming desire by most customers for a safer alternative to the toxic chemicals that required flag notification at the end of a treatment.
- Traditional lawn treatment companies are wed to the past and have little opportunity to change methods because of equipment investment and reliance on old ways.
- Mr. Wentworth studied the organic trend closely and experimented with it extensively. He became convinced that his expertise, drive, and customer knowledge would stack the cards in his favor.

Business History

Evergreen is a start-up company. Mr. Wentworth has recently resigned from his position with GreenThumb to start his venture. To date, he has invested approximately $5,000 of his own capital.

Growth and Financial Objectives

The first year goal of Evergreen is to have 275 customers by the end of the first 12 months with subsequent annual growth in revenues equal to the national projected rate of 20 percent per year.

FIVE YEAR SALES FORECAST (all numbers in 000)

	2000	2001	2002	2003	2004
Lawn Feed and Weed	$156	$187	$224	$269	$323
Tree and Shrub Care	48	58	70	84	101
Other	12	14	17	20	24
Total Sales	$216	$259	$311	$373	$448

FIVE YEAR SALES FORECAST (all numbers in $000)

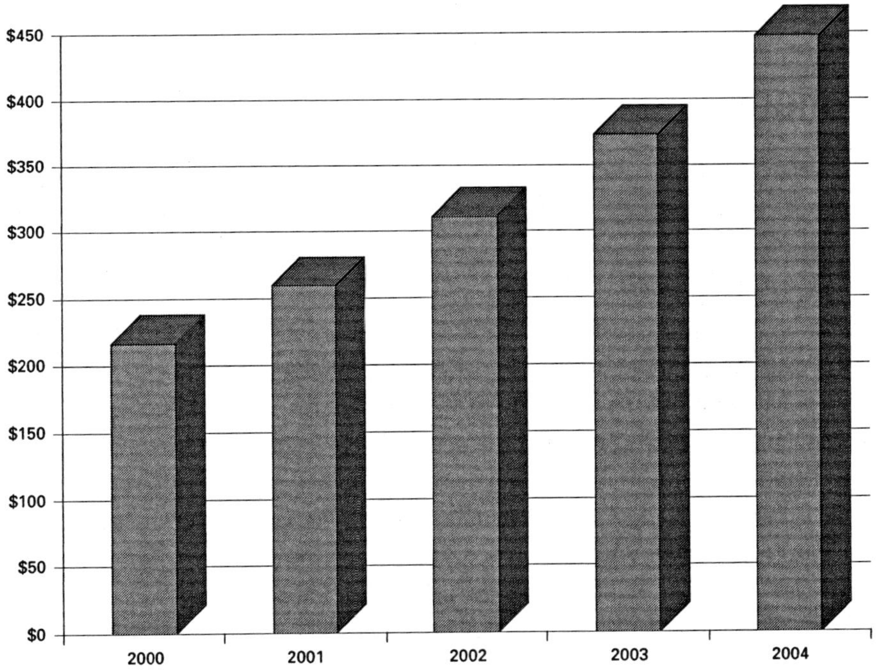

Sales forecast based on 275 customers the first year, followed by 20% growth

Legal Structure and Ownership

The company is organized as a sole proprietorship. Mr. Wentworth has filed all the necessary paperwork to gain a d.b.a. certificate and all appropriate permits.

Company Location and Facilities

Mr. Wentworth will conduct the business from his home office at 101 Wet Stone Hill Road, Wakefield, Rhode Island. The home office is equipped with a personal computer, laser printer, and fax machine. Mr. Wentworth has erected a 2,500 square foot barn on this residential property that will be used to store supplies and equipment, including the company truck.

Plans for Financing the Business

Mr. Wentworth has contributed $5,000 of his personal funds to the business venture. He plans to contribute an additional $20,000 from a maturing CD and another $10,000 from a loan from his father-in law. He will need an additional $75,000, in the form of a five year business loan, to purchase supplies, equipment, and a truck. The loan can be collateralized, at least to some extent, with the title to the truck and the equipment. The truck and equipment will have a combined cost of $65,000.

OWNER'S BACKGROUND

Since the business is organized as a sole proprietorship, there is no management team. Mr. Wentworth will be the sole manager.

Background on Mr. Wentworth

Nolan Wentworth, who will run the business, is a graduate of the University of Rhode Island's Turf Sciences program. He has also had excellent practical experience, with much of this related to lawn care. Mr. Wentworth worked for five years as a greenskeeper at a large public golf course in Massachusetts and worked for another five years as a landscape architect for a nursery in Rhode Island. For the last two years, Mr. Wentworth worked for GreenThumb as a lawn specialist, a position for which he had to become company certified. While he was with GreenThumb, Mr. Wentworth worked under the direction of an agronomist for over six months.

Mr. Wentworth also keeps up with developments in the industry. He is very much aware of the April 1990 public hearings held by the U.S. Senate to acquire information on the environmental impact of the use of chemical insecticides and fertilizers. He is keenly aware that the government may impose increased government regulation on this business, and is constantly reevaluating any impact this might have on the industry. He has researched new fertilizers and insecticides that are not harmful to the environment and is very much interested in organically based fertilizers. Mr. Wentworth plans to stay on top of the effects of new products on the environment through books, magazines, conferences, and workshops. His business knowledge will become a public relations tool.

Other Employees

The company will have two part-time employees. Evergreen will utilize the skills of two other family members:

- Mr. Wentworth's wife, Jane, will manage the books for the company and manage customer renewal process.
- In the summer, Mr. Wentworth will employ his son Jimmy (age 20), who is attending the University of Massachusetts Amherst. Jimmy is studying Architectural Landscape Design.

MARKET ANALYSIS

Summary

From all indications, the South County lawn care market is large enough to support several companies. At this time only one major player is in the market. The lack of competition in the market combined with Evergreen's unique expertise and approach make success highly probable. The overall market seems large enough and is growing fast enough to provide plenty of business to a company that can successfully service its target market. Evergreen's target market has three factors that will also contribute to success.

- They are sold on the idea that a beautiful lawn and fine looking shrubs and trees add significant value to a property.
- They lack the time needed to conduct their own lawn care program.
- They have the economic resources to afford a six step application program.
- While not essential, Wentworth believes that the large majority of customers will select the Evergreen alternative because of its organic approach.

Industry Analysis

It is estimated that more than 15 million homes nationwide use lawn care services. The size of the South County, Rhode Island market for lawn care is estimated to be potentially $750,000 per year. This estimate is based on the industry statistics that disclose the number of suburban households per thousand that contracts for lawn care. Evergreen's projected share of the market is modest, at approximately 14 percent of the market by the end of year one.

Target Market

The market that Evergreen will be targeting is the suburban upper-middle to upper-class market with household annual incomes that range from $60,000 to $100,000 and higher. In South County, Rhode Island, there are approximately 22,000 households with annual incomes in the range defined above. The six application per year lawn care maintenance program, which costs an average of $360 (for a 7,000 square foot area), is affordable for this market. The defined market can be easily convinced of or already sees the merit of the six application process as a way of assuring a beautiful lawn. Statistics show that in neighborhoods where the average household income is $60,000 or above, one out of every three homes has a lawn care provider. However, market penetration in the South County area has not been great up till now with only one local vendor providing service. Estimates show that only one out of ten homes in this demographic segment currently contract lawn care services.

Customer Profile

The demographics of the homeowner market that Evergreen will serve are as follows:

- Income Level: $60,000 + annual household income
- Occupation: Executive and professional
- Median property values: $130,000 +
- Neighborhoods: Suburban, upper-middle class
- More likely to have at least one child

Major Competitors and Participants

The only major competitor at this time is GreenThumb. Other competitors are lawn maintenance (grass cutting) and landscapers who offer lawn care as secondary to their primary business. GreenThumb is a national company that has had a South County franchise for the past four years. GreenThumb has had the market virtually to itself. Evergreen will be in direct competition with GreenThumb. Mr. Wentworth was employed by GreenThumb for the last two years and will attempt to persuade GreenThumb customers to convert to Evergreen at 5 percent below their GreenThumb cost. GreenThumb has over 2,000 customers.

Projected Market Growth and Market Share Objectives

Mr. Wentworth's sales goals are very modest with a target of 275 customers by the end of year one. It is estimated that Evergreen's market share will be approximately 14 percent of the existing market but under 5 percent of the potential market. Mr. Wentworth is predicting that half of these customers will come from the existing GreenThumb base and half will be new customers. Annual growth is assumed to be at least at the national projection of 20 percent for each of the next five years. These goals seem to be modest and achievable when compared with the customer list of over 2,000 customers from GreenThumb.

PRODUCT/SERVICE OFFERING

Product/Service Summary

The service that Evergreen will offer is a six step lawn care program that involves fertilizing for growth and color and applications that will control weeds and insects. Each program will be custom designed based on a 14-point, no charge, evaluation.

Product/Service Uniqueness

Evergreen's service is also unique because of the skill and knowledge that Mr. Wentworth brings to the business. In addition, Mr. Wentworth's customer relation skills help to make this venture unique and give a definite competitive advantage to the firm. Mr. Wentworth knows that being courteous to the clients and his expert qualifications are the most critical issues for this business. If a lawn care firm is unable to maintain a friendly, courteous relationship with its customers, it will not be successful.

Product/Service Descriptions

Evergreen will be in the business of selling a six part application process that will give the homeowner a beautiful lawn. The service consists of a six specifically designed and seasonally scheduled service visits (applications).

- *Early season.* The first visit of the year involves an application that will promote spring green-up and lawn recovery from winter stress. The application will also help control weeds and crabgrass.
- *Spring.* This application is designed to give your lawn extra nutrients which will result in a greener and thicker lawn. Weed and crabgrass control will be applied, only if necessary.
- *Early summer.* This fertilizer application gets your lawn ready for the possible stressful summer (heat and draught) ahead. The lawn will be checked for isolated weed and insect problems and treated accordingly.
- *Late summer.* Like application 3, this is a fertilizer that will help promote color without pushing growth. Again, the lawn will be checked for isolated weed and insect problems and treated accordingly.

- *Early fall.* This application is designed to help thicken the lawn and to promote new root growth. Since weeds and insects can be present in fall lawns, the technician will check for those problems and treat the lawn accordingly.
- *Late fall.* This application consists of a special fertilizer that will promote root growth and food storage for the winter ahead. This application is critical for winter survival and will help bring about a healthier lawn for the following spring.

Competitive Comparisons

Many of the services offered by Evergreen are comparable in price and value to that of GreenThumb. However, there are four differences.

Evergreen will offer a free 14-point evaluation that will help the technician design an appropriate program and will give the homeowner a better understanding of his or her lawn's needs. The 14-point evaluation is in writing (in a checklist format) and examines the following: grass type, turf density, color, thatch, diseases, soil type, weeds, mowing, insects, shade, watering, problem grasses, potential, and present conditions.

Another distinct difference between GreenThumb and Evergreen is that Evergreen will give the homeowner the option of using organic and environmentally safe fertilizers. The homeowner will be told, in writing, the pros and cons of organic versus non-organic fertilizers and the difference in cost between the two will be clearly disclosed.

The third competitive difference is that Evergreen will not charge an additional amount for grub control, as is the case with GreenThumb.

Finally, another competitive advantage is Mr. Wentworth who is well known in the community and has already developed rapport with many of GreenThumb's customers. In addition to working with many homeowners in South County, Mr. Wentworth is a frequent guest on a local talk radio home and garden show. The benefits Evergreen can sell because of Mr. Wentworth's background, reputation, and experience include many intangibles: confidence, reliability, and answers to questions about lawn care.

Competition Comparison

The following chart summarizes the key differences between GreenThumb and Evergreen Lawn Care:

Feature	EverGreen	GreenThumb
Seasonal cost	$10.00 per 1,000 sq. ft.	$9.75 per 1,000 sq. ft.
Customer satisfaction	Money Back Guarantee	Money Back Guarantee
Treatment	Organic	Toxic Chemicals
Child and pet safe	Yes	No
Grub control	Included	Extra Charge
Effective long term treatment	Yes	No (Requires more and more chemicals)

Research and Development

Evergreen has access to a regional agronomist who is employed by Grass Roots, Inc., Evergreen's fertilizer supplier. Grass Roots, Inc. spends in excess of $500,000 annually on R&D and freely shares its findings with its customers. Grass Roots, Inc. also conducts quarterly seminars on lawn care at its Montvale, New Jersey, headquarters. In his study of the organic treatments, Mr. Wentworth spent a lot of time with Grass Roots, Inc. and has a strong working relationship with its research team.

Patents and Trademarks

Evergreen does not own any patents or trademarks.

MARKETING PLAN

Creating and Maintaining Customers

Evergreen will attract and maintain its customer base by competitively pricing the service and demonstrating, through hard work and a customer driven approach, that the company can take the time and hassle out of lawn care. Evergreen will position itself as the busy person's safe and natural way to a beautiful lawn. Customers will quickly recognize that the company's main "asset" is its founder, Mr. Nolan Wentworth. And as is often the case with service oriented businesses, new customers will be created as current customers begin to appreciate the skill, expertise, and knowledge of Mr. Wentworth. Those customers will recommend Evergreen to their family and friends and will help to broaden the customer base.

Product Pricing Strategy

Evergreen's service will be priced to be competitive with the marketplace. Mr. Wentworth understands the pricing strategy of the competitor and he will monitor its pricing to stay competitive. GreenThumb's basic price is $9.75 per 1,000 square feet (with discounts given, because of economies of scale, when total square footage is greater than 12,000 feet).

Evergreen's sales literature tells customers that Evergreen will meet the price or promotional appeals of any competitor, as long as the customer has documented proof — such as a competitor's bid sheet, program estimate, or coupon. Existing GreenThumb customers will be given a one year 10 percent discount enticement to convert their lawn care service to Evergreen. Mr. Wentworth is happy to give these discounts for the first year in order to establish the business base. He is confident that he will be able to retain the customer over a several year period.

Product Positioning

While Mr. Wentworth brings some clear skills to the business, the most important positioning of the business is its safe, natural and longer lasting approach. There have been many negative reports on the use of lawn chemicals. Evergreen has contracted with a local artist to design a truck that will communicate this message loud and clear to the customer. The company has also secured a local telephone number that spells NATURAL. Call NATURAL to find out more will be one of the messages on the truck.

The Evergreen service will be positioned as the professional and executive solution to expert lawn care. Advertising will discuss how just about every homeowner could perform their own lawn care program but the time and hassle of the task are a barrier. Emphasis will also be placed on the value of expert service. Mr. Wentworth's background and reputation and the 14-point evaluation will help substantiate the expert claim.

Sales and Service Delivery

The sales cycle in this service business is very seasonal. Seventy-five percent of all purchase decisions are made between February 15th and April 15th. The service delivery begins on May 1st. There are three main ways to get a new client and the chances of success are in this order:

- Friend referral
- Article or other public relations opportunity
- Direct mail
- Newspaper advertisement
- Prospect notices truck in neighborhood

The promotional plan below is designed to complement this sales cycle and customer buying mentality.

Mr. Wentworth will perform much of the direct calls on sales prospects and lead the follow-up efforts. He will also use the services of freelancers in the area to perform telemarketing. Mr. Wentworth's wife, Jane, will handle the books, manage the billing and sign up customers from one year to the next.

The service will be delivered to the customer using a variety of equipment and tools. Evergreen will initially purchase a GMC small flat bed truck that will be retrofitted with a tank and pump system used to apply the fertilizer and weed control. The truck, tank, and pump system is the key equipment of the business. The estimated cost of the system is $65,000.

Promotional Strategy

The promotional strategy will consist of telemarketing calls to existing GreenThumb customers who will be told about Mr. Wentworth's service and who will be offered the one year 10 percent discount. In addition, any customer who refers two customers to Evergreen will receive one of the applications free. On average, the free application represents a $60 value. A telemarketing service will also be utilized to set up appointments for the 14-point lawn evaluation. Homeowners will be contacted and informed that an Evergreen technician will be in the area conducting free, no obligation, lawn analysis. The calls will clearly differentiate the service from Evergreen's chemical unfriendly competitor.

Evergreen will also use a local bulk mail coupon service that will mail monthly coupon savers and offers for the free 14-point lawn evaluation to households with median incomes of $60,000 or more. The mailing will include a special offer for 1,000 frequent flier miles on American or United airlines, the two most frequently held affinity programs. Mr. Wentworth recently attended a convention that discussed the value of these programs when services of over $500 are offered to high income purchasers.

Newspaper advertising campaigns, both in traditional hometown papers and in the free "shopper papers," will be executed in late winter/early spring and in early fall.

The service truck for the company will bear the company logo and a brief listing of services offered, along with the NATURAL business telephone number.

A brochure will be given to each potential customer when the written estimate is completed. The brochure will describe Mr. Wentworth's skills and experience and the type of service the customer will receive. In addition, after a service is rendered, a brochure describing what the customer needs to do to maintain the grass will be given.

Special prices in the spring will be offered and discounts to regular customers who contract for year-long services.

Mr. Wentworth plans to spend a reasonable part of his time working with local newspapers and radio shows to place articles about the advantages of natural lawn care. He has enlisted the services of some local college journalism students to write some example articles that will be distributed to the media.

FINANCIAL PLAN AND ANALYSIS

Initial Capital Requirements

The initial start-up capital requirements of the business are expected to be about $110,000. A large portion of the initial capital (76 percent) is for the upfront costs for equipment and supplies. The remaining amount (24 percent) is for the monthly expenses needed to launch the business.

Financial Highlights

Key financial ratios have been calculated for the five-year planning period and are shown below. Although the Debt/Equity ratio is a bit high at the end of year one, it improves significantly during years two through five. Please note that since this is a service business, the gross margin is 100 percent because there is no cost of sales, just operating expenses.

Five-Year Income Statement

The projected operating results for the five-year planning period are shown below in the pro-forma income statements. Net profits range from $8,000 for the first full year of operation to $36,000 by the fifth year.

Five-Year Balance Sheet

The projected financial position as of the end of each fiscal year in the planning period is shown below.

Cash Budgets

Cash budgets have been prepared using two formats: a 12-month cash budget for year one and annual budgets for each of the five planning periods. Both reports are shown below.

Break-Even Analysis

The monthly break-even point of about $5,200 in sales translates to about $62,400 annually. According to income statement projections, the store will operate above the break-even point for all five years in the planning period.

ESTIMATED START-UP CAPITAL

	Monthly Expenses	Cash Needed to Start	% of Total
MONTHLY COSTS			
Salary of owner-manager	$1,000	$3,000	2.7%
All other salaries and wages	833	2,499	2.3%
Rent		0	0.0%
Advertising	250	3,000	2.7%
Delivery expense		0	0.0%
Supplies	1,250	15,000	13.6%
Telephone		0	0.0%
Other utilities		0	0.0%
Insurance	250	3,000	2.7%
Taxes, including social security		0	0.0%
Interest		0	0.0%
Maintenance		0	0.0%
Legal and other professional fees		0	0.0%
Miscellaneous		0	0.0%
Subtotal		$26,499	24%
ONE-TIME COSTS			
Fixtures and equipment		$65,000	59.1%
Decorating and remodeling			0.0%
Installation charges			0.0%
Starting inventory		10,000	9.1%
Deposits with public utilities			0.0%
Legal and other professional fees		1,000	0.9%
Licenses and permits		500	0.5%
Advertising and promotion for opening		2,000	1.8%
Cash		5,000	4.5%
Other			0.0%
Subtotal		$83,500	76%
TOTAL ESTIMATED START-UP CAPITAL		**$109,999**	

FINANCIAL HIGHLIGHTS

	2000	2001	2002	2003	2004
Liquidity					
Current Ratio	8.62	11.00	18.69	23.15	29.00
Acid-Test Ratio	6.31	8.31	14.85	19.31	24.38
Leverage					
Debt Ratio	27.86%	14.10%	8.07%	4.55%	2.39%
Debt/Equity Ratio	38.62%	16.41%	8.78%	4.77%	2.45%
Times Interest Earned	20.43	25.00	30.86	37.14	45.14
Efficiency					
Inventory Turnover	0.70	0.71	0.58	0.70	0.70
Average Collection Period	16.90	28.19	23.47	29.36	32.59
Total Asset Turnover	0.82	0.69	0.58	0.51	0.47
Profitability					
Gross Margin	90.28%	90.35%	90.68%	90.62%	90.63%
Return on Assets	51.91%	44.68%	39.21%	34.90%	32.12%
Return on Equity	71.96%	52.01%	42.65%	36.56%	32.91%

INCOME STATEMENT

For the Years 2000 through 2004
(all numbers in $000)

REVENUE	**2000**	**2001**	**2002**	**2003**	**2004**
Gross sales	$216	$259	$311	$373	$448
Less returns and allowances	0	0	0	0	0
Net Sales	$216	$259	$311	$373	$448
COST OF SALES					
Total Cost of Goods Sold	$21	$25	$29	$35	$42
Gross Profit (Loss)	$195	$234	$282	$338	$406
OPERATING EXPENSES					
Selling					
Salaries and wages	$3	$3	$3	$3	$3
Commissions					
Advertising	$5	$5	$5	$5	$5
Depreciation	$3	$3	$3	$3	$3
Other	$1	$1	$1	$1	$1
Total Selling Expenses	$12	$12	$12	$12	$12
General & Administrative					
Salaries and wages	$20	$25	$30	$40	$50
Employee benefits	$3	$4	$5	$6	$7
Payroll taxes	$3	$4	$5	$6	$7
Insurance	$4	$4	$4	$4	$4
Rent					
Utilities	$2	$2	$2	$2	$2
Depreciation & amortization	$5	$5	$5	$5	$5
Office supplies	$1	$1	$1	$1	$1
Travel & entertainment	$1	$1	$1	$1	$1
Postage	$1	$1	$1	$1	$1
Interest	$7	$7	$7	$7	$7
Furniture & equipment					
Total G&A Expenses	$47	$54	$61	$73	$85
Total Operating Expenses	$59	$66	$73	$85	$97
Net Income Before Taxes	$136	$168	$209	$253	$309
Taxes on income	0	0	0	0	0
Net Income After Taxes	$136	$168	$209	$253	$309
Extraordinary gain or loss					
Income tax on extraordinary gain					
NET INCOME (LOSS)	**$136**	**$168**	**$209**	**$253**	**$309**

BALANCE SHEET—YEARS ONE THROUGH FIVE

For the Year End 2000 through 2004
(all numbers in $000)

ASSETS	2000	2001	2002	2003	2004
Current Assets					
Cash	$53	$68	$148	$191	$237
Net accounts receivable	10	20	20	30	40
Inventory	30	35	50	50	60
Temporary investment	9	10	10	10	20
Prepaid expenses	10	10	15	20	20
Total Current Assets	$112	$143	$243	$301	$377
Fixed Assets					
Long-term investments	$30	$45	$80	$54	$65
Land					130
Buildings (net of depreciation)				150	170
Plant & equipment (net)	110	178	200	200	200
Furniture & fixtures (net)	10	10	10	20	20
Total Net Fixed Assets	$150	$233	$290	$424	$585
TOTAL ASSETS	$262	$376	$533	$725	$962
LIABILITIES					
Current Liabilities					
Accounts payable	$10	$10	$10	$10	$10
Short-term notes					
Current portion of long-term notes					
Accruals & other payables	3	3	3	3	3
Total Current Liabilities	$13	$13	$13	$13	$13
Long-Term Liabilities					
Mortgage					
Other long-term liabilities	60	40	30	20	10
Total Long-Term Liabilities	$60	$40	$30	$20	$10
Shareholders' Equity					
Capital stock	$80	$80	$80	$80	$80
Retained earnings	109	243	410	612	859
Total Shareholders' Equity	$189	$323	$490	$692	$939
TOTAL LIABILITIES & EQUITY	**$262**	**$376**	**$533**	**$725**	**$962**

CASH BUDGET—FIRST 12 MONTHS

For the Year 2000
(all numbers in $000)

	Jan	Feb	Mar	Apr	May	Jun	Jul	Aug	Sep	Oct	Nov	Dec
Beginning cash balance	$2	$22	$25	$26	$30	$34	$35	$39	$42	$45	$47	$51
Cash from operations	10	10	10	10	10	10	10	10	10	10	10	10
Total Available Cash	$12	$32	$35	$36	$40	$44	$45	$49	$52	$55	$57	$61
Less:												
Capital expenditures	$84											
Operating Expenses	$15	$6	$6	$5	$5	$6	$5	$6	$6	$5	$5	$5
Interest			2			2				2		2
Dividends												
Debt retirement	1	1	1	1	1	1	1	1	1	1	1	1
Other												
Total Disbursements	$100	$7	$9	$6	$6	$9	$6	$7	$7	$8	$6	$8
Cash Surplus (Deficit)	($88)	$25	$26	$30	$34	$35	$39	$42	$45	$47	$51	$53
Add:												
Short-term loans												
Long-term loans	75											
Capital stock issues	35											
Total Additions	$110	$0	$0	$0	$0	$0	$0	$0	$0	$0	$0	$0
Ending Cash Balance	**$22**	**$25**	**$26**	**$30**	**$34**	**$35**	**$39**	**$42**	**$45**	**$47**	**$51**	**$53**

CASH BUDGET ACTIVITY—FIRST 12 MONTHS (all numbers in $000)

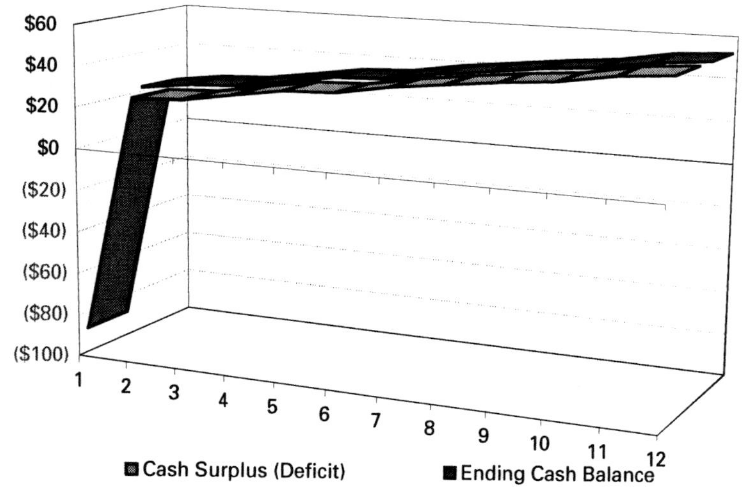

CASH BUDGET—YEARS ONE THROUGH FIVE

For the Years 2000 through 2004
(all numbers in $000)

	2000	2001	2002	2003	2004
Beginning cash balance	$2	$53	$68	$148	$191
Cash from operations	120	112	185	190	190
Total Available Cash	$122	$165	$253	$338	$381
Less:					
Capital expenditures	$84				
Operating Expenses	75	79	90	131	130
Interest	8	5	4	3	2
Dividends	0				
Debt retirement	12	13	11	13	12
Other	0				
Total Disbursements	$179	$97	$105	$147	$144
Cash Surplus (Deficit)	($57)	$68	$148	$191	$237
Add:					
Short-term loans	$0				
Long-term loans	75				
Capital stock issues	35				
Total Additions	$110	$0	$0	$0	$0
Ending Cash Balance	**$53**	**$68**	**$148**	**$191**	**$237**

CASH BUDGET ACTIVITY—FIVE YEARS (all numbers in $000)

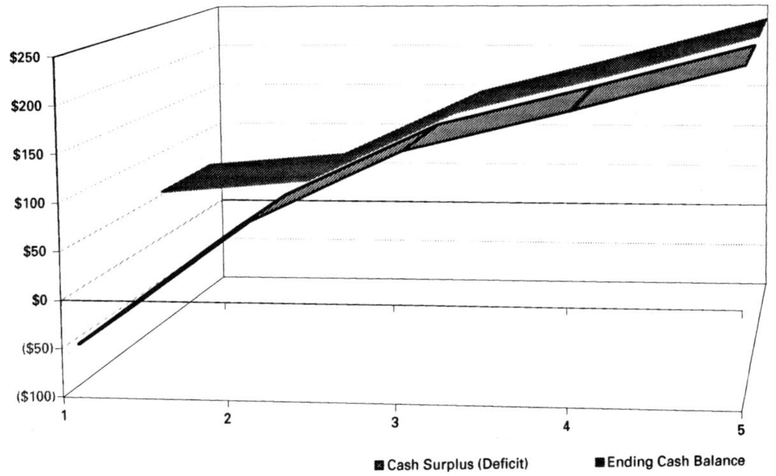

BREAK-EVEN ANALYSIS

	Fixed Costs	Variable Costs
Product costs		
Average cost of product		$15.00
Monthly selling expenses		
Sales salaries & commissions	$1,000	
Advertising	$500	
Miscellaneous selling expense	$400	
Monthly general expenses		
Office salaries	$0	
Supplies	$1,000	
Miscellaneous general expense	$1,000	
Totals	$3,900	$15.00
Average selling price per unit		$60.00
Results		
Contribution margin per unit		$45.00
Monthly unit sales at break-even point		87
Monthly sales dollars at break-even point		$5,200

BREAK-EVEN ANALYSIS (all numbers in $000)

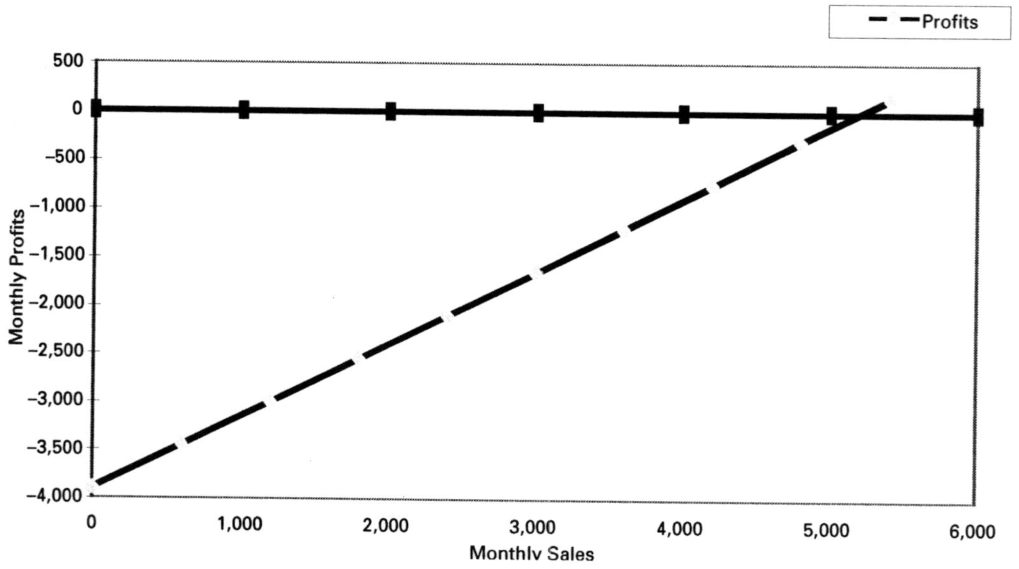

CHAPTER 8

Obtaining the Financing You Need

Business ownership can bring many new challenges to your life. Many of these challenges center around having enough money to help you stay afloat in down times and keep you riding high during times of profitability. As a startup, you will need to consider how you will obtain financing for many aspects of your venture. For instance, unless you are a homebased business, you will need to purchase a building or rent office space to operate your business. More than likely, you will need equipment or machinery—even if all you need is a computer and a fax machine. And, until your profits can carry your business, you will need working capital to sustain your business' life.

This chapter explores the world of financing and teaches you how to accomplish the following:

- Understand the basic types of funding and to learn which one might be best for you;
- Deal with your local bank;
- Approach the often elusive venture capital community; and
- Find out more about the numerous federal, state, and private loan programs available to today's small businesses.

You may be fortunate enough to have family members, friends, or local associates who can lend you money. You may even be able to rely completely on your personal savings. For the majority of both new and existing small business owners, however, obtaining financing from outside sources is a must.

Some Factors a Lender Will Consider

Obtaining financing for your small business will ultimately depend on two major factors:

1. Your business' ability to repay the loan, and
2. The ability of the principal owners or management team of the business.

Funding a new business venture from outside sources can be difficult to obtain for one overriding reason: A start-up business usually has no track record that will show its ability to repay a loan. The owners or managers may not have a proven track record either. Risks are very high for untested ideas and untested owners and managers. Just because you were a manager for a large corporation doesn't necessarily mean you can successfully run a small business. In fact, you may find it easier to obtain financing for an existing business than for one that you start from scratch.

For the majority of both new and existing small business owners obtaining financing from outside sources is a must.

The time to look for start-up or expansion funds from prospective lenders is when you have completed your business plan. As you read in the previous chapter, a business plan can make or break your business. And, in the case of securing financing, this is especially true.

Basic Types of Funding

Before you approach a lender, make sure you understand the basic types of funding. The two most common types of funding are:

1. Debt financing, usually asset-based loans, and
2. Venture (equity) financing.

Lenders will fund asset-based loans on the probability of obtaining repayment of the loan and the type and marketability of the collateral you have. Your collateral may be in the form of stocks or bonds, a home or automobile, or any other items that have a value and can be easily sold by the holder of the collateral if you fail to make your loan payments. Equity financing usually does not require collateral but the lender will probably put a performance requirement on your business.

If your business does not meet the requirement(s), you may lose management say-so in the business and, in some cases, your stake in the venture.

Most equity funding is based on a participation in ownership of the business with the expectation of getting a multiple of the investment during a fixed period—usually five years. This compares to debt financing where the lender makes no provision for participation in your business. In this case, the lender simply expects a payback of the amount borrowed, plus interest (or rent on the money), for the period of the loan. The loan can normally be paid in installments or a lump sum or a combination of both.

Most debt lenders want to rent money to you at a rate that is higher than what they can get by investing in safer investments, such as treasuries, municipal bonds, or other businesses. Most lenders do not want to risk their money—it is to get a good interest return on it, with a reasonable risk. They do not want to own your collateral and collect their money by the sale of the collateral; they want to receive payment on the scheduled dates with both interest and principal. Most lenders will require you to guarantee the loan with other assets you may have other than the collateral that is pledged for the loan. Therefore, your entire net worth may be at risk if your business fails.

Most lenders will require you to guarantee the loan with other assets you may have other than the collateral that is pledged for the loan.

Alternative Types of Funding

In addition to the above traditional methods of funding, alternative types of financing exist, including:

- Lines of credit
- Letters of credit
- Factoring
- Floor planning

Take a moment to learn about these nontraditional financing forms to see if one might apply to your business situation.

LINE OF CREDIT

If your business is in need of a quick infusion of cash to maintain a positive cash flow, you may want to consider using a line of credit. Most commercial banks will give revolving lines of credit—where a fixed amount is available with the ability to draw down on funds under the line, repay the funds on receipt of invoiced sales, and redraw the funds again when you need them. This prearranged amount of credit can be used to meet expected increases in inventory and receivables that may be caused by seasonal fluctuations. Keep in mind, a line of credit needs to be paid to a zero balance as soon as you have an inflow of cash from collecting receivables. Lines of credit are not to be used for long-term capital purposes nor to fund a continuing operating deficit.

Letter of Credit

If you find yourself dealing with a new vendor who is not assured of your company's creditworthiness, you may want to look into a letter of credit. A letter of credit is a guarantee from a bank that a specific obligation will be honored by a bank if a borrower fails to pay. Because your bank knows you and your ability to pay—from cash, collateral, or some prearranged credit facility—it will put its own credit standing in place of your credit standing. A bank will normally charge a fee to grant a letter of credit.

A letter of credit is a guarantee from a bank that a specific obligation will be honored by a bank if a borrower fails to pay.

Factoring

You can acquire cash based on the value of your receivables not in the form of a loan, but rather by selling your account to a lender. In this situation the lender is referred to as a factor and the factor is responsible (not you) for collecting on the account. As a result, your customers pay their bills directly to the factor, and the factor reduces the loan as money is collected. This way, the factor bases all credit decisions on the credit of your customer, not on your business' credit.

Floor Planning

Floor planning is a relatively new financing tool that uses an asset-based lending approach. In this situation, a company would finance its inventory and the purchased inventory would act as collateral until the sale is made. Floor planning is ideal for businesses that have large ticket retail items, such as furniture, appliances, and automobiles. Floor planning allows these businesses to maintain a high level of inventory so their customers have many choices. As items are purchased, the business repays the inventory cost to the lender.

Lending Sources

There are many sources of assistance for obtaining funding. Some possible sources of capital include banks, credit unions, loan companies, family, friends, credit cards, venture capitalists, private investors, small business loan consortiums, and even government loans and grants. Start with your bank or local small business development center (SBDC).

Your Local Bank

Like all businesses, your venture will need banking services to maintain a checking account, conduct credit card transactions, and handle other specialized services. It is only natural to go to a local bank for business financing. Unfortunately, banks rarely finance new businesses because they have yet to establish their ability to repay, they have little collateral, and the ownership or management is often inexperienced.

It is only natural to go to a local bank for business financing.

Frequently, banks will not finance you unless your business has been established for several years and shows a history of clear profitability. Even then, very small businesses may have difficulty obtaining conventional financing. Banks notoriously shy away from funding ongoing operations, and prefer giving loans for expansion or improvements where significant collateral and a large safety margin play a big role.

Not all banks cater to small businesses. Some banks specialize in handling consumer accounts and generally avoid small businesses altogether. Fortunately, the reverse is also true and there is probably a bank in your area that is experienced in small business loans.

Select and Develop a Good Banking Relationship

To establish good banking relations, be honest and provide your banker with knowledge about your business and industry. A good banker will become interested in your business and keep abreast of your problems and successes. If you only see your banker when you need a loan, you are not developing a good relationship. Your banker is much like your attorney and accountant. He or she should be kept up-to-date about your business and is an integral part of helping you solve problems in your business.

It is extremely important that you understand your bank's lending philosophy. Most bankers require two sources of repayment. For instance, your bank may give you a loan as long as you agree to a lien on your accounts receivables, inventory, fixed assets, or real property. In addition to this, a bank will require your personal guaranty—a situation that fosters a psychological commitment to the success of your business.

If you are not willing to personally sign and stand behind your business, your banker may hesitate to give you a loan.

Once you have established a relationship with your banker and have earned a reputation for fiscal responsibility, sound management, and trustworthiness, your banker will begin to consider you a valued customer. This distinction carries significant advantages to your small business, including easier financing in the future. When you present your banker with a loan request and your business plan, your proposal undergoes an evaluation process. Your banker will look for the following information:

- The requested amount of the loan
- The purpose of the loan
- The source and ability of repayment
- Sources and type of collateral
- Management abilities

When you present your banker with a loan request and your business plan, your proposal undergoes an evaluation process.

You can easily remember the loan evaluation process by learning the "five C method." Your bank will look at all five Cs, including:

- *Conditions.* What is the current status of the economy and your business' industry?
- *Collateral.* What will be your secondary source of repayment?
- *Capacity.* Are you prepared for others to take a cold, hard look at your financial track record?
- *Capital.* Do you or your business have any equity?
- *Character.* A key to the lending process, do you have the ability to convey your trustworthiness and integrity?

If you've done your homework, your business plan will contain all of this information in a highly readable and readily understandable format.

Foster your banking relationship by avoiding some actions that will send red-flag danger signals. Don't request another loan after you have spent the money from your first loan. Don't change banks to get a better interest rate. Don't approach a bank if you are undercapitalized or have a history of bad management or serious profit losses. Above all, stay in close communication with your banker—presenting both the good and bad sides of your business.

Venture Capitalists

Whereas banks use past performance as primary criteria when evaluating a loan proposal, venture capitalists focus mainly on the future prospects of a company. Venture capital is a major source of funding for high-tech companies that have the potential of going public or being sold to another company at a large profit in a relatively short period of time. According to *Venture Economics* and the National Venture Capital Association, in 1999 venture investments increased funding for Internet-related investments, biotechnology, and medical services.

If your business is part of an industry segment that is poised for rapid growth and exceptional profits then you may want to pursue venture capital funding. Venture investors seek to earn between five to ten times their initial investment within a five- to eight-year investment horizon. Looking at it another way, venture capitalists seek markets that are sufficiently large to achieve $100 million or greater in value. The primary goal of the venture capitalists is rapid capital appreciation. This goal is usually achieved through a sale of a company to a strategic buyer or through an initial public stock offering (IPO). Keep in mind, sustained growth and profitability beyond a five-year horizon are essential for creating top value when the venture capitalist takes your company public or sells it.

Most companies will not qualify for venture capital funding. As a rule, over 100 investment proposals are reviewed for every one company that receives venture funding. But if you think your idea has potential for funding, you should seek help in developing your plan to make presentations to venture capitalists.

If you do decide to seek venture capital funding, be prepared to give up a portion of your ownership in your company's equity. Equity ownership will have a direct relationship to the amount a venture capitalist invests in your business and the risk that firm assumes if your company fails. As an example, suppose you want to start a business and only have 10 percent of the $100,000 you need to start the business. A venture capitalist may fund the other 90 percent, but you will probably be expected to turn over 90 percent of the ownership in your company as equity. This percentage ownership varies depending on the business type, business plan, competition, your management expertise, projected profits, and the overall investment risk. If this issue scares you, look into obtaining venture capital through small business investment companies (SBICs)—investors that use long-term debt guaranteed by the Small Business Administration (SBA) to supplement their private capital. A detailed discussion of SBICs is located later in this chapter.

If you do decide to seek venture capital funding, be prepared to give up a portion of your ownership in your company's equity.

Finding a venture capitalist that may be interested in your business takes a lot of effort on your part. You will need to identify a list of venture capitalists whose investment preferences match your needs and business profile. Look for firms that are looking for businesses like yours—relative to investment size, development stage, and industry and geographic location. Then, narrow your search to a manageable number of investor candidates, preferably six or less. After you have narrowed your search, you will need to write a well-documented financing proposal. There are several types of proposals you can use to raise venture capital and loans, including a private placement circular, a prospectus, and a limited partnership offering.

For sources of venture capital, check your library, ask your banker, and discuss your project with your local SBDC or business department at a college near you. Seek out resource guides that list venture capitalists. One helpful book is *Pratt's Guide to Venture Capital Sources*. This guide lists each firm's location, investment preferences, contact persons, and available capital pools.

Finding a venture capitalist that may be interested in your business takes a lot of effort on your part.

If you have access to the Internet, you may want to check out the Angel Capital Electronic Network (ACE-Net). This Internet-based listing service, sponsored by the U.S. Small Business Administration's Office of Advocacy, provides information to angel investors on small businesses that are seeking to raise $250,000 to $5 million in equity financing. Angel investors are typically wealthy individuals with significant business experience—thus providing invaluable advice to the companies in which they invest. Using ACE-Net, an enrolled investor can anonymously view, via the Internet, executive summaries and additional investment information provided by participating entrepreneurs. Thus, an investor in California and an entrepreneur in Maine, can seem as close to each other as next door. To find out more, contact ACE-Net at its Internet Web site, www.ace-net.org.

Private Loan Companies

In the past, most small businesses steered away from private loan companies because they were known for high interest rates and were the lender of last resort. This situation has changed during the 1970s. Thanks to the SBA, private loan companies, working as small business lending companies (SBLCs), have become one of the most important SBA loan sources today.

There are some advantages to using an SBLC rather than a traditional bank lender. First, an SBLC is regulated only by the SBA whereas other lenders must report to other regulatory authorities as well. Second, SBLCs specialize in SBA-guaranteed loans. Therefore, your loan request is processed in an expeditious and professional manner.

To be eligible for an SBA loan, your business must meet the size standards established by the SBA regarding your industry type.

Federal Government Programs

Although most small businesses are funded from private sources, there are numerous sources of state and federal help.

Most federal loan programs are processed by the Small Business Administration (SBA). In fact, up to one-third of all small business loans are guaranteed through the SBA. The SBA does not fund the loan but guarantees it through a bank or other institution. If a borrower defaults on a loan, then the SBA will reimburse the bank for a percentage of the loan loss. Thus, banks are more apt to make loans with the SBA's guarantee then on terms it would otherwise not be able to make available.

To be eligible for an SBA loan, your business must meet the size standards established by the SBA regarding your industry type. Further, there are other loans for specific purposes, such as to assist the disabled or for minority or economically disadvantaged individuals, provide incentives for energy savings, pollution control, or doing business in a specific location.

Loan Guaranty

The 7(a) loan guaranty program is the SBA's primary business loan program. It provides loans to small businesses that are unable to secure financing on reasonable terms through normal lending channels.

The program operates through private-sector lenders that provide loans that are guaranteed by the SBA. The lenders, not the SBA, approve and service the loans and request the SBA guaranties. Lenders look favorably on the 7(a) loan guaranty program. The guaranties reduce the risks to the lenders, thus expanding their abilities to make small business loans.

For most SBA loans there is no legislated limit to the total amount of a loan that you may request from a lender. Generally, the SBA will guarantee up to $750,000. Under the program, the SBA can guarantee as much as 75 percent of a commercial loan. For instance, on a $50,000 loan, the SBA guarantees to repay the lender up to 75 percent of the unpaid balance if the borrower defaults. The lender's liability, then, is 25 percent, or $12,500. For its guaranty, the SBA will charge the lender a one-time guaranty fee of 2 percent of the guaranteed portion of the loan.

The interest rate on loans of more than seven years may not exceed 2.75 percent over *The Wall Street Journal's* published prime lending rate and may not exceed 2.25 percent over the prime lending rate for loans under seven years.

The maximum SBA loan maturity is 25 years. However, your loan's maturity will be based on the cash flow and ability of your business to repay it without hardship. Generally, the maturity will vary according to the purpose of the loan and can be up to ten years for working capital and 25 years for fixed assets, the purchase of machinery or equipment, or the purchase or construction of plant facilities. You can use the proceeds of an SBA loan for most business purposes including:

- Purchasing real estate to house your business operations;
- Funding construction, renovation, or leasehold improvements;
- Acquiring furniture, fixtures, machinery, and equipment;
- Purchasing inventory; or
- Financing receivables and augmenting working capital.

The maximum SBA loan maturity is 25 years.

You cannot use the proceeds of an SBA loan for any of the following:

- Financing floor plan needs;
- Purchasing real estate where the participant has issued a forward commitment to the builder/developer or where the real estate will be held primarily for investment purposes;
- Making payments to owners or paying delinquent withholding taxes; or
- Paying an existing debt unless you can show that the refinancing will benefit your business and that the need to refinance is not a sign of bad management on your part.

Several loan programs under the 7(a) program address specific needs and include:

- *Low Documentation Loan (LowDoc).* If your business needs a loan of $150,000 or less, applying for the loan under LowDoc could be as easy as completing a one-page SBA application.
- *CAPLines.* Under this program, loan proceeds generally will be advanced against a borrower's existing or anticipated inventory or accounts receivable to meet the cyclical working capital needs of small business.

- *Women's and Minority Prequalification.* If you are a woman or minority owned business, you could meet with an SBA-designated intermediary, such as an SBDC counselor, to obtain prequalification from the SBA before approaching a lender.
- *504 Certified Development Company Program.* This program could allow you to get long-term, fixed-asset financing through certified development companies.

SBICs are privately owned and managed investment firms that make capital investment in small businesses.

Small Business Investment Company (SBIC)

Licensed and regulated by the SBA, SBICs are privately owned and managed investment firms that make capital investment in small businesses. They use their own funds plus funds obtained at favorable rates with an SBA guaranty or by selling their preferred stock to the SBA. This vital partnership between government and the private sector economy has resulted in more than $9 billion in loans to more than 65,000 small business throughout the United States.

The SBIC program provides funding to all types of manufacturing and service industries. Some investment companies specialize in certain fields, while others seek out small businesses with new products or services because of the strong growth potential. Your business is qualified for SBIC financing if it has a net worth of less than $18 million and average after-tax earnings of less than $6 million during the previous two years. If your business does not meet this test, it may still qualify as a small business under either an employment standard or amount-of-annual-sales standard.

Both of these standards vary from industry to industry. Keep in mind, SBICs differ in size and investment philosophy. Each SBIC has a policy on the type of financing it prefers, size preferences, industry preferences, and geographic requirements.

If your business qualifies under the SBIC program, you may be able to receive equity capital, long-term loans, and expert management assistance. SBICs may invest only in qualifying small business concerns. SBICs may not invest in:

- Other SBICs;
- Finance and investment companies or finance-type leasing companies;
- Unimproved real estate;
- Companies with less than one-half of their assets and operation in the United States;

- Passive or casual businesses (those not engaged in a regular and continuous business operation); or
- Companies that will use the proceeds to acquire farm land.

You should understand the differences between the two types of SBICs. You may encounter a "regular" SBIC, or a firm that is known as a "specialized" small business investment company (SSBIC). SSBICs are specifically targeted toward the needs of entrepreneurs who have been denied the opportunity to own and operate a business because of social or economic disadvantage. To qualify, your business must be 51 percent owned by socially or economically disadvantaged persons. More than 100 SSBICs operate in the United States. For a complete list of SBICs and SSBICs, contact the National Association of Small Business Investment Companies (NASBIC). The address and phone number of this agency is listed in Appendix C.

It has been very difficult to get loans of a few thousand dollars because they are not profitable to most lenders and generally are of a higher risk.

Microloan Program

One of the most difficult types of loans to obtain are for small amounts of debt. It has been very difficult to get loans of a few thousand dollars because they are not profitable to most lenders and generally are of a higher risk. In response to this issue, the SBA created the Microloan Program. Under this program, the SBA makes funds available to non-profit intermediaries who in turn make loans to eligible borrowers. The amounts of the microloans can range anywhere from $100 to a maximum of $25,000. The average microloan is for $10,000.

Another advantage of the microloan is that a completed application can be processed by a nonprofit intermediary in less than one week. Although each lending organization has its own loan requirements, an intermediary is required to take as collateral any assets that you bought with the microloan. Further, your personal guaranty will be required.

Recently microloans have become more available through entrepreneur associations and some state agencies. Check with your chamber of commerce or small business development center if you are considering a business that needs a small amount of capital to get started. Often you will be required to have a mentor who is in business and possibly attend classes that discuss developing a plan and managing your prospective business.

SMALL BUSINESS INNOVATION RESEARCH (SBIR) PROGRAM

Since 1982, the SBA has used the Small Business Innovation Research (SBIR) program to accomplish the following objectives:

- Stimulate technological innovation;
- Fund projects initiated by high-tech small business to help meet federal research and development needs;
- Foster and encourage participation by minority and disadvantaged persons in technological innovation; and
- Increase the commercialization of innovations from federal research and development.

Eleven federal agencies—from the Department of Agriculture to the Nuclear Regulatory Commission—participate in the SBIR program. Under the program, these federal agencies request highly competitive proposals from small businesses in response to solicitations outlining their research and development needs. Awards are granted after an evaluation of the technical feasibility of the research and development concept. For more information, contact the Office of Technology as listed in Appendix B.

CERTIFIED AND PREFERRED LENDERS

The SBA recently streamlined its guarantee program, expediting loans through its Certified and Preferred Lending program. Only the most active and expert lenders qualify for this program.

Certified lenders make up nearly one-third of all SBA business loan guaranties. Certified lenders are those who have been heavily involved in regular SBA loan guaranty processing and have met certain other criteria. The SBA delegates partial authority to certified lenders and processes loan applications with a three-day turnaround. Preferred lenders are the SBA's best lenders and have been given full lending authority in exchange for a lower rate of guaranty.

Check with your bank to be sure it is a certified or preferred lender to make the approval process faster.

Certified lenders make up nearly one-third of all SBA business loan guaranties.

TIPS FOR OBTAINING AN SBA LOAN

The most important thing you can do in your attempts at getting an SBA loan is to be prepared. Your second most important task is to find the right lender. You must know your needs and have a ready explanation for how you arrived at the amount you are requesting. Ideally, you will use your business plan to show the past, present, and future condition of your business.

As a reminder, make sure you include the financial history, management background, and monthly cash flow projections of your business.

You will probably be required to submit personal financial statement and tax returns also.

State Government Programs

Most states have economic development agencies that encourage the development of new businesses. The loans may be to encourage starting a business in a target area or expanding a business by building new facilities or adding equipment. Often the amount of the loan is tied to the number of new jobs to be created in the area.

Check Appendix D for a list of some state sources of funding. Funding of the programs often is insufficient to respond to a large percentage of applicants. However, it is well worth your time to check to see if there are loans for which your business qualifies.

CAUTION: You may hear of loans offered at very low rates of interest through federal or state agencies. If this is information is available by buying a tape or video or going to a seminar, beware. You will find that there are no such loans: the lending requirements are similar for all businesses. You may also be directed to companies that charge much higher rates of interest than banks charge if you have a high risk venture. Beware of such loans because you must repay a much larger share of your business income to repay the loan, and you will increase the chances of failure of your business.

Most states have economic development agencies that encourage the development of new businesses.

Chapter Wrap-Up

One of the worst situations you can get into as a business owner is not having enough money to run your business. Top on your priority list should be a clear picture of your business and personal financial needs before you make your first sale.

To assist you, first estimate the money you will need to set up your business—from office set up expenses to production equipment needs; from utilities deposits to insurance; from withholding taxes to licensing fees. Review chapters 2, 3, and 4 and make a list of the fees for which you will be responsible—both in the short-term as well as the long-term.

Next, establish a business bank account. The key here is to find the right banker for your business' needs. Compare fees and credit card arrangements. Inquire about floor planning, factoring, lines of credit, and accounts receivable financing. Gain a thorough understanding of a bank's policies, procedures, and personalities of the major players before you choose to do business with it.

Last, but certainly not least, know which lenders to approach and which ones to avoid. Stay informed about the federal and state loan programs available to your small business. Lenders will notice how educated you are and respond with a greater respect and appreciation. Keep your financial records up-to-date. Be ready to show proforma (projected) financial statements for at least the next three years. Maintain easy access to your business' cash flow projections, balance sheets, and profit and loss (P&L) statements. (These and other critical finance and accounting terms are fully covered in the next chapter.) Show your prospective lenders that you mean business—be prepared with a completed business plan before you approach a lender. Make sure you use the tips for creating a smart business plan from the previous chapter.

Stay informed about the federal and state loan programs available to your small business.

CHAPTER 9

Essential Finance and Accounting Methods

Every business owner will benefit from a better understanding of finance and accounting. Admittedly, these tasks are the last things most business owners care to spend time working with on a regular basis. In fact, many feel that a once-a-year accounting at tax time provides sufficient financial information to guide them through the year. Unfortunately, this is unlikely to be true except for the smallest businesses.

Approximately one million new businesses are started every year in the United States. Many of them will fail, leaving the owners and investors poorer, but wiser, about how to operate a business successfully. One of the primary reasons for any business failure is insufficient financial resources.

Some start-up companies have enough money to operate for years without making a profit from the business. Most businesses are not that fortunate and must generate enough revenue from the business to pay creditors, employees (including themselves), and vendors. Some businesses are even so successful they grow faster than they can afford to and go out of business because of too much success.

The secret to remaining in business is being able to monitor the lifeblood of the business—the cash flow. There are many indicators of the health of a business. They include the income statement, the balance sheet, the cash flow analysis, and a multitude of ratios and other indicators that monitor the daily, weekly, monthly, and annual success of a business.

Having a full understanding of basic finance and accounting could mean the difference between the success or failure of your business. Even if you hire an accountant or bookkeeper to maintain your business accounts, you still need to understand the significance of the numbers they generate in order to manage your business.

Types of Accounting Systems

This chapter will introduce you to the main types of accounting methods, including:

- Cash based accounting
- Accrual based accounting
- Tax accounting
- Financial accounting
- Management accounting

You should understand each of these to get a full picture of your company's financial position. Also, you will learn some basic accounting documentation procedures and payment acceptance methods.

> Cash based accounting is the easiest and most popular method for sole proprietorships.

Cash Based Accounting

Cash based accounting is the easiest and most popular method for sole proprietorships. Cash enters and leaves an account as income and expense.

Cash based accounting in its simplest form is similar to a checkbook ledger with a running balance. The balance gives you a snapshot view of the health of your business—the larger the balance at any given moment, the healthier your state of affairs. However, a snapshot view such as this clearly has a limited value. A healthy balance now means nothing if you have to pay an expense tomorrow that is three times that amount. In addition, the ledger cannot show the value vested in inventory, equipment, or accounts receivable.

Cash based accounting is used internally by smaller businesses to maintain the most accurate picture of their business' cash flow; however, the government requires you to report your yearly earnings using accrual based accounting. You may want to use both methods.

Accrual Based Accounting

Accrual based accounting gives a more accurate picture of the state of your business' financial health and more closely conforms to generally accepted accounting practices. Suppose you have a grounds maintenance business and you charge a flat fee of $600 for six month's worth of work. Even though you collect and deposit your fee in April, a more accurate picture of your business is produced by amortizing—taking the monthly value of the fee and applying it to monthly income and expenses—rather than showing it as income in the month it was collected. For example, if you collect the fee in April and apply it to your account at the rate of $100 per month, you will amortize the fee over six months. If you make a sale in December and don't receive the cash for it until the following year, the sale is recorded as occurring in the year it was recorded—not the year the cash was received. This can seriously affect your income tax if a large sale at the end of the year will create a larger profit than you would without the sale.

The effects of accrual accounting may cause an expense to be booked in one year, but paid for in the following year. Be aware of the accrual accounting rules—as well as the cash based accounting rules—especially at the end of a year when you can dramatically affect your profit by delaying or accelerating a sale or expense.

Accrual based accounting gives a more accurate picture of the state of your business' financial health and more closely conforms to generally accepted accounting practices.

Tax Accounting

The IRS has developed its own set of rules for accounting, and the information required to compile and pay your taxes differs from the information you need to manage your business. Further, the IRS rules you must follow may be different from the rules you choose to follow for your banker. While you may keep two sets of books—one for tax purposes and one for business operations—most small business owners simply maintain one set of books and comply with the IRS' requirements. For example, you may have a piece of equipment that you can depreciate according to IRS rules in five years. But the actual useful life of the equipment may be ten years. For tax purposes you would depreciate it as rapidly as the law allows, but for your own accounting you would know that it would not have to be replaced for 20 years. Thus, you would depreciate it over a longer period for your internal calculations.

Most new business owners are confused by the rules and meaning of depreciation. If a machine is purchased with cash or a loan, it is paid for and most business owners would expect that they could deduct the cost of the machine from the current year's expenses. This is not the case when it comes to IRS requirements. Since there is a useful life to the machine, the IRS may require that you write it off over a period of years. IRS groups different equipment into different categories for depreciation purposes. It is wise to consult with an accountant to be sure you select the correct depreciation period for equipment you purchase.

To help you use the tax accounting method, you may want to look into using a software program to get you started. Some popular tax software comes close to achieving expert level advice and works directly with files from your bookkeeping or existing accounting software. These programs often include interactive video clips and sound files from top tax advisors, can generate completed IRS forms for filing, and have the capability of filing your taxes electronically. If you decide to use these tools, shop the market carefully. The software should meet these following minimum requirements:

- It should be updated annually;
- It should be able to use your existing accounting program files; and
- It should be endorsed by one of the "Big Six" accounting firms.

As your business grows in both size and revenue, you will benefit more and more from the advice of a knowledgeable tax accountant.

Be cautious in relying on your computer and your wits in computing your taxes. While you are likely to file a return that meets the IRS' requirements and expectations by using these methods, you are just as likely to end up paying too much.

The IRS allows small businesses to deduct a certain amount of new capital purchases in a single year. Check with the current IRS requirements to determine how much you can deduct.

Get Expert Help

As your business grows in both size and revenue, you will benefit more and more from the advice of a knowledgeable tax accountant. Tax law is complicated and changes on a yearly basis. Without expert help, you could end up paying thousands of dollars in excess taxes or be penalized for not paying sufficient taxes or taking deductions that are not acceptable to the IRS.

A valuable source of timely information that offers hints on avoiding a tax crunch is *Small Business Computing*. This monthly magazine—and its cousin *Home Office Computing*—provides current information on a variety of business topics via its Internet Web site. To learn more about this helpful resource, log on at www.smalloffice.com. Even the IRS has its own user-friendly publication. As a new business owner you can get IRS Publication 1558—a series of 12 newsletters that contains tax tips and explanations of new tax legislation. The address and phone number of the nearest IRS services office is listed in Appendix B.

Financial Accounting

Financial accounting is the basis for all entry level accounting classes and textbooks. It is used to prepare financial reports, such as income statements, balance sheets, and cash flow statements. Most often, these reports are generated using accrual based methods so that income is recorded as it is earned instead of as it is collected and expenses are recorded as they occur instead of as payment is made for them. To better understand financial accounting, take a moment to become familiar with three essential financial reports. Samples of each of the statements are included in Appendix A.

> An income statement provides detailed information about your expenses broken down into as many categories as you feel are necessary.

Income Statement

An income statement is sometimes called a profit and loss (P&L) statement. It is used to determine current profitability and is based on the most current information available. It is the basis for determining income tax obligations and levels of supportable debt by lending institutions.

An income statement provides detailed information about your expenses broken down into as many categories as you feel are necessary. For example, you may choose to list a single utilities expense or you may choose to break utilities down into gas for heat, electricity for lighting, and water. The more information available to you, the more able you are to make informed decisions about expenses in the future. Don't collect more information than you will use, however.

Income statements may also be used to track expenses against a budget. By comparing actual costs against projections, you can decide where you need to place more controls or where unexpected expenses occurred. This process will allow you to better plan your operating budget for the following year.

It is not unusual for your income statement to show that you have a profit for a given period, but you wonder where the profit is because your bank account is much lower than the income statement indicates. This situation occurs because you show depreciation of equipment which adds to the income but does not produce an equivalent amount of cash. You may also be building inventory, using available cash, but the income statement will reflect the cost of what you sold during the period, but will not add the additional inventory to the profit or loss situation.

You can see that while your income statement is useful to explain how much profit you made relative to your cost of goods and other expenses, it does not describe accurately the state of your business. If you want a snapshot view of your business regarding its overall condition on a specific day, use a balance sheet.

Balance Sheet

Balance sheets are prepared periodically, usually on a monthly, quarterly, or yearly basis. They are used to summarize your business' net worth, taking into account all assets, liabilities, and equity at a given moment in time. Assets include everything the business owns—cash, accounts receivable, fixed assets, and inventory. Liabilities are everything the business owes—such as accounts payable, payroll, and tax liabilities. Total equity is equal to the sum of all assets minus the sum of all liabilities. If you operate your business as a corporation, then equity is the current value of all capital stock as well as the total profit or loss since the start of your corporation.

> Balance sheets provide a numerical bottom line that is useful in evaluating business growth or decline and creditworthiness.

Balance sheets provide a numerical bottom line that is useful in evaluating business growth or decline and creditworthiness. By comparing a current period with previous periods, you can observe trends. While the income statement and balance sheet are the typical indicators of the condition of a business, the cash flow statement will explain why you do not have the cash in your bank account that you might expect. When projected for the following months or years, it will help you plan for critical cash need periods if your business is seasonal or cyclical.

Cash Flow Statement

A cash flow statement will help you understand where cash has been used and where and why cash is short or in abundance. A cash flow statement is basically an accounting of available cash, plus cash income minus cash disbursements, for each period forecast.

As you become more experienced in looking at your historical cash flow, you should project your cash flow for at least a year in advance. A projection will provide a clear picture of your ability to meet expenses over the forecast period. If you will need a loan in the future, start before the need is upon you; most lenders are suspicious of a business owner who suddenly realizes that there will be a cash shortage and must obtain a loan within the next week or two.

Once established, use your cash flow statement to compare against actual performance during a forecast period. This comparison provides crucial feedback that will allow you to predict potential cash shortfalls and prevent them before they occur. Comparing predicted performance with actual performance also allows you to adjust basic assumptions and thereby more accurately prepare future cash flow forecasts.

The information produced by management accounting will give you timely, detailed feedback about your operations.

Management Accounting

Management accounting, also called cost accounting, is a specialized form of internal accounting that provides managers and owners detailed operating information about production processes. This type of reporting is particularly useful in manufacturing businesses and may include such information as unit production cost, product line profitability breakdowns, and sales performance by region or by store.

The information produced by management accounting will give you timely, detailed feedback about your operations. This feedback will allow you to draw conclusions about efficiency, cost, inventory valuation, quality control, product turnover, return or repair rates, warranty issues, and the cost effectiveness of design changes. Anything that can be measured will provide potential fodder for management accounting. Management accounting can be complex and labor-intensive depending on the amount and type of information gathered. So, it is important to place controls on how much and how often management accounting is needed to adequately control your business.

Track Key Indicators

Your business may benefit from simply tracking a few key indicators instead of a wide array of information. Economy analysts, for instance, often rely on key economic indicators to predict how the economy is reacting to world events. They rely on these indicators instead of the numerous other factors that affect the economy. If they were to analyze all factors, their reports would be out-of-date and completely useless. Similarly, your business can rely on key indicators to predict its performance.

For instance, suppose you have a small retail business and are concerned about losses to shoplifting. So you start to collect information about profit versus sales and inventory data on a monthly basis to determine the rate of losses incurred and to test the effectiveness of the control methods you employ to deter shoplifters. This same concept can be applied to other types of businesses. A manufacturer will measure quality control reject ratios to evaluate the effectiveness of their job training program. And a service station will compare storage tank inventory data to sales to determine whether its underground tanks are leaking.

There are many internal sources of information that will tell you how your business is fairing. Don't depend solely on the end of quarter or year accounting to provide you with the information you need to determine if your business has a problem.

Accounting Documentation

As a small business owner, you need to know how to use standardized forms to document sales transactions.

All businesses need to develop ways to process and account for their purchases and sales. When you start your business you may be able to remember what you have ordered and how much cash it will take when it is received. As your business grows and you hire employees, you will need to develop procedures that track income and expenses. In addition, the IRS demands that you have documentation relating to what you report in your income tax return for the business. A paper trail of sales and expenses will help you better understand the true cost of doing business and your profit. It can make an IRS auditor happier, if you have the unpleasant experience of having an audit. The two simplest methods for documenting income and expenses involve using purchase orders and invoices.

Purchase Orders

Regardless of which method of accounting you use, you will need to have a means to collect data. As a small business owner, you need to know how to use standardized forms to document sales transactions. One of these standard forms is the purchase order.

A purchase order is used to place an order with a supplier or a manufacturer. It acts as official authorization for the supplier to ship the merchandise being ordered. Since it functions as a permanent record of a transaction, prepare a purchase order even when placing orders by telephone or by letter.

A purchase order is traditionally designed as a three-part form—that is, an original and two copies. The original is sent to the supplier as the transaction approval document. The first copy is forwarded to the accounting department for payment processing once an invoice is received. The second copy is retained by the purchasing department as a record that the required merchandise was ordered. An optional third copy, used in larger companies, is returned to the requisitioning department as documentation that purchasing action was taken. Very small businesses—fewer than five employees—may require only the original and a single file copy.

If your business ships merchandise, you will receive purchase orders from customers as a normal part of business. These purchase orders will contain the same information as the purchase orders that you prepare. These purchase orders are a promise to pay for goods shipped. They also provide the shipping department with an accurate location address, phone number, and mailing address. A well-designed purchase order is essential for accurate recordkeeping. At a minimum, the purchase orders you use should include the following information:

If your business ships merchandise, you will receive purchase orders from customers as a normal part of business.

- Your company's name, address, phone number, fax number, and e-mail address, if available;
- A purchase order number to allow future tracking and filing of the purchase;
- The supplier's address and a "ship to" address (keep in mind, this may be different from the actual physical address of the business);
- The date the purchase order was prepared;
- The quantity, product code number, description, unit price, and extended price of the merchandise (unit price multiplied by quantity less any discounts) being ordered;
- A column listing the line item costs, applicable sales tax, shipping and handling costs, and final total for the purchase order;
- Your internal accounting information that identifies which account the purchase is to be charged against;
- An authorization signature line; and
- Any other information you may require including conditions of the purchase and special instructions to the supplier.

You will want your purchase orders to project the same degree of professionalism as all other paperwork that leaves your company.

Beyond the value of the tracking and internal control, purchase orders are important legal documents. If you disagree with a supplier as to what was supplied or the terms under which the item was shipped or produced, a purchase order which spells out the exact details of the expected purchase can provide you with a legal document and probably will help resolve an issue before it gets to the lawyer level.

Invoices

Another business form that you will use to collect accounting data is an invoice. An invoice is an itemized list of the merchandise shipped to you and an accounting of the costs associated with it. It is used to document merchandise shipped to you. As delivery is made, you will use the invoice to inventory what you receive and verify that everything that was shipped to you arrived in good condition. The invoice is then forwarded to the accounting department for approval and filing. The accounting department will routinely compare the invoices to the originating purchase order to verify that no errors were made, and that actual costs were in line with expected costs.

An invoice is an itemized list of the merchandise shipped to you and an accounting of the costs associated with it.

As a supplier, you will prepare a shipping invoice or packing list to send with the merchandise that you ship out to your customers. Like a purchase order, an invoice will contain specific information about your company such as your company name, address, and phone number. An invoice will reference a specific purchase order or purchase agreement and will contain an itemized listing of goods shipped and may contain information about costs of the items and the aggregate costs.

A copy of an invoice is sent to your customer as a billing invoice. Additionally, a copy of the outgoing invoice is forwarded to the accounting department where it is verified and filed. An outgoing invoice is filed as an account receivable, while an incoming invoice is filed as an account payable.

Standardized forms—like purchase orders and invoices—are available through mail order business supply companies, from your local printer, or from office supply stores. Another helpful resource is *The Ultimate Small Buisness Advisor* by Andi Axman (Entrepreneur Press), which contains sample forms in the book and on CD that you can adapt to your business. Also, most of the popular business software includes standardized templates that you can use in your business. Merely fill in the blanks on your computer screen and the program will prepare completed purchase orders for you. For your convenience, a sample purchase order and an invoice are included in Appendix A.

Payment Methods

Every business needs cash to operate. How you collect the cash will differ greatly between the type of business and custom within your industry. If you are in an industry that traditionally gives credit for 30 or 60 days, you will be at a disadvantage if you can't provide the same to your potential customers. If you don't offer to take checks or credit cards, but your competitors do, you can bet that many customers will buy your product or use your service only once. However, there are downside risks on all types of payment options except cash, and even with cash, there is a greater chance that you will be robbed or that employees can siphon off some of the receipts.

You need to develop payment acceptance policies and procedures. If you sell with the expectation of receiving payment within 30 days after billing, you will need to have a cash reserve to help you get through your initial months of business. Some companies do not pay from invoices—they expect to receive a statement at the end of the month that summarizes their account and will pay at the end of the month or sometime during the following month.

You need to develop payment acceptance policies and procedures.

If you do accept checks, you run the risk of receiving bad checks for which there is little chance you will collect at a later time. Take some time now to familiarize yourself with the various methods of payment. Then, make a decision on what will work best for your business' situation.

Paying by Check

One of the first financial actions you should take after deciding to get into business is to open a checking account under your business name. Many banks will not open an account unless you have documentation that a business has been legally formed.

Although you can operate a sole proprietorship from your personal checking account, it is advisable to have a separate checking account for all business transactions. If you form a corporation it is imperative that you do not mix your personal funds with your business funds. Nothing raises a red flag quicker than lack of responsibility with your business finances and your personal finances. Having separate bank accounts will help you avoid future accounting and accountability problems. Banks will probably demand some proof that you operate as a corporation and will expect to see documentation from a state authority that the corporation operates legally in your state.

Once an incoming invoice is received, verified, routed and filed, all that remains is to pay for the transaction. By convention, most all invoices are paid by check, allowing you to easily track expenditures and simplify bookkeeping tasks. However, you will want to establish a petty cash account that will enable you to purchase some items with cash. It is important to keep track of the use of petty cash purchases. If you can't show they were used for business purposes, you will not be able to deduct the expenses and may pay additional taxes because of a higher profit. Billing invoices generally indicate a specific due date, and you will prepare payments based on that date. A check provides you with a record of payment, and it should reference the purchase order number or invoice number on the memo line. Send the check to the supplier along with a copy of the invoice so as to arrive on or just before the payment due date.

Billing invoices generally indicate a specific due date, and you will prepare payments based on that date.

ACCEPTING CHECKS

Accepting checks as payment for goods or services is a generally accepted practice, but it is unwise to accept checks indiscriminately, particularly from new or potentially unreliable customers. A check can be thought of as a promise to pay, and it is only as good as the word of the person or entity issuing it. Some problems that can occur when accepting a check include fraud, insufficient funds, and stop payments.

- *Fraud.* This occurs when a check is intentionally written against a dormant, empty, or closed account or against an account that the customer does not own. Frequently, the checks have been stolen or illegally reproduced, but in all cases the customer has no intention of ever making the check good.
- *Nonsufficient funds (NSF).* When a customer's check is returned marked NSF, you should immediately call the issuing bank to see if the funds might now exist to cover the check. If so, immediately send the check through again or take the check directly to the bank and cash it. If there are still insufficient funds, you will have to take steps to collect from the customer directly.
- *Stop payments.* By law, your customers can put a stop payment on their checks if they have good reason to do so, such as dissatisfaction with the product or the service. Having an adjustment and returns policy in place will help you collect on the account if it comes into dispute.

You can protect yourself against bad checks through local and national services that verify checks as you accept them. They may also guarantee reimbursement if the check is bad. However, you may find that the cost of such a service is greater than the potential or real loss you will incur if you take a few precautions.

You can protect yourself against bad checks through local and national services that verify checks as you accept them.

Verifying Checks

A few basic precautions will reduce the chances of getting stuck with a bad check. The effort expended to verify a check before you accept it will pay dividends in the long run.

- *Proper identification.* Make sure the check is properly signed and that the signature matches the signature on the driver's license or other identification. The check should be made out to your business.
- *Check the amount.* The amount of the check should be written legibly in two places. The amount in both places should match exactly.
- *No "starter" checks.* The check should have a preprinted address and phone number. Do not accept "starter" checks.
- *No two-person checks.* Checks that are written by someone else to your customer are usually not accepted by a business. You cannot obtain information about the originator of the check, only the person to whom the check is written.
- *Verification.* If the sale is especially large or the customer is unknown to you, call the bank to verify the check before providing the service or merchandise.
- *Check guarantees.* Require your customer to present a check verification card when writing a check or subscribe to an electronic check verification service accessed during the point of sale.
- *Waiting periods.* If your business is a mail-order business, you may decide to hold some checks before shipping the ordered item. You will need to determine how long it will take for a check to reach the bank on which it was written and be returned if the check is bad.

When you receive your monthly bank statement, immediately compare the cleared checks against those you issued to be certain that the signatures match. Banks generally do not look to see if a check is signed or if the signature matches those on the signature cards they require you to provide.

If you find a check with no signature—or a forged or improper signature—you have between 30 to 60 days to return the check to the bank and receive credit. The liability for forged checks is generally deemed the responsibility of the account holder if not presented to the bank within this time period. However, if you fail to notice an improper check, be aware that the account to which it was deposited may be closed by the bank before you can obtain a credit.

There are three helpful rules when it comes to protecting yourself from internal fraud: One, make sure that a person other than the person who writes the checks reconciles your checking account. Two, never accept a check reconciliation using a copy of the statement—always use the original. Three, consult with your accountant on additional methods for protecting your assets.

Credit Cards

Accepting credit cards for your business transactions represents a significant advantage to potential customers.

Accepting credit cards for your business transactions represents a significant advantage to potential customers. But the practice has a downside in addition to the expense and paperwork. You must take several basic steps before you can accept credit cards from customers. You must establish merchant discount agreements with each major credit card you decide to accept. You must establish a working agreement with your bank to handle the transactions. And you must learn how to process credit vouchers.

Some private companies handle all parts of the credit card transaction for you by establishing agreements with the appropriate credit card companies, conducting the credit transactions, and verifying available credit electronically before completing the sale. However, the one-step convenience comes at the cost of considerably higher processing fees. As electronic transactions become more commonplace, fees for these services will drop considerably.

Credit card transactions are subject to many of the same problems that check transactions present. Credit card fraud is a growing concern. If you accept a card that has been lost, stolen, altered, or counterfeited, you will lose any income from that sale as well as the cost of the merchandise.

Even if the sale and the card are valid, a customer could return merchandise or dispute a charge, resulting in a chargeback to your account and lost income for your business. You have rights regarding chargeback but you should clearly understand how the credit card company handles complaints and be certain to respond to the credit card company's inquiry about the chargeback within the time indicated by the credit card company.

You can avoid many of the problems associated with accepting credit card transactions by taking these few extra precautions at the time of the sale.

- Check the card against an invalid card list provided by the credit card company.
- Certify the card electronically through a card verification service.
- Verify the signature on the card against the signature on the driver's license or other valid identification.
- Record additional information on the credit card invoice, such as address, phone number, and driver's license number.
- Have the customer sign an adjustment and return agreement to help you collect on the account if a chargeback is made to your account.

The debit card is similar to a credit card in appearance and operation, but operates on an entirely different principle.

Debit Cards

Many banks are turning to a debit card as a means of controlling overdraft on checking accounts. The debit card is similar to a credit card in appearance and operation, but operates on an entirely different principle. Instead of drawing funds for the transaction against a line of credit the way a credit card does, the debit card draws funds directly from the customer's checking or savings account.

This system provides significant advantages to the retailer. Funds are verified as being available at the point of sale, eliminating bounced checks and failed transactions. Also, a personal code, which must be entered electronically by the customer, virtually eliminates fraudulent use of the debit card. Since no cash changes hands, the opportunity for theft is reduced as well as the impact on the business if theft does occur. Finally, funds are frequently transferred from the customer's account to your business account within one working day.

Chapter Wrap-Up

Now that you are familiar with the basic accounting methods, you may even be more convinced of your desire to steer clear of the books and let an accountant manage your finances. Hiring a financial professional is a wise management decision. However, controlling your business' financial health is the difference between success and failure.

Work toward a personal involvement with your business' finances and educate yourself as much as possible so you can better understand the cash flow needs of your business. Establish internal controls—like purchase orders and invoices to help track income and expenses. In addition, establish procedures that apply to all customers across-the-board. You may change your procedures as you learn more about your customers and customs within your industry. Also, it is essential to have procedures if you hire employees because they cannot guess what your procedures may be from customer to customer or from day to day.

If you want to stay in business you must be able to collect on your accounts receivable.

Finally, get a firm grasp on which collection techniques your business will employ. Collecting the cash that is owed you, either immediately upon culmination of the sale or within 30 or 60 days, is what will make your business work successfully. You may feel uneasy about calling customers to remind them that a bill has not been paid. You will find customers who will take advantage of your unwillingness to call and ask for payment if it is overdue. If you want to stay in business you must be able to collect on your accounts receivable.

CHAPTER 10

Effective Human Resources Management

As federal, state, and local governments focus more on the rights of employees, no employer can afford to be unaware of the laws affecting selection, hiring, and dismissal. In Chapter 4 you were introduced to the various duties of an employer, including fair employment, minimum wage, reporting wages, and anti-discrimination practices. This chapter gets into the nitty gritty of managing your personnel program and establishing and enforcing company policies. In short, this chapter tells you the basics of managing your human resources. From writing a job description to interviewing prospective applicants; from conducting performance reviews to dealing with disciplinary issues; from establishing a benefits package for your small business to developing a company policy handbook—this chapter gives you a beginner's look at the oftentimes elusive subject of human resources management. Even if you don't plan on hiring employees right away, make sure you know what laws pertain to you when and if you do decide to post that first job opening.

Hiring

Eventually you will face the task of hiring new employees. This important process will have an enormous impact on the success of your business. Your employees are a representation of your business and it is natural to want to select the best candidate possible for each position in your company. Select well and you will add an effective team member to your organization. Select poorly and you will lose valuable time and money attempting to correct your mistake.

The most common method of recruitment is to first clearly define the job position by writing a job description and then take applications. If you have done your homework, you will end up selecting the best candidate. Even this simple scenario contains hidden pitfalls. As a small business owner, you must strictly base the decision to hire one applicant over another on the individual's relative qualifications and suitability for the position. Failure to be aware of the various laws regulating hiring practices leaves you open to litigation. The Americans with Disabilities Act of 1990 (ADA) and the Civil Rights Act of 1964 (CRA) contain specific guidance in hiring individuals. Both acts prohibit discrimination in hiring based on race, sex, national origin, color, religion, age, marital status, sexual preference, or physical or mental disabilities. Both apply to employers having 15 or more employees for 20 weeks or more per year. For additional information, see www.eeoc.gov.

> Your employees are a representation of your business and it is natural to want to select the best candidate possible for each position in your company.

As guidance for complying with the requirements of the ADA and the CRA, the Equal Employment Opportunity Commission (EEOC) and other federal agencies adopted the 1978 Guidelines on Uniform Employee Selection Procedures. To learn more about these guidelines, contact your state's employment agency. For additional information, see www.dol.gov.

Writing a Job Description

The key to selecting well-qualified people for your employees is to clearly spell out their job positions. Make sure your job descriptions include job qualifications, assigned duties, responsibilities, knowledge, coordination, reporting requirements, and physical working conditions. Good position descriptions will help your employees understand what their jobs entail and what your company expects from them. Good job descriptions will also help your company's organization and serve as a blueprint for a well-structured operation. For a sample job description, see Appendix A.

Advertising a Job Position

Advertising a job position is the first step in the recruitment process. A well-thought-out ad will draw a diverse group of applicants who meet the qualifications of the position. Before writing the ad copy, consider the requirements of the position you are filling. Will the position require interaction with the public, your customers, or both? Will your new employee require a valid driver's license to fulfill his or her duties? Does the job require any special skills or abilities? What experience level are you seeking?

A well-thought-out ad will draw a diverse group of applicants who meet the qualifications of the position.

Review your ad for discriminatory language. Make sure the wording does not unintentionally exclude a segment of the population. Place your ad in as many places as necessary to ensure that everyone has the same opportunity to see it and apply for the position. Include a phone number and physical address in each ad to avoid discriminating against hearing or visually impaired applicants. Consider listing the position with the unemployment agency in your state as a means to ensure that all potential applicants are aware of the opening in your business. Select a closing date and time for the position. Require that all applications be submitted before that time expires, or specifically state in your ad that you will accept applications until the position fills.

The Job Application

A well-prepared application form is your first line of defense in preventing hiring discrimination lawsuits. It is also your best tool for reducing a large pool of applicants to a group of the best qualified. Use a standardized application form for your company, ensuring that you collect the same information for each applicant. Because it must conform to the requirements of the ADA and the CRA, it serves as a guide to prevent collecting data that might become the basis for discrimination.

The application package should include a company statement of equal opportunity, a privacy act statement, and a release allowing your business to investigate the accuracy of the application. Appendix A contains a sample application. You must ensure that all applicants understand these special provisions of the application, and that the wording or layout of the application is not discriminatory. Extra fine print, for instance, discriminates against someone with weak or impaired vision.

You may optionally elect to have applicants provide you with a resume along with a completed application. Other sources of information may include letters of recommendation and copies of awards, transcripts, and professional citations. While these documents can be helpful in deciding between two equally qualified candidates, they are no substitute for a completed application form in protecting you against claims of hiring discrimination.

The Screening Process

Review application packages as you receive them. Place those that do not meet the advertised qualifications in a separate pile from those that do meet the selection criteria. Record which qualifications the applicant did not meet. When the closing date has passed, review the qualified applicants objectively. Select the five or six best qualified applicants to schedule for interviews. Record the reasons why you didn't select the other applicants. Ensure that your reasoning is as objective as possible and based solely on selecting the best qualified applicant for the job. For example, do not discriminate against applicants who are from a town that rivals your high school's football team.

Once you have selected which applicants to interview, contact each of them to verify their continued interest in the position, and to set a date and time for their interviews.

Once you have selected which applicants to interview, contact each of them to verify their continued interest in the position, and to set a date and time for their interviews. While one or more applicants may withdraw for various reasons, try to interview at least three to allow an objective comparison of each person's qualifications.

How to Conduct an Interview

Interview each applicant under the same conditions and in the same way. Conduct the interviews in a place where there will be no interruptions or distractions. Make sure the atmosphere is nonthreatening to allow a free flow of communication. It is a good idea to have a third party present during the interview to prevent accusations of sexual harassment or misconduct. Use the job description to direct you through the interview process as you become familiar with the qualifications and strengths of each applicant in relation to the specific job.

Prepare for the interviews by deciding what questions to ask and what types of information to elicit from the applicant. Determine exactly what you need to know and avoid asking forbidden questions that could become the basis for hiring discrimination. Use a checklist, if necessary, to ensure that you stay in focus during the interview. Ask each applicant the same general questions. You can use one of four basic types of interview—the structured, informal, stress, or panel interview.

A structured interview relies on preselected questions asked of each applicant. It is quick and consistent, but lacks flexibility. It is suitable as an initial screening interview.

An informal interview occurs in a far more relaxed atmosphere and can be nearly conversational in manner. This type of interview requires more skill and usually takes a great deal more time than a structured interview. By asking open-ended, nonjudgmental questions, you can establish a flow of information from your applicants about their expectations, qualifications, and abilities. In this type of interview, you can gain information from applicants that you cannot legally request.

Use a stress interview to screen applicants for jobs where calmness under pressure is particularly desirable. Such an interview may be useful in eliminating candidates from consideration. The questions asked in a stress interview require the applicants to respond to hypothetical situations, describe past experiences, or discuss their relative strengths or weaknesses. Successful applicants usually require a follow-up interview to further determine their qualifications.

> Use a stress interview to screen applicants for jobs where calmness under pressure is particularly desirable.

A panel interview is efficient when a group or committee is responsible for filling a position. The panel is headed by a single individual who keeps the panel focused. Appearing before a panel allows all hiring members to see each applicant under similar conditions.

After you have finished an interview, take the time to record what happened. Using notes you took during the interview as a guide, record the applicant's responses to your questions as well as your observations about the applicant's demeanor and characteristics. Include an appraisal of that individual's qualifications for the position and suitability for employment with your company. Also make note of negative characteristics, if any.

Handling the Background Check

After the interview, you will want to do a background check. Obtain permission to contact past employers, educators, family members, and references from the applicant early in the selection process. Most employers include an authorization statement in the application form. Refusal to grant permission for the employer to investigate can be reason to reject an application for employment.

The best approach in verifying application information and checking references is to call past employers and references directly. Speaking to a person on the telephone usually results in more detailed information with less likelihood of misunderstanding. Restrict your questions to verifying information given on the application and to gaining impressions of the applicant's work habits and qualifications. Collect information only from sources authorized by the applicant, and take care to avoid questions relating to the applicant's physical or mental health.

Generally, references provided by past employers, educators, and coworkers are more useful than those obtained from friends, neighbors, and relatives. The former are more likely to have observed the applicant's work habits while the latter may simply be doing the applicant a favor rather than providing an objective appraisal.

Keep in mind, you assume liability for information that your receive during the background checks. Therefore, avoid basing your hiring decision solely on information given during the verification process.

When Testing a Job Applicant

Avoid basing your hiring decision solely on information given during the verification process.

Occasionally, it may be appropriate to include testing as a part of the applicant screening process. When using testing as part of the recruitment process, all applicants must take the same test under the same conditions. Some types of testing may include aptitude, achievement, situational, personality, drug, polygraph, and honesty testing. You must carefully consider which types of testing you will conduct, if any. It is not always appropriate to test applicants.

Testing is sometimes useful in filling certain positions. For instance, you may wish to test an applicant's typing speed if a specific typing proficiency is a job requirement. Drug testing is allowable provided the test cannot detect prescribed medication. If it can, you must make an offer of employment before conducted the testing. You may require a test for HIV only when there is reasonable risk of an exchange of bodily fluids between employees. Remember that it is illegal to discriminate against persons with HIV. You may use "paper-and-pencil honesty" testing when prospective employees will handle money or have access to pilferable equipment. Testing is always inappropriate when it results in hiring discrimination. You must always administer it fairly and apply it correctly and appropriately. Only allow qualified professionals to conduct testing. Ensure all testing conforms to the 1978 Guidelines on Uniform Employment Selection Procedures as adopted by the Equal Employment Opportunity Commission.

Alternatives to Hiring Employees

There are alternatives to hiring through applications and interviews, including contracting to independent agents, hiring temporaries from an agency, or leasing employees. Each method offers advantages over conventional methods, including handling less paperwork and lower employee costs.

> A rule of thumb is that a contractor provides a service or a product while an employee provides labor in a structured way.

Using Independent Contractors

If the work you need done can be accomplished away from your business or outside normal business hours, an independent contractor may work best for you. For instance, suppose you need standard bookkeeping accomplished each week. A private bookkeeper can complete this work at his or her place of business on a weekly basis—usually for a set fee. You save the expense of providing the bookkeeper with office space and equipment. The fee you pay is your only expense. All overhead employee costs such as federal, state, and Social Security taxes as well as the paperwork required to collect and deposit those taxes are borne by the contractor. You need only file IRS Form MISC-1099 as required by the IRS.

The Fair Labor Standards Act (FLSA) defines employer-employee relationships. The distinction between employee and contractor is important and you are required to properly classify such workers. For instance, if you provide office space or equipment and set specific work hours, the IRS may consider the contractor to be an employee. You must then collect and file taxes for that person. A rule of thumb is that a contractor provides a service or a product while an employee provides labor in a structured way. Refer back to Chapter 4 for more information on dealing with independent contractors in your state.

Temporary Agencies to the Rescue

Temporary agencies rent employees, typically for periods from half a day to several years. A temporary employee frequently possesses characteristics not found in a regular employee. They possess qualifications beyond their job description. They possess a wide range of experience. They can be available on very short notice.

Situations that warrant hiring temporary employees include conducting inventory for tax purposes, sudden increases in business production, or the temporary loss of a permanent employee due to illness, pregnancy, or military recall. The temporary agency will normally bill you on a weekly basis. The fee you pay to an agency usually covers all employee expenses.

Employee Leasing as an Option

Employee leasing, also called contract staffing, is a relatively new idea in business. An agency provides your business with all employees and handles all personnel management concerns from hiring to firing. You start to realize savings over the normal hiring process when you lease more than five employees. The benefit to the employee is that the leasing agency typically manages a much larger workforce than your business will and, therefore, is able to provide a better, more diverse benefits package.

Keep in mind, when you hire an employee, provide a federal Form W-4, Employee Withholding Allowance Certificate for the employee to complete and return to you prior to paying the first payroll for the employee. You may obtain forms from your IRS district office. You will receive copies of the forms and tax withholding tables and instructions from the IRS when you register with your state's employment office.

A sample of Form W-4 is located in Appendix A. Refer to Appendix B for the address and phone number of the IRS district office nearest you.

Policy and procedures are predetermined responses to employee-related problems.

Your Company's Policy and Procedures

Policy and procedures are predetermined responses to employee-related problems. Important advantages are gained by setting and writing company policies before a problem occurs that requires policy response. This handbook will help you do the following:

- Provide written guidance for handling employees;
- Communicate your business rules and expectations to your employees;
- Communicate your business approach and philosophy;
- Protect your business from litigation; and
- Ensure all problems are handled consistently.

The process of developing a cohesive set of policies and procedures for your business will lead you to firmly review your goals and business philosophy. This process will be particularly helpful if you haven't yet considered a set of policies. Some policies will be required by law. Others will be extensions of your personal approach to business. In either case, you will want to be certain that each policy is accurate, complete, and reflects the best interests of you and your company.

While nearly any issue can be addressed as a matter of policy, there are a few that are basic to any policy manual or handbook. In most cases, these policies were developed in response to federal regulations, so it is prudent to use them as the foundation of your policy manual. Some of these "hot" policies include:

- Equal employment opportunity
- Equal pay
- Sexual harassment
- Substance abuse
- Smoking
- Safety
- Termination
- Leaves of absence
- Use of company time, equipment, or resources

Your company policy should prohibit discriminatory practices in hiring, promoting, demoting, or firing employees.

Equal Employment Opportunity

Equal employment opportunity is mandated by federal law under the Civil Rights Act of 1964 (CRA) and the Americans with Disabilities Act of 1990 (ADA), as well as other clarifying legislation. These laws prohibit employment discrimination based on race, religion, color, national origin, age, gender, or sexual orientation, and physical or mental disability. Your company policy should address these issues directly and prohibit discriminatory practices in hiring, promoting, demoting, or firing employees. Additionally, this policy should prohibit discrimination in pay, compensation, working conditions, and working assignments.

Equal Pay

The Equal Pay Act of 1963 is an amendment to the Fair Labor Standards Act of 1938 (FLSA). It prohibits unequal pay for equal work to members of the opposite sex. For instance, paying a male supervisor a higher wage than a female supervisor when both possess similar skills, tenure, experience, and performance levels constitutes wage or sexual discrimination under this act. This is equally true of the reverse scenario.

When preparing company policy statements regarding equal pay and equal opportunity, seek the advice from professional sources to ensure that you are complying with all federal, state, and local guidelines.

Sexual Harassment

There are two types of sexual harassment, quid pro quo and hostile environment. In a quid pro quo sexual harassment case, employment conditions are based on the individual submitting to sexual harassment, abuse or conditions. Employment conditions include promotions, demotions, hiring, firing, and preferential treatment in job assignments, opportunities, and perks.

On the other hand, hostile environment sexual harassment includes behavior that is unwelcome to the recipient which includes requests for sexual favors, exposure to sexually explicit jokes, innuendoes, telephone calls, faxes, email or other forms of visual, aural or written communication. When these conditions are so prevalent they produce an uncomfortable working environment for the recipient, sexual harassment exists.

Sexual harassment is not gender specific; both men and women can be victimized by sexual harassment, usually by members of the opposite sex, but also by same-sex coworkers. In the case of quid pro quo sexual harassment, the employer is liable regardless of whether or not he or she knew what was happening.

Employers are usually free of liability for hostile environment sexual harassment unless it can be shown they knew or should have known that a hostile environment existed.

Your company policy should clearly state a zero-tolerance for sexual harassment.

Your company policy should clearly state a zero-tolerance for sexual harassment. You may want to address punitive and corrective measures in the event a claim of sexual harassment occurs. Make a clear channel for reporting abuses to the appropriate management resource. Consider formal training for your employees during orientation and on a periodic basis thereafter.

Office romances and flirtations do not constitute sexual harassment provided the following conditions are met:

- The romance is consensual,
- The romance does not spill over into the work environment, and
- No quid pro quo condition can be inferred or implied.

Even meeting these conditions is not a guarantee that accusations of sexual harassment will not be made if the relationship ends poorly. As an employer, any interference in the personal lives of your employees may be considered an invasion of privacy. Thus, word your policy to insist on professionalism and decorum in the workplace.

Substance Abuse

Drug or alcohol impairment results in lowered performance levels, production losses, and higher rates of absenteeism. Employees who engage in substance abuse are four times more likely to have accidents and five times more likely to file workers' compensation claims.

If an employee is impaired while on the job, he or she represents a safety risk to themselves as well as to other employees. In addition, if they represent your company to the public or to customers, your business is not being presented in the best light. Your company's personal liability insurance may not protect in the case of the former, and no insurance coverage exists to protect you from the latter.

If an employee is impaired while on the job, he or she represents a safety risk to themselves as well as to other employees.

Company-sponsored events, such as picnics, dinners, and outings, may invite abuse, particularly if alcohol is served. Your policy must address these issues to protect your company from litigation. In addition, your policy must clearly define behavior that is unacceptable on the job, such as:

- Drug or alcohol impairment while on the job,
- Possession or use of drugs or alcohol on the job, and
- Sale of drugs or alcohol on business property during business hours.

Clearly explain disciplinary actions for violations of substance abuse policy. Be careful not to discipline an employee for addiction. Addiction is a medical condition beyond the employee's control that requires outside, professional assistance to correct.

Consider drug and alcohol awareness training for managers or for all employees as a method to prevent substance abuse. Require managers to be aware of substance abuse indicators and to intervene when appropriate, even if substance abuse is not specifically suspected. You may even require that employees inform you when they are taking prescribed medication that may cause drowsiness or interfere with the operation of machinery.

Smoking

Smoking reform laws have dramatically changed the way America works. While smoking on the job was once the norm, most companies now prohibit it and require smokers to either go outside or retire to a specially ventilated area to smoke. These policies were largely enacted in response to legislation, despite vigorous opposition from smokers. The majority of legislation has been based on clinical studies linking second-hand smoke to health risks for nonsmokers. But smoking also presents risks to the smoker in the workplace beyond the health risk of smoking itself.

Smokers have a higher absentee rate and get sick more often than nonsmokers. Smoking on the job diverts attention from the task at hand, increasing the risk of accidents. Smoking takes time, resulting in a lower productivity rate when compared to nonsmokers. Smokers statistically file more workers' compensation and health insurance claims than nonsmokers. Taken in aggregate, smokers represent a significantly higher expense than nonsmokers. Yet many states specifically prohibit discrimination against smokers.

Smoking on the job diverts attention from the task at hand, increasing the risk of accidents.

In your company policy handbook, address smoking as a health risk that violates the rights of nonsmokers while preserving smokers' rights. Use company policy to define the rights of each group. Ensure that designated smoking areas are adequately ventilated. Designate specific areas and times for smoking which do not interfere with productivity. Ensure that nonsmokers receive a comparable amount of time away from their workstations so smoking is not perceived to be a privilege.

Safety

As an employer, you have a duty to provide a safe working environment for your employees. This duty has both an ethical and a legal basis. As discussed in Chapter 4, the Occupational Safety and Health Act (OSHA) as well as similar laws at the federal, state, and local level regulate many aspects of business safety and require reporting of workplace accidents and illnesses.

Your business may present specific risks to your employees that may result in physical dangers, hazardous or toxic materials, or environmental conditions such as excessive heat or noise. You must provide protective equipment and training to employees exposed to these risks.

Most risks can be identified through careful evaluation of the workplace by an objective individual. Professional evaluations are available at little or no cost. Your insurance carrier, state department of labor office, or even local OSHA office can provide assistance. Further, the local office of the U.S. Small Business Administration (SBA) or small business development center (SBDC) can provide you with referrals to safety professionals. Finally, professional safety consultants can be found in most metropolitan areas. Keep in mind, however, that hiring a consultant can be expensive. Refer to Appendix B and Appendix C to learn how you can contact your local SBA office or nearest SBDC.

You can word your safety policy so that unsafe practices by any employee are strictly prohibited. Accident report forms should be readily available to all employees and filled out promptly after each on-the-job accident. Your policy should also define disciplinary actions as well as provide a means for reporting unsafe conditions or practices.

Many companies have formed active safety committees whose duties include safety monitoring, accident investigation, and recommendations for handling unsafe practices or conditions. Further, large companies are incorporating wellness topics into the training programs that address such issues as alcoholism, smoking cessation, and stress reduction.

Termination

A well-written termination policy may save you from unnecessary litigation at the hands of a former, disgruntled employee. Sadly, not all employees are models of perfection and, sooner or later, you will encounter an employee who is a frequent discipline problem.

Your termination policy should specifically define which behaviors will result in immediate termination, such as:

- Theft of company property
- Crime on company property
- Violence against another employee

> A well-written termination policy may save you from unnecessary litigation at the hands of a former, disgruntled employee.

You might also want your company policy to include an employment-at-will clause. Employment-at-will means employment can be terminated at any time by either the employer or the employee for any reason.

Your termination policy should also address lesser infractions that could lead to termination if a behavior isn't corrected. This part of the policy must define procedures to be followed to correct inadequate or errant behavior. Then, strictly follow these procedures to protect your company from litigation.

Ironically, there is a longer list of unlawful reasons for terminating employment, most of which have developed from legal precedents. These include, but are not limited to retaliatory discharge, breach of contract, discrimination, and bad faith. The National Labor Relations Act (NLRA), as well as numerous other pieces of legislation, are increasingly protecting employees from wrongful discharge. You should consult with an attorney prior to terminating an employee whenever legal precedents are unclear.

Certain laws apply to terminated employees with some minor variations from state to state. You should pay a terminated employee up-to-date at the time of termination, including all money owed for accrued vacation time or sick time. This is a good time to collect keys, identification cards, and company property.

Leaves of Absence

Employees may encounter various reasons for requiring extended leaves of absence. Keep in mind, brief absences of ten days or less should be considered personal leave rather than a leave of absence.

FAMILY LEAVE

The Family and Medical Leave Act of 1993 (FMLA) permits employees to take up to 12 weeks of unpaid leave each year for the birth or adoption of a child; to attend to a seriously ill child, spouse, or parent; or for serious personal illness. As an employer you must guarantee that your employees can return to their same jobs or a comparable job and must continue health care coverage, if provided, during the leave period. This law is regulated by the Equal Employment Opportunity Commission (EEOC) and applies to employers with 50 or more employees within a 75-mile radius. The law does not apply to employees with less than one year on the job or who have not worked at least 1,250 hours or at least 25 hours per week in the past year. Workers who are on family leave are not eligible for unemployment benefits or other government compensation. To learn how your state handles family and medical leaves, refer to Chapter 4.

Workers who are on family leave are not eligible for unemployment benefits or other government compensation.

MILITARY LEAVE

The Uniformed Services Employment and Re-employment Rights Act of 1994 requires that military leave must be granted for up to five years. The employer must rehire the employee if that person was inducted into or voluntarily enlisted in the armed forces of the United States. The law also protects reservists and National Guard members who are called to active duty. See Appendix C for the address of Employer Support of the Guard and Reserve. The national organization can either help you or direct you to a local representative who can answer questions about employer and employee rights and responsibilities.

Use of Company Time, Equipment, or Resources

The temptation to use company property or equipment for personal benefit is fairly understandable. Your business is likely to be able to afford equipment that is bigger, faster, stronger, or better than home equipment. The employee who types a garage sale flyer and makes 50 copies during his or her lunch hour has still imposed some degree of wear and tear on company equipment. Similarly, sending or receiving personal faxes, using the company phone for personal business, or borrowing a tool set to work on the family car all constitute misuse of company property for personal gain.

You may decide to take a no-harm-done approach to some of these abuses, but small abuses invite larger ones, and a thousand minor expenses add up to a significant loss over the course of a year. Conversely, you don't want to impose a harsh, prohibitive atmosphere that makes employees feel uncomfortable working for you.

Your policy should make it clear that all equipment, supplies, and services were purchased for the benefit of the company and that minor theft of services or supplies is not in the company's best interest. At your discretion, you may allow provision for employees to check equipment out over night for personal use. However, such practices invite theft and make tax depreciation of eligible equipment difficult to determine.

Employee Orientation

Now that you have a good idea of the major issues to include in your company policy manual, you will want to ensure that your employees understand the importance of adhering to these procedures. One way to open up a clear line of communication is to formally acquaint each new employee on the day the employee joins your business. As part of your employee orientation make sure you discuss the following with them:

- The driving force—overall vision and spirit—of your business;
- The structure and organization of your business, identifying the key players and major divisions;
- The various employee policies, with a focus on essentials like starting and quitting times, breaks, meal times, sick days, vacation days, and timecards; and
- The benefits package your business offers and its participation eligibility dates.

By establishing this open line of communication upfront, your employees will feel more valued and will get a clear picture of where they fit in.

One way to open up a clear line of communication is to formally acquaint each new employee on the day the employee joins your business.

Monitoring Your Employees' Performance

A performance review and improvement plan are valuable tools to ensure that employees stay on the job and remain a productive and viable part of your workforce. Firing employees is costly to your business. Your losses include the time and effort expended in training, making them a part of your workforce, and attempting to assist them in overcoming deficiencies. Finally, the time you spend when terminating an employee represents a significant loss.

The Importance of Performance Reviews

A performance review is a process used by business managers or owners to evaluate and document an employee's job performance. To be effective, performance reviews must be fair and impartial. Administer them following the schedule set forth in your employee handbook or other company policy document.

> A performance review is a process used by business managers or owners to evaluate and document an employee's job performance.

Effective performance reviews, based on job requirements, provide a systematic record of an employee's job performance. This continuous record gives the employee valuable feedback and encourages improvement. It provides fair documentation of strengths and weaknesses, simplifies management decisions regarding raises, promotions, transfers, demotions, and terminations. Complete records may even protect a company in the event of legal actions initiated by a discontented or former employee.

It is important to use standardized methods and formats for all performance reviews. You will want to rate all employees according to a set of consistent standards. The 1978 Guidelines on Uniform Employee Selection Procedures prohibits basing performance reviews on discriminatory practices or biases concerning racial, ethnic, religious, or gender preferences.

Most employers conduct performance reviews annually, usually during the anniversary month of the employee's start date, while a few prefer scheduling them semiannually. Schedule several reviews during, and one at the end of, the employee's initial probationary period. These reviews provide feedback to the new employee on his or her conformance with job requirements as well as company policy, and serve to identify problem areas early in the employer-employee relationship. They also provide information on which to base a decision to terminate a new employee, if necessary, at the end of a probationary period.

Preventing Performance Review Problems

When properly and fairly administered, performance reviews are a valuable management tool. However, even a well-designed program is subject to problems resulting from human error. An awareness of these potential problems will allow you to take steps to prevent them, and will help maintain the consistency and fairness of your program.

When properly and fairly administered, performance reviews are a valuable management tool.

Managers Rate Employees Differently

Managers will not rate employees in the same way. Some tend to see all employees in the most positive light, while others take a more negative approach. Ideally, you want everyone involved in rating employees to do so in a balanced, even-handed way that uniformly recognizes strengths as well as weaknesses. Periodic discussion of the review process with your managers is the best method of ensuring fairness and objectivity in the performance review process. Some employers use a dual review method. The employee's supervisor and a supervisor from another area who is familiar with the employee's work each evaluate the employee separately.

Unclear Rating Standards

Unclear rating standards result in an inconsistent performance review program. Poorly defined standards result in a situation where one manager defines good attendance as zero absenteeism, and another manager defines good attendance as no more than three absences. Performance standards must be clear to supervisors and workers alike. Define all terms and avoid vague generalities when defining standards.

Last In, First Out

It is natural for reviewers to remember recent events best; therefore, rating an employee's performance based on work accomplished during recent months rather than during the entire evaluation period. A significant improvement in performance as evaluation time approaches is a good indication that this problem exists in your review process. To prevent that from happening, encourage supervisors to frequently notice performance trends and to collect performance data throughout the evaluation period. Examples of pertinent information include letters of recommendation or congratulation, voluntary participation on committees, taking on new leadership positions, and completing additional training. Also, make note of minor infractions, tardiness, and informal counseling.

THE HALO EFFECT

An employee who is neat, well-mannered, and cheerful seems to be brighter and more capable than a casually dressed, introverted employee. This "halo effect" is a hindrance to objective performance appraisal. Reviewers must be alert to this and ensure that they are evaluating real performance rather than perceived performance. Train your reviewers to be aware of the halo effect and provide them with clear-cut standards to use in appraising performance.

The Documentation Process

Document all performance reviews consistently using a standardized performance review report. The performance review report provides a permanent record of the performance review, its timeliness, and its fairness. It is best to use a standardized form when conducting performance reviews. The report form should be general enough to be applicable to all employees, yet specific enough to provide a clear appraisal that generates useful management information. Most forms combine a scaled rating system with space for amplifying comments. A sample performance review is located in Appendix A for your use.

The performance review report provides a permanent record of the performance review, its timeliness, and its fairness.

The employee and the supervisor fill out the performance review report through cooperative effort. The employee should sign the report to indicate that he or she has read it and understands its content. Keep in mind, signing does not necessarily indicate that the employee agrees with the report. After completing and signing the report, the supervisor forwards it to upper management for review, if applicable. After review, file the report in the employee's personnel record.

In cases where the employee disagrees with the content of the performance appraisal, you should have a procedure in place that allows fair rebuttal. Typically, an employee can rebut in written form to an upper manager. After review, the rebuttal becomes a part of the employee's personnel file.

Counseling—An Opportunity to Improve

Counseling is similar to the performance review, but differs in that it occurs as a result of a change in performance. Generally, employees view counseling as being negative because it most often occurs as a result of poor job performance. Management's role when this happens is to help the employee understand how his or her performance is inadequate.

Then, you can work with that individual to identify the source of the problem and recommend ways to correct it.

Ideally, both management and the employee will approach counseling as an opportunity to improve rather than as a punitive measure. It is important to state the goal of the counseling at the beginning of the meeting. Remember that your employee is a valued asset who has contributed time and effort to your business. Your goal is to keep all your employees productive and motivated.

Ideally, both management and the employee will approach counseling as an opportunity to improve rather than as a punitive measure.

Poor performance may be job related as a result of poorly defined policy, personality conflict, politics, or environment. An employee suffering from eye strain from his or her computer terminal may perceive that management is uncaring, particularly if the condition has persisted over time. Timely counseling in an open and supportive atmosphere will allow you to identify these problems and correct them.

Management will rarely intervene directly when degraded performance is the result of external problems, such as family difficulties, substance abuse, or financial woes. In these cases, refer the employee to an outside professional agency. A referral gives the employee the clear message that he or she is a valued asset. Arrange for a follow-up meeting to inquire about the employee's progress in coping with the problem and provide feedback on performance issues.

Your Disciplinary Action Policy

The time to decide how to handle a discipline problem comes long before it occurs. Disciplinary actions must follow a prescribed format in accordance with your company policy manual. This is a case where preparation will save you a great deal of trouble in the long run. Decide which behaviors you will consider as minor infractions and which ones you will consider to be grounds for immediate suspension or termination. Develop a policy for dealing with each of these two types of infraction.

Typical minor infractions include tardiness, waste of supplies, arguing with coworkers, or violating company policy. While your company policy manual is the basis for determining infractions, leave room in your discipline policy for supervisors to use good judgment in determining when violations have occurred.

Your disciplinary action policy is a series of specific steps. Those steps include, but are not limited to a verbal warning, counseling with a written warning, an improvement plan, review, suspension, and termination. The process takes time, but when compared to the cost of training and nurturing a new employee, it is worth the effort to save an otherwise good employee.

Giving Warnings

As part of your disciplinary action policy, you will need to decide the basis and process of giving warnings. Warnings can come in a verbal or written form. A verbal warning given when an infraction occurs will send a clear message to your employee that the specified behavior is inappropriate and unacceptable. Give verbal warnings in a friendly, yet firm manner. Most people want to do well and will respond immediately to friendly guidance. When a behavior ends with a verbal warning, place a note to that effect in the employee's personnel file.

A written warning is the next step in the process. It is a formal counseling session with the employee, documented on a standardized company form. The form will include a detailed explanation of the infraction and the expected behavior. It will provide space for the employee to explain extenuating or mitigating circumstances. It will suggest methods for the employee to correct the deficiency, set a time limit for improvement, and explain the consequences for failure to improve. As a supervisor or manager, you will discuss the written warning with your employee and clearly explain each portion. At the conclusion of the counseling session, the employee should sign the warning to indicate that he or she completely understands it. Then, forward the warning to upper management for review, if applicable, and file it in the employee's personnel record.

As part of your disciplinary action policy, you will need to decide the basis and process of giving warnings.

Handling Suspensions

When an employee does not respond to warnings, suspension should follow. Suspension of an employee is a serious matter and is reserved for only the most serious disciplinary problems. Suspension without pay is a clear message to the employee that he or she must change problem behavior or risk termination. Your goal is to retain otherwise valuable employees by giving them every opportunity to change.

As with counseling and written warnings, it is important to keep detailed records of your personnel actions. Remember, you are attempting to correct a performance problem, not a personality problem.

Detailed records will clearly show that you acted appropriately and dealt with the problem fairly and professionally. Use a formal suspension notice to record this action.

A suspension notice is a standardized form that should be completed, dated, and signed by an employee's supervisor. A notice should include:

- A description of the suspension action,
- A statement of the reason for the suspension, and
- A list of the corrective actions required.

The form should include space for the employee to sign to acknowledge understanding and receipt of the suspension notice. File the original in the employee's personnel folder and provide copies to the employee and the employee's supervisor.

A suspension is not a substitute for termination.

A suspension is not a substitute for termination. You cannot suspend an employee indefinitely. So be certain that you include a specific ending point for the suspension in the description of the suspension action, usually a period lasting from several days to several weeks. After the employee returns to work following suspension, any further infractions normally lead to termination.

Take Caution with Disciplinary Terminations

The practice of employment-at-will and the right to terminate an employee for good or just cause are being increasingly challenged in the courts. There is a growing list of legal precedents for wrongful discharge of an employee. The list includes such concepts as retaliatory discharge, breach of written contract, breach of implied contract, and discrimination based on sex, age, or disability.

As an employer, your best defense is to ensure that your employee handbook and company policies make the employment at will doctrine perfectly clear. Further, ensure that the wording of these documents does not imply permanent employment.

Observe the following guidelines when terminating an employee.

- Only terminate an employee based on documented substandard performance or misconduct and only in accordance with established equal opportunity doctrine.
- Handle terminations discreetly, privately, and professionally.
- Ensure the employee receives all pay earned to date.
- Make sure that all company policies, including performance review, counseling, grievance, and appeal policies are followed, when applicable.

Use a standardized company form to document the termination. Make sure the form includes the reason for termination and refers to supporting records and documents. Provide a checklist on the form to ensure that correct termination procedures are followed and that the employee's rights are observed. Following these recommendations does not guarantee protection from a wrongful discharge suit. The law is changing continuously and your best insurance is to consult with your attorney when you prepare your company policy manual. Stay abreast of changes in the law and keep your manual current with legislation.

Write a separate policy in your personnel manual for handling termination due to misconduct, such as theft or destruction of company property, fighting, criminal activity, or continuous unexcused absence. Carefully define those conditions that will result in either immediate termination or termination following suspension. When you terminate someone for misconduct, take care to observe all the precautions and requirements of normal termination procedures. Fully document the termination decision and process, including a description of the type of misconduct that occurred. Include documentation that proves or supports the determination of misconduct.

Require resigning employees to give notice of their intent to resign whenever possible.

Other Types of Terminations

Termination also results from other actions such as resignation and layoff due to restructuring or the elimination of a position. These terminations follow the same basic procedures as other types of termination. Fully document the circumstances of the termination, treat the departing employee with dignity and professionalism, and provide the employee with all earned pay before his or her departure.

Require resigning employees to give notice of their intent to resign whenever possible. Sufficient notice allows you time to complete all administrative paperwork, verify pay and benefit requirements, conduct an exit interview, and start looking for a replacement employee. Generally, two weeks or ten working days is sufficient notice. A departing employee frequently feels more free to express dissatisfaction with working conditions, and an exit interview is a valuable means of getting feedback about the company, the working environment, and management practices.

Layoffs result from a reduction in the workforce and the elimination of a position through restructuring. Notify employees of an impending layoff and the reasons for it as far in advance as possible. Carefully consider which employees will be laid off, following established policy guidelines. Consider company needs, seniority issues, and the abilities of individual employees. When possible, consider reassigning individuals to other areas for which they are qualified.

Benefits Packages

Benefits fall into two categories: those that are legally required and those at the discretion of the employer. Legally required benefits include payment of Social Security taxes, workers' compensation insurance, and unemployment insurance. Discretionary benefits include anything from medical insurance to free tickets to sporting events. Virtually anything of value that you provide or make available to your workforce qualifies as a discretionary benefit. The only limitation is your imagination.

Benefits fall into two categories: those that are legally required and those at the discretion of the employer.

Keep in mind, in today's job market, employees expect a benefits package along with their salary or hourly wage. Typical benefits include medical insurance coverage, accidental death and disability coverage, and some form of retirement plan. The cost of these benefits increases each year, but you can generally expect to pay approximately 25 to 35 percent of the wage expenses for each employee. This means that an employee who earns $7.50 per hour will represent an hourly expense of as much as $10.15. Generally, employees are not aware of the costs associated with providing benefits.

You may decide that the nature of your business does not support the cost of providing employee benefits. This is particularly true under the following conditions:

- Your workforce is largely unskilled;
- All or most of your employees are part-time or temporary; or
- Your nearest competitors are not providing a benefits package.

However, as your business grows and you require a larger, more skilled workforce, a comprehensive benefits package will help to attract the best qualified employees to your business.

If you decide to include a retirement plan as part of your employee benefits package, make sure it is in sync with the Employee Retirement Income Security Act (ERISA). This act governs how certain pension plans and welfare plans are administered. Pension plans include certain retirement plans, profit sharing, stock option plans, and individual retirement accounts (IRAs). Welfare plans include most types of employee insurance such as health, disability, life, and accidental death coverage.

Recent shifts in cultural values are subtly changing the way today's workforce views benefits. Tomorrow's employees are likely to value a clean and pleasant working environment, state-of-the-art equipment, and a four-day workweek over tickets to the next big game. So before planning a benefits package, take the time to survey the needs and desires of your employees.

Chapter Wrap-Up

If your business will have employees, you will need to carefully manage the people you hire. Just like other critical investments for your business, the time you take to hire and retain top-quality employees is an investment that can pay huge dividends or seriously affect your ability to make a profit.

Effective human resources management is a multi-faceted process, which requires you to stay informed and proactive

- Develop thorough job descriptions before you announce an opening.
- Understand anti-discrimination laws, so you know which questions to avoid on written applications and during interviews.
- Know how to screen job applicants and track your evaluations after both formal and informal interviews.
- Properly acquaint and train new employees, so they know exactly what your business expects of them.
- Review and monitor your employees' performance and foster their existing skills support their developing new ones.

A good human resources package means having well-defined company policies and procedures.

A good human resources package means having well-defined company policies and procedures. In short, create a company policy and procedures manual or an employee handbook and make sure each employee gets a copy. Document that employees have read your handbook by having them sign a paper indicating they understand all the policies and procedures outlined in the manual. In general, make sure your company policy manual covers the following:

- Benefits
- Career opportunities
- Company background
- Employee evaluation procedures
- Employee grievance procedures

- Employee safety
- Employee/nanagement relations
- General policies and procedures
- Pay rates and schedules

Remember, the people who will work for you will communicate the character and quality of your business and its product or service. Build a team that will help you and your employees make the most of your enterprise. For specific state and federal government regulations related to your business, refer back to Chapter 4.

Build a team that will help you and your employees make the most of your enterprise.

CHAPTER 11

Insurance Matters

Getting into business is inherently a risk. There is no guarantee of success. However, you can reduce risks by making informed decisions which can reduce the possibility of loss due to the risk, eliminate the chance of a particular risk, or insure against loss due to a risk. The most common way to guard against many risks is by obtaining insurance.

Insurance is a necessary business expense. You need insurance to protect you and your business from hazards, such as fire or other disasters, crime, general liability, or an interruption of business. As an employer, you are required to purchase workers' compensation insurance and may additionally choose to provide health, life, or disability benefits for your employees. This chapter introduces you to the numerous type of insurance coverage to help you make an informed decision.

Not all risks are insurable and, in some cases, the cost of insuring is too great. You will assume the risk and hope that you do not have a loss that is not covered by insurance. Your first step in evaluating your need for insurance is to assess the risks to your business.

What Is Risk Assessment?

Risk assessment is the process of determining the risks your business has and what you should do about them. You will have to strike a balance between the expense of being covered against every eventuality and the risks associated with having insufficient insurance coverage. By critically evaluating each aspect of your business and considering its relative importance to your business, you will lay the groundwork for determining your insurance needs. This will save you a great deal of time and money as you shop for the best coverage at the best price.

To assess risk you must determine where losses can occur by reviewing every aspect of your business to identify which people, property, or conditions you need to continue to operate. Evaluate safety issues and concerns, your crime risk, and the potential for fire or other disaster. Evaluate the financial condition of your business and decide how much loss your business can absorb without risking failure. Consider temporary closures, downtime, inventory, cash flow, borrowing power, and other pertinent variables. Prioritize and categorize each potential loss based on its severity and potential frequency.

Risk assessment is the process of determining the risks your business has and what you should do about them.

Four Ways to Handle Risks

You will handle risks in one of four ways: elimination, reduction, retention, and transference.

- *Elimination.* This means that you decide to drop a product or service that exposed you to a particular risk. For example, you would eliminate the potential for a delivery van accident with potential damage to your vehicle, driver, another driver and other property if you no longer delivered your product or only provided service for items that would be brought to your place of business by a customer.
- *Reduction.* This entails modifying a potential loss by continuing to assume the risk. However, you change an element of the risk that would reduce the likelihood or the severity of a loss.
- *Retention.* You understand the potentials for the risk, but because the likelihood of a loss or because the cost of insuring against the loss or changing your business are higher than you can afford or want to pay, you assume the full consequences of the potential loss.
- *Transference.* When you obtain insurance to cover a risk, you transfer the risk to the insurance company. The company is insuring

many risks and thus spreads the cost of the consequences of a loss across many insured companies or individuals.

Each alternative imposes different levels of cost or potential cost. Your task is to weigh the cost of each method against the potential risk to your business. The example below, while simplistic, clearly demonstrates the application of each method.

For example, suppose your business is a feed and grain store. You determine that one of your risks is loss of inventory due to spoilage from mice. So, you choose to eliminate a frequent and severe mouse problem by periodically hiring an exterminator. If mice are frequent visitors, but don't spoil much inventory, you may choose to reduce the risk instead by investing in one or more cats. When infestation is infrequent and does not result in much spoilage, you will probably retain the risk and absorb the losses as part of the cost of doing business. A rare, devastating invasion resulting in complete loss of your inventory will lead you to transfer the risk to an insurance carrier. To better understand the four methods of handling risks, consider the following scenario.

> You may have risks that are not insurable.

You own a food processing company with more than 100 products. One of the products requires much more care in preparation than the others because of past problems with a fungus in the food. The food item accounts for only 1 percent of the total sales and less than 1 percent of the profit of the company. To solve the problem, you have several options to choose between.

- *Eliminate the risk.* Discontinue the product; thus, you eliminate the extra care that is required to offer a product that is marginal in profit.
- *Reduce the risk.* Install new equipment that is easier to maintain and monitor and is more reliable than your other equipment.
- *Retain the risk.* Assume that with constant vigilance you will not have a problem with the food item.
- *Transfer the risk.* Purchase a liability insurance policy that will cover the consequences of bad food being purchased and making people sick as well as a recall of the product if such a problem should occur.

The above scenario assumes you have all four options regarding how to handle risks. In many cases, you may have risks that are not insurable. For example, You may be at the end of a road where a flood may cause the road to be impassable during certain times of the year. Although you may obtain flood insurance, the risk is not that you are flooded, only that you can't reach your business because of a flood. Although you may be able to obtain special insurance for such an eventuality, most insurance will not cover this risk.

You may also find that although you can obtain insurance for certain risks, the costs associated with insuring certain risks may be more than the potential loss over a given period. For example, if you want to insure against theft and you believe that the greatest loss you would incur due to theft would be $10,000 you may have to pay $2,000 in premiums per year if you were insuring all items that could be stolen. If you have a loss more than every five years, you would be financially ahead to insure the loss. However, if a loss might occur only once in ten years, you can cover the loss with what you would pay in insurance premiums. Of course, you don't know how often a loss will occur. Be certain that if your business is prone to losses often, either your insurance will be canceled or the premium will be increased.

Insurance is very cost effective if you can obtain low premiums for potentially high losses as in liability insurance.

Insurance is very cost effective if you can obtain low premiums for potentially high losses as in liability insurance. However, the insurance companies will determine if your business has a high potential for liability claims and will charge on the basis of the industry experience for such claims and may even refuse to write insurance because of the potential of high losses.

Other risks normally associated with running your business are not insurable, such as losing a major customer or the cost of raw materials increasing after you have made a bid or set a price for an item you produce. In such cases, you need to determine the potential risks and include solutions into contracts or pricing policies.

Types of Insurance

To start, understand the unique characteristics involved with the two broad classes of insurance—property-casualty insurance and life insurance.

- *Property-casualty insurance.* This type includes property insurance for fire and other hazards and casualty insurance. Workers' compensation is a casualty insurance but also covered under this type of insurance is auto liability, general liability, credit insurance, bonds, boiler and machinery, crime and other miscellaneous casualty.
- *Life insurance.* Both term and whole life policies are available. These types of insurance are used in business where two partners

take insurance out for the other partner so each can buy the other partner's share in case of his or her death.

Property Insurance

As a new business owner, the chances are high that you will need some form of property insurance. If you lease an office or warehouse the lease will probably require you to obtain some type of fire policy. If your product is transported ship via truck or marine vessel you may want a policy to cover potential loss.

Fire insurance is generally thought of as property insurance. There are many types of property insurance. Some are for a direct loss such as the loss due to a fire; others are for consequential losses such as being out of business for a couple of months due to a fire.

> As a new business owner, the chances are high that you will need some form of property insurance.

There are many ways policies can be written and interpreted, but you must determine which of the following you want from your policy:

- Replacement cost (replacing an old item with a new one with no deductions for depreciation);
- A stated loss amount; or
- Actual cash value (what you paid less an amount for depreciation).

There is also a provision in some insurance policies called coinsurance. If you do not insure for at least 80 percent (sometimes 90 percent or 100 percent) of your potential loss, the insurance will only pay the percentage of loss that you have insured of the total potential loss. For example, you may insure a building that has a value of $1,000,000 for $500,000 (thinking that you would not suffer a complete loss of the building and would be willing to take the chance that it would not be a complete loss. If a fire occurred which caused $50,000 damage, the insurer would only pay 50 percent of the $50,000 loss ($500,000 divided by $1,000,000).

In addition, if your building increased in value while you occupied it, and the value at the time of loss was considerably more than when you took out the insurance, the insurer may invoke the coinsurance provision based on the value of the building at the time of loss, not when you became insured. Therefore, you should review your policies regarding the values you insure on an annual basis when the policy is renewed.

If you operate your business out of your home your coverage for losses to your business will be limited with usual homeowners insurance.

In addition, if you conduct part of your business from buildings other than the home, but on the same property as your home, the other buildings and contents will probably not be covered unless you have a separate business policy for them.

Casualty Insurance

Insurance that is not life insurance or property insurance is normally considered casualty insurance. Workers' compensation is a form of casualty insurance and was described above. Other casualty insurance includes automobile and liability insurance.

AUTOMOBILE INSURANCE

If you own or lease a vehicle for your business you should be aware that there are different rules for a business policy than for your personally owned vehicles. As an individual, automobile insurance covers the individual (the named insured) for whatever vehicle the person drives, including rental vehicles. For business insurance, the vehicle is covered for drivers who have permission to use the vehicle. There is also coverage called Drive Other Car Endorsement (B.F.D.O.C.)—which you can get on your company policy to cover you when you are driving a noncompany vehicle if you do not have other personal insurance. As a part of automobile insurance, liability insurance pays for bodily injury or property damage to others due to the use of the automobile.

Insurance that is not life insurance or property insurance is normally considered casualty insurance.

Physical damage insurance is composed of two types of classifications: comprehensive and collision. Comprehensive covers most losses except those caused by collision. It includes vandalism, theft, and broken windshields. Collision covers a loss due to collision of the vehicle with another object.

A third element of automobile insurance is for medical payments. It includes the occupants of either or both vehicles and normally covers medical, dental, surgical, ambulance, and funeral services.

In many states you can obtain uninsured motorist coverage to protect the company against loss due to the lack of insurance of another driver.

A type of insurance called employers nonowned auto and hired auto coverage will protect your company in the event an employee, while on company business, has an accident and may be held liable.

LIABILITY INSURANCE

Liability for a situation occurs in one of three ways:

1. Negligence
2. Statutory law
3. Assumption by contract

There are legal requirements for acts to be defined as negligent and a discussion of the requirements is not in the scope of this book. Virtually every business has a potential for being sued for a negligent act. Therefore, you should carefully determine your potential exposure in this area and locate an insurance company that can insure what might be devastating loss to your company. As an employer you can be held responsible for the actions of one of your employees even though you have taken steps to prevent a situation from occurring.

Statutory law liability occurs when a law has been enacted that creates a legal obligation, such as the requirement to carry workers' compensation insurance or liability regarding products that may be inherently dangerous.

Assumption by contract refers to a hold-harmless agreement in a contract. For example, your lease agreement probably will contain a hold-harmless agreement that requires you to maintain liability insurance and hold the landlord harmless for any accident that may occur on the premises.

There are several forms of liability insurance coverage but many can be combined into one policy or insured individually. Check with your agent regarding potential liability that your company may have and see if the cost of insurance is reasonable for the level of coverage you will receive. If you have a home office and have a homeowners policy with liability coverage, the policy may not cover liability for anyone hurt at your place of business. Check with your agent to see if you need a separate policy for your home office.

There are several forms of liability insurance coverage but many can be combined into one policy or insured individually.

Crime Coverage

Crime is a real threat to many businesses. Virtually all businesses must be aware of employee dishonesty, theft, bad checks, vandalism, and personal injury as daily occurrences. Some businesses have a higher potential for one type of loss rather than another so there are different types of coverage that meet individual needs.

One of the most frequently used coverage for loss of money by employees or others handling cash or accounts in business is through the use of bonds. There are various types of bonds available that protect against theft, embezzlement, loss of money on or off the premises, counterfeit money, and forging. The cost of coverage for such problems may exceed the value of the coverage or you may decide to implement company policies that protect you from such loss. For example, some retail establishments do not accept checks without the customer having a check guarantee card, or they may not accept checks at all.

Even if you have a policy for theft, you many not be able to collect the amount of loss. The policies will generally limit the types of theft for which you can claim against the policy. For example, you probably will not be able to collect on a theft policy if you find that your inventory is actually $10,000 lower than you expected according to your computerized inventory. You may suspect a theft, but there is little likelihood that the insurance company will pay for the loss.

Theft policies also have coinsurance provisions, described previously, so be careful that you are aware of the potential payoff if there is a claim.

Life Insurance

Life insurance is probably the best known of all insurance policies. There are two major types of life insurance: term and whole life. There are variations of the policies but basically they insure against a person's life rather than against other hazards.

> Life insurance is probably the best known of all insurance policies.

Term insurance pays a benefit if an insured person dies during the term of the policy. If the person does not die, there is no remainder value of the policy. It is similar to other casualty policies that expire with no payment made if no claim arises. Term insurance is less expensive and the most widely used form of life insurance.

Whole life policies are designed to pay the beneficiary the face amount of the policy in case of death. If the insured decides to terminate the policy there may be some cash value to the policy.

There are many variations of both types of policies. Their applications in business generally are designed for retirement, purchase of partners' shares of the business or in some cases, the cash value of the whole life policy can be borrowed from the insurance company or used as collateral to make a loan to the business.

When You Have Employees

In addition to property-casualty and life insurance choices, you will need to explore other types of insurance should you have employees. Some of these employer insurance considerations include:

- State mandated workers' compensation
- Optional health, disability, and accidental death insurance

If you offer insurance as part of your employee compensation package, be aware of certain recent legislation that affects how you administer that insurance.

As an employer you are required to purchase workers' compensation insurance if you have a certain number of employees.

Workers' Compensation Insurance

As an employer you are required to purchase workers' compensation insurance if you have a certain number of employees. The requirements vary from state to state. Make sure you read Chapter 4 to understand the workers' compensation laws applicable to your state. Workers' compensation coverage pays benefits for job-related illnesses, injuries, and death. Paid benefits may include medical expenses, death benefits, lost wages, and vocational rehabilitation. Failure to carry coverage for your employees could leave you liable for payment of all benefits and subject to fines.

To better understand your role in carrying workers' compensation insurance, make sure you know how your premium is calculated. Premiums are calculated by dividing an employee's annual payroll by 100 and multiplying the result by a factor based on the employee's classification rating. Classification ratings vary from occupation to occupation and from state to state. The insurance industry in your state has classified hundreds of occupations according to the risk of injury suggested by the occupations' loss histories. For instance, cashiers experience lower job-related injury risks than mill workers, and thus have a much lower rating factor. Accordingly, workers' compensation insurance coverage for a cashier is much less expensive than for a mill worker.

Premiums are further modified by an experience factor based on a business' claim history. For example, a business with a good workers' compensation claim history will have a lower experience modification factor—resulting in lower premiums. The reverse is also true. Thus, as a purchaser of workers' compensation insurance, you must ensure that all your employees are correctly classified and their claim histories have been considered in the final premium calculations. These simple checks could save you a considerable amount of money each year.

You can reduce your insurance costs in other ways. Purchase a type of policy called a participating policy, which pays dividends to companies with low loss records. Another good service to look for is loss control assistance. Your insurance company's loss control department can help you prevent or reduce claims by providing free published materials and guidance as well as evaluation and troubleshooting. Work environment and safety program evaluations are expensive to purchase independently, but may be provided as a free service by your insurance company.

Investing in safety will usually produce a positive return on your investment. You can lower your compensation payments if claims are low. It usually takes three years to develop a rate, called experience modification. This rating can be higher or lower than the standard rate, based on claims. Remember, if the rate goes up, you pay the increase on all employees based on their payroll for the entire year. Thus, a small increase or decrease in a rate can mean a substantial savings or additional payment at the end of the year.

> Investing in safety will usually produce a positive return on your investment.

Some states require companies to have employee committees that review safety issues in the workplace. Even if your state does not require it, it is a good idea to obtain ideas from employees regarding workplace safety. You can have a formal policy or a suggestion box. Employees are good at anticipating safety problems because of their close proximity to potentially dangerous situations. Not all industrial accidents involve heavy machinery. Individuals may slip on the floor or over wires or obstacles. Lighting or seating can cause long term problems that will cost you much more money than correcting the problem would cost. In addition, accidents cost you in terms of time due to an employee's absence. If an employee has an accident you either must do without his or her services or get a temporary who is not as familiar with your business as the employee who is off, and spend time training the new employee.

If you are a home-based business, you will find it helpful to obtain information from your workers' compensation company regarding how it handles injuries when workers are at your home. Your insurance company's policies may affect your policies regarding working at home.

Health Insurance

Recent national debate concerning health insurance has made businesses the major provider of health insurance for most workers in the United States. There are two basic types of health insurance: disability insurance and medical insurance.

DISABILITY INSURANCE

Disability insurance can be used in a business to assist an owner to hire a manager in the case of the owner's disability. It may also be used to pay off a partner if the person who is disabled is unlikely to be able to return to work.

Whatever kind of disability insurance you obtain, be certain to get the following information:

- The income per month that the policy will pay;
- The number of months payments will be made; and
- The period of time you are disabled and other conditions necessary for payment to be made.

MEDICAL INSURANCE

Most people will identify their primary source of medical insurance as the place where they are employed. Whether you are the owner of a business or an employee, medical insurance will likely be one of the first and most sought after benefits derived from the business.

If you incorporate, your corporation will be able to deduct the full cost of medical insurance premiums as a business expense. If you are a sole proprietor or partner, only a portion of the expense will be deductible. If your business is not a corporation, be sure to check the changing percentages with your accountant.

There are two major elements of medical insurance: major medical and comprehensive coverage. Major medical is coverage for hospital and recuperation expenses. Comprehensive is used for hospital and outpatient treatment, office visits, testing, and other health treatment.

There are many ways to purchase medical insurance that reflect higher or lower costs and benefits. The amount of deductible is one of the major sources of price differential in plans. By having a higher deductible, thus insuring for major medical problems, you will be able to keep the cost per employee lower than with higher deductible amounts.

Check with your industry association to see if insurance is offered as part of its benefit plan.

Check with your industry association to see if insurance is offered as part of its benefit plan. You should also check with your insurance agent regarding the coverage period for a policy. If you change insurance companies and a claim is filed for the period when you were with the previous company, you may not be covered. It is best to know how you are covered especially if there is a chance that a claim can occur after you change your insurance company.

Follow ERISA Guidelines

If you provide employees with insurance other than workers' compensation or if you give other benefits such as a profit sharing or retirement plans, you will need to comply with the Employment

Retirement Income Security Act of 1974 (ERISA). ERISA requires that you have a summary plan description (SPD) for each welfare plan in effect. Then, you must distribute a copy of each SPD to all covered employees. Each SPD must include specific information as well as an ERISA rights statement as specified by U.S. Department of Labor regulations. Insurance companies will often supply you with an SPD for each plan as a part of their service.

When your company grows to 100 or more employees, ERISA requirements become much more complex, involving several annual reports to the U.S. Department of Labor and an annual report to all employees. You should consult an expert in these regulations. Most insurance and investment companies have experts who are available to help you.

Consolidated Omnibus Reconciliation Act (COBRA)

Recent legislation applies to businesses with 20 or more employees. This legislation, the Consolidated Omnibus Reconciliation Act (COBRA), requires you to offer the same group health benefits as you offer regular eligible employees to the following:

- Employees who have been terminated (for reasons other than gross misconduct), laid off, or resigned;
- Employees whose hours have been reduced;
- The widowed, divorced, or separated spouses of employees;
- Employees eligible for Medicare; and
- The children of employees who have lost dependent status.

Eligibility for this coverage begins as soon as a sponsoring employee becomes eligible for coverage under the group health plan. Then, that employee and his or her dependents are eligible for continued benefits for up to 36 months thereafter. Your company can charge the employee up to 100 percent of the coverage cost plus a 2 percent surcharge.

If you fail to comply with the requirements of this act, your company cannot deduct health plan contributions from its taxes. Further, COBRA does not prevent your company from terminating your group health care plan.

Should you have employees, make sure you understand your responsibilities under COBRA. Consult with a knowledgeable insurance specialist; most insurance companies can provide up-to-date information about COBRA.

Should you have employees, make sure you understand your responsibilities under COBRA.

Shopping for Coverage

Becoming an expert on insurance matters is probably the last thing on your mind as you attempt to start your business. However, high on your priority list during startup should be finding the best coverage for the best price. Your best option is to find a reputable agent or broker you can trust. Finding an agent may not be as difficult as it sounds. Ask for referrals from friends, your lawyer, your accountant, or friendly competitors.

Once you have several referrals, your next step is to narrow your search by selecting agents who have earned Chartered Life Underwriter (CLU) or Chartered Property/Casualty Underwriter (CPCU) designations. These professionals are generally more experienced and capable than agents without one of these designations. The Certified Insurance Counselor (CID) agent is a professional designation very popular among agents and keeps the agent up to date on a current basis.

If you are unable to locate a suitable agent, you can choose to hire an insurance consultant instead. An insurance consultant is an expert in insurance matters and will provide an objective analysis of your risk management and insurance needs. Hiring an insurance consultant is similar to seeing a doctor or an attorney. Follow your consultant's advice carefully when selecting coverage from your agent or broker. The hourly fees for consultants are usually quite high but can result in significant savings in annual premiums. Billing is usually broken down into quarter-hour segments. Be wary of consultants who attempt to pad their fees by offering extended services that you may not need or that you can get elsewhere at a far less expensive cost.

If you hire a consultant, make sure he or she is a member of the Society of Risk Management Consultants. To be a member of this society, a consultant cannot be an insurance broker. This stipulation prevents potential conflicts of interest and reduces the risk of unethical behavior. To contact the society, use the address and phone number listed in Appendix C.

An insurance consultant is an expert in insurance matters and will provide an objective analysis of your risk management and insurance needs.

Chapter Wrap-Up

A smartstart for new entrepreneurs involves a close look at their business insurance needs. It might seem unusual to plan for a major loss or potential disaster while at the same time you are planning to open your doors for business. However, countless business owners—even relatively new businesses—have benefited from a solid insurance package.

The way you problemsolve includes being prepared for emergencies.

The tasks of getting insurance quotes and making contacts with agents, brokers, and insurance companies are not high on anyone's list of favorite things to do. You can simplify the process by informing yourself of the various types of insurance available. Then, look at your business as a whole and assess the potential risks. Know how you want to handle these risks—whether you will transfer, reduce, retain, or eliminate—before you approach an insurance agent.

To be able to get the best quote, you will need to decide which types of coverage are necessary for your type of business. If crime is a real threat, then you will need to consider some form of crime coverage. If potential negligence as a result of using your product or service is likely, then you will want to explore liability coverage. Of course, as an employer you will have to comply with workers' compensation issues for the state in which you will operate. Also, you must evaluate the need to include disability and medical insurance as part of your employee benefits package.

One thing you can be sure of as you start your business: problems will surface on a regular basis. The way you problemsolve includes being prepared for emergencies. Risk assessment and insurance will protect your assets and help you stay in business.

CHAPTER 12

Setting Up Your Office

New business owners tend to view office work as something to be handled later, when they get the time. This is generally a mistake. The adage that "no job is finished until the paperwork is done" has been presented humorously, yet it is based on a fundamental truth. Somewhere amid the excitement of producing and selling a new product hides the simple fact that you are engaged in a business. Businesses are managed from an office setting.

To lessen the pain of dealing with records and paperwork, it is vital to be as organized as possible. This chapter will help you:

- Organize your incoming mail,
- Improve your telephone answering techniques,
- Establish a homebased office,
- Choose the right furniture and equipment for your operation, and
- Select the best location for your business.

The effort put forth in becoming organized will pay off a hundredfold as your business grows and demands more of your time and energy. Luckily, there are well-established tools to help you handle these chores until you can hire someone to handle them for you.

Managing Your Incoming Mail

Handling mail and other correspondence is the nuts and bolts of office management. Mail procedures are fairly simple to put into place. It takes a little self-discipline to follow these procedures, but the payoff is a headache-free office.

The easiest way to handle incoming mail is by using the one-touch approach. With the one-touch approach you only handle each piece of mail once as you go through your incoming mailbox. You may handle some of it again later as you respond to it, but only once as it comes in. Incoming mail goes to one of three places after you have screened it:

- The wastebasket
- The interesting mail basket
- The action mail basket

Handling mail and other correspondence is the nuts and bolts of office management.

E-mail must also be handled efficiently. Each morning, go through the incoming mail and forward, respond, save, or delete each new piece of mail. Set aside 10 to 15 minutes each morning to reviewing and sorting your e-mail correspondence.

Wastebasket Mail

When handling incoming mail, the wastebasket is your friend. By throwing away the mail that you don't need as soon as possible, you eliminate time lost in rereading junk mail and your desk stays clean and uncluttered.

One small business owner automatically throws bulk mail away without even opening it. Her feeling is that no important material will be sent out bulk rate. She may be right. Her business is thriving. On the other hand, junk mail is fun to read and can be a source of marketplace intelligence unavailable anywhere else. Either way, unless you find that you can't live without the touted product, throw it out.

Interesting Mail

Occasionally, mail will arrive that has the potential for being useful at some future point. Some possibilities include equipment catalogs for your type of business, trade magazines, and business propositions.

Place this type of mail in the interesting mail basket. Interesting mail always does one of two things with time: it becomes junk mail or it becomes invaluable. Sort through it every week or so as you get the time to find the valuable parts. Keep your wastebasket at hand for the rest of it.

Telephone technology has continued to advance rapidly in the wake of personal computer technology.

Action Mail

Action mail requires a response of some sort on your part. Your action mail box should be kept as empty as possible. Write the type of response required and a due date on the outside of the envelope. Make a similar notation on your calendar or in your computer. Computerized personal information managers (PIMs) can help you stay organized. To learn more about PIMs, see the discussion later in this chapter. Respond to this type of mail as soon as possible, preferably long before the due date and definitely not after it. As a general rule, do not take more than one week to respond to action mail.

Set aside a time in your workweek to handle action mail. Use this time to pay bills, respond to inquiries, and schedule appointments. As you respond to each piece of action mail, try to handle each item only once. Mail that is handled many times before acted upon can waste huge amounts of office time.

Avoiding the Telephone Traffic Jam

The telephone has been called the lifeline of business. With it, you can reach the world, and the world can reach you. But as anyone starting out in business can tell you, the phone will always ring at the worst possible time and you can become so busy handling telephone calls that you never get anything done. But the telephone is basic to business. One popular policy manual workbook makes 16 different references to the use of the telephone.

Telephone technology has continued to advance rapidly in the wake of personal computer technology. Today's "smart phones" and associated phone company services perform a wide variety of functions including:

- Call waiting
- Call forwarding
- Conference calls
- Voice mail
- Data and voice differentiation

- Full duplex speakerphone technology

These features combined will allow today's small business owner unprecedented flexibility in handling telephone traffic. Recent innovations in computer technology allow you to handle many of these functions directly from your computer terminal.

With the help of a personal computer, you can eliminate most of the hassles associated with business phones, while preserving many of the advantages. The technology to do this has been getting steadily less costly and more accessible to the average person starting out in business. Many people are beginning to place telephone handling features above word processing and bookkeeping convenience as the number one reason for purchasing a business computer.

A good message includes a greeting, the name of your company, the hours you are available, and how to leave a message.

Answering Machines and Voice Mail

If you have decided that a computer is not in your start-up budget, technology is still on your side. Today's telephones incorporate some of the features of computer-based phone technology—such as answering machines and voice mail—at a fraction of the cost. Spend your phone dollars on the quality of features rather than quantity, and test telephones and answering machines in the store before you buy. A bargain buy is not a bargain if it makes your voice sound odd or unintelligible.

You may be tempted to record a cute or humorous message on your answering machine. Resist the urge to do so unless you know your customers and potential customers very well. Your message should be short and straightforward; avoid extraneous or superfluous information. A good message includes a greeting, the name of your company, the hours you are available, and how to leave a message. Avoid saying that you are unable to answer the phone right now. The caller will have already figured that out. Including the hours you are open is especially effective for a retail business where fully half of the incoming callers want to know how late the store is open. An appropriate message might sound something like this:

> Hello. Thank you for calling ABC Mousetraps. Our hours are from 8:00 A.M. to 5:00 P.M., Monday through Friday. Please leave a message after the tone.

Many people use their answering machine to screen calls to pick up only those that require an immediate response. This approach is far more appropriate in a private setting. Your personal telephone is in place largely for your convenience. In a business setting, the tables become partially turned. You probably installed your business phone for the convenience of your customers, as well as for your own convenience. When customers take the time to call you, they generally deserve some of your time in return. So, in a business setting, take care to screen out only those calls that don't have the potential to result in a sale.

Similarly, make sure your system is as efficient and professional as possible. Give the same basic information and briefly describe the options available to the caller. Avoid, if at all possible, forcing the caller through a maze of multilayered menu options. Most customers will not be pleased at the prospect of having a lot of their time wasted just to leave a message. The basic elements of a good voice mail message are included in this example:

> Thank you for calling. This is the ABC Mousetraps' voice mail messaging system. You may enter the extension you wish to contact now, or leave a message for the marketing department by pressing one, a message for the production department by pressing two, or a message for management systems by pressing three. Press four to listen to a general information message about ABC Mousetraps. Press zero to speak to an operator.

You will want to delete the last sentence for the after-hours version of your message. This message format is effective for even the smallest business. Today's technology will enable you and your business to establish a professional line of communication with your clients, vendors, and suppliers.

For those times when you are not available by phone, an answering machine or voice mail allows your customers to leave messages for you. Your job, then, is to check your machine frequently for important calls and return them as soon as possible. Make note of who called you, when they placed the call, and from where they placed the call.

For those times when you are not available by phone, an answering machine or voice mail allows your customers to leave messages for you.

The Homebased Office

A homebased office presents many difficulties that you may have never considered in a structured work environment. The greatest risk is a complete loss of organization as paperwork slowly spreads from your home office desk to the floor and out into the next room, or even throughout the house. Before you decide to go out and lease space in a new office, learn how you can easily keep track of the growing mounds of paperwork. Keep in mind, the suggestions that follow apply to a business office as well as a home office.

When setting up their home office, many people take a haphazard approach when selecting furniture, equipment, and location. If successful in business, these people end up rebuilding their home office at great trouble and expense, or they end up entering *Home Office Computing* magazine's annual contest for a makeover of the most disorganized office.

The best time to set up your home office is before you hang out your shingle. The slightest care at this point will pay dividends later. The most obvious benefit to careful setup is avoiding the back pain and muscle aches associated with improperly fitted furniture. Careless placement of keyboards, monitors, tables, and chairs can lead to a whole series of repetitive stress injuries, including the dreaded Carpal Tunnel Syndrome and bursitis as the most well-known. There are dozens of these disorders. Some are permanently debilitating; all are painful and preventable.

Setting up your home office need not be an expensive proposition.

Setting up your home office need not be an expensive proposition. Unless you will be receiving customers in your office, try using used furniture and fixtures for your office. Create an environment that is cheerful and motivates you to produce. An office composed of gray metal desks, files, and cabinets from a military surplus depot, while undeniably cheap, may have a withering effect on your productivity.

Basement, Garage, or Spare Room?

Where you decide to locate your office in your home may be dictated by available space. Hopefully, your home office isn't relegated to a corner of the dining room, even though some successful home businesses are operated from that very location. It is more common, however, to have use of a separate room such as a spare bedroom, the corner of a basement, a converted porch, or an attic loft or garret. Some home business owners convert a section of the garage or build an office over the garage. And a very few make their office from a garden cottage or gazebo.

If you have a choice of locations, there are a number of factors that you may want to consider before choosing one over the other. Some of these factors are practical, some are environmental, some merely a matter of personal taste.

PRACTICAL CONSIDERATIONS

A primary influence on choosing the location of your home office is accessibility. If customers or clients will be regularly coming to your office, a location with or near a separate outside entrance is desirable. However, that is not always possible. When clients must travel through your home to get to your office, it is important that this part of your house is neat and orderly. Keeping areas of the home orderly can be especially difficult when there are very young or teenage children living there.

If at all possible, your home office should not be located in your bedroom. As many new business owners will attest, a start-up business demands a great deal of time, and rest comes dearly enough as it is without unfinished details calling to you in the middle of the night. Conversely, it is probably not a good idea to have your bed just a few steps away as your energy levels wane in the afternoon or as you face the dreaded tedium of bookkeeping or routine correspondence.

Locating your office away from the living area of your home provides specific psychological benefits. A basement, attic, or garage office allows you the illusion of working away from home, helping you to tune out the distraction of waiting chores, visiting neighbors, and personal calls. In addition, having a remote office helps to maintain your home as a refuge from the demands of your business.

Locating your office away from the living area of your home provides specific psychological benefits.

ENVIRONMENTAL CONCERNS

Environmental concerns, in this case, refer to the office environment rather than where rabbits and coyotes play. Creating a good working environment is a challenge to any home worker, but choosing the wrong office location can make that challenge far more difficult.

Consider the vivid images invoked by the following descriptive phrases of the following home office locations:

- A dark, damp basement;
- A hot, dusty attic;
- A cold garage; or
- A cramped loft.

These locations require special treatment to be effective workplaces. You will need to pay more attention to extra lighting and heating, cooling, and ventilation. More than other places in the home, these will benefit from the installation of natural light sources.

An attic or over-the-garage office will benefit greatly from the installation of skylights or large gable windows. They will need extra cooling and ventilation during summer heat and a source of heat when it is cool. Basement offices will require improved ventilation and extra light to make up for the lack of natural light.

Noise is another environmental consideration. A typical home office is much quieter than its corporate counterpart, and many corporate refugees find the change disconcerting at first. Soft music in the background may help ease the transition. If music is a distraction in itself, consider buying a noise machine, an electronic device that produces white noises, such as static, ocean waves, running water, rustling leaves, or rainfall. Other noise producers include aquariums, small tabletop fountains or burbles, and wooden or bamboo wind chimes.

Some home office workers have complained of the opposite effect. Playing children, running lawn mowers, and the general hubbub of today's busy world seem to filter more easily through the walls of your home than through the walls of the office building you may leave behind. Simple fixes for this problem include installing acoustical tile ceilings, sound absorbing materials on walls and floors, and double or triple glazed windows.

Consider those things unique to your home and personality that will distract you the most and prevent you from accomplishing the work you need to get done.

OTHER OFFICE LOCATION CONSIDERATIONS

Everything else considered, the decision on where to locate your home office may boil down to personal considerations. Consider the following:

- Will office work conflict with children watching television or vice versa?
- Is your office so close to the refrigerator that you will indulge in excessive or frequent snacking?
- Do doorbells and telephone calls from the house intrude into the office?

In short, consider those things unique to your home and personality that will distract you the most and prevent you from accomplishing the work you need to get done. Conversely, consider those things about working at home that you value the most, such as being in regular contact with your family and integrating your work life and your home life. Then select the location of your office with these factors in mind.

Office on a Budget

Many start-up businesses are concerned with trimming costs wherever possible, and balk at equipping a home office with expensive equipment and furnishings. A few are successful at creating a functional work environment that is efficient, productive, and inexpensive. In general, setting up an office on a budget requires more room and more work. Important ergonomic, comfort, and lighting characteristics can be short-changed only at the expense of productivity, health, or well-being.

Setting Up Basic Furniture, Equipment, and Fixtures

Now that you have chosen the right location for your home office, take the time to choose its furnishings. To begin with, consider the basic office furniture complement of desk, chair, and filing cabinet. Then, evaluate your needs for equipment, lighting, and location. Arguably, the most important piece of office furniture is the office chair. But, even the most perfectly fitted chair will be of little benefit if the desk is at the wrong height. So, when setting up your home office, be particularly sensitive to the various dimensions suggested, and make fine adjustments as necessary to suit your particular size and configuration.

THE OFFICE CHAIR

If your tendency is to either use whatever you have on hand, such as a spare kitchen chair or to buy a used swivel chair, you may want to think twice. Many people even splurge on a new office chair. The decision to purchase office chairs is far more important than for mere convenience. When you consider that up to three-quarters of your workday will be spent sitting in your office chair, your personal comfort and efficiency take on meaningful proportions.

The best approach to selecting the proper chair for your office is to sit in it with a "Goldilocks" mindset. The chair cannot be too big, too small, too soft, or too hard. It must be just right. Often this feeling of being just right is the result of an intangible set of conditions, but there are characteristics that you can look for while sitting in the prospective chair.

- *Height of the seat.* Make sure your thighs are parallel to the floor and your feet rest flat on the floor. If the chair isn't naturally at this height, it should be fully adjustable and, ideally, should be fully height adjustable from a sitting position so that you can easily change it to accomplish different tasks. You may require an ergonomic footrest if your legs are too short to rest comfortably on the floor.
- *Choose a comfortable chair seat.* Your chair should have a firm cushion and be contoured so as not to cut into your legs. The chair back should extend from the lumbar region of your lower back to

If your tendency is to either use whatever you have on hand, such as a spare kitchen chair or to buy a used swivel chair, you may want to think twice.

mid-shoulder blade, providing firm, adjustable support to your entire back while in a normal sitting position. The armrests, if any, should be positioned at or just below the point of your elbow.

- *Make sure it's accident proofed.* The base of the chair should extend beyond the dimensions of the seat for stability and, if on casters, should be designed with five points to prevent the chance of an accidental tipping.

To meet these requirements, you can spend up to $1,000 or more for a fully adjustable, designer, ergonomic chair. Or, as one home office worker did, slightly modify a wooden kitchen chair for less than $20. In either case, be certain that the chair fits you and that you can spend six to ten or more hours each day sitting in it. Remember, even a perfect chair will become uncomfortable with time, so make sure your daily routine includes occasional breaks away from your chair to prevent stiffness and fatigue.

YOUR DESK

Different office tasks demand different working surface heights relative to your chair height.

Different office tasks demand different working surface heights relative to your chair height. For instance, the ideal writing surface height may be 30 inches, while the ideal height for a keyboard (typewriter or computer) may be 26 inches. Actual heights will, of course, vary from individual to individual. Luckily, there are ready solutions to this varying height problem in most workstations available on the market today.

Your best strategy in purchasing a workstation or desk is to test it out in the showroom first. This requires no small effort on your part as you must first locate a suitable chair and get it properly adjusted. Sit at the workstation and test the writing table height, the typing height, and the reading height for comfort. Ideally, each of these surfaces will be slightly adjustable to allow for variations in your body proportions from national averages. Many higher quality workstations today offer several work surfaces with adjustable heights and positions. Some workstations will even alert you if you have worked from one position too long for comfort!

Other considerations besides working height include depth and width of the desk. Obviously, it must fit in your available office space without overpowering it or making the remaining space awkward or cramped in either function or appearance. Many mass-marketed manufacturers are cutting costs by making the desktop shorter and narrower. Frequently, the result is a computer monitor positioned so closely that eyestrain is inevitable with the remaining desktop space orphaned to the sides where it becomes unusable for reading and writing tasks.

Finally, in selecting your desk or workstations, consider the ease of shifting from one task to another. You should be able to easily shift from typing correspondence to answering the phone to checking your calendar; to writing a short memo; to pulling a file and back again without making a series of trips about your office. The transition from task to task should be smooth and seamless and accomplishable with the least effort possible.

Office automation has had a profound and positive impact on the feasibility of working from a home office.

FILING CABINETS

Surprisingly, you will find that you can't stay in business for long without a filing system. Your system may be as simple as having stacks of paperwork organized into piles around your office, or as complex as banks of filing cabinets lining the wall or anywhere in between. If you are like most people, however, you are likely to end up with at least one filing cabinet to hold the paperwork you will accumulate as your business grows.

New, well-made filing cabinets are expensive. However, it pays to seek quality in this purchase. Inexpensive, poorly made filing cabinets constructed of lightweight materials will inevitably become inadequate for your business needs. The drawer guides on cheaper filing cabinets can break or jam under heavy loads or repeated usage. A full file drawer can weigh as much as 100 pounds or more. Inexpensive cabinets are not designed to handle these loads safely.

There are many variations on the standard filing cabinet design. The drawers can be of standard width, or wide enough to accommodate legal-sized files. Lateral filing cabinets on wheels are growing in popularity, but don't make as efficient use of floor space as vertical cabinets. Finally, the number of drawers in each cabinet can vary from two to six. Most quality filing cabinets are lockable.

Equipment

Office automation has had a profound and positive impact on the feasibility of working from a home office. Tasks such as routine correspondence and bookkeeping, which used to require a new business to hire at least a part-time office assistant, may now be accomplished by a sole proprietor as a part of the daily routine.

Fax machines, answering machines, copiers, and printers are being replaced by business computers with special features to handle faxes, voice mail, and routine paperwork tasks. While not yet inexpensive, the costs of these computer systems are rapidly falling and have already dropped well below the cost of purchasing individual office equipment components.

Just a few years ago it cost upwards from $6,000 to equip an office with a copier, fax machine, answering machine, and basic desktop computer for word processing and bookkeeping purposes. In today's business environment, a single business computer workstation can accomplish the same tasks for approximately half the expense, and do them simultaneously. Indeed, the personal computer has begun to fulfill early industry predictions as being an all-encompassing single tool office machine.

Personal Information Managers

If you have and use a personal computer in managing your business, there are dozens of programs on the market that will help you organize your time and efforts. These programs—called personal information managers (PIMs)—track business contacts, suppliers, customers, phone numbers, appointments, action items, and "to-do" lists. Many of these programs perform additional functions that may or may not be useful to you. Several good PIMs are available as shareware—that allows you to try the program before buying it. Choose one that is easy to use and you will come to depend upon it.

A personal computer will automate many tasks and help you to produce consistently high-quality correspondence.

A personal computer will automate many tasks and help you to produce consistently high-quality correspondence. When it comes to handling stock and production records, payroll, and general ledger bookkeeping, a desktop computer shines. However, in-baskets, out-baskets, paperweights, and rotary card files are still basic office tools that will do much to handle the initial paper glut.

Surprisingly, today's office automated technology is easy to use. Hardware components require little maintenance, and recent advances allow the user to simply plug most components in and turn them on. The computer does the rest automatically, prompting you on what to do and how to do it. Much software has become similarly user-friendly and features automatic installation programs, interactive tutorials to teach you the ropes. There are even special deinstallation routines if you want to remove the software from your computer at some future date. Perhaps more importantly, most of the software marketed today features a look-alike appearance to other programs on the market. Drop-down menus, toolbars, and mouse-driven pointers allow new users to rapidly learn the ins and outs of new programs.

One downside of all-in-one technology is the risk, however remote, of equipment failure. While a complete loss of function is rare, it is important to purchase warranty plans and to have a qualified repair technician available should the need arise. Make sure you consider this as part of your risk assessment plans. Refer back to Chapter 11 to get up-to-date information on insurance issues. Many insurance companies will provide a rider to your policy that covers your hardware and software against theft, fire, and accidental damage.

Many insurance companies will provide a rider to your policy that covers your hardware and software against theft, fire, and accidental damage.

You can do other things to reduce the impact of equipment failure:

- *Keep paper copies of all documents on file.* The paperless office predicted about ten years ago is not yet a reality for most businesses. Relying on a single storage method for important business documents invites disaster.
- *Save work in progress frequently.* At least once every ten minutes is a good rule of thumb. Most quality software incorporates an autosave feature, which can be customized as to the number of minutes between saves. The best approach, however, remains disciplining yourself to manually save your work. One unexpected power outage just as you reach the end of two hours of unsaved work will make a believer of you.
- *Make daily or weekly back-up copies.* Include all data files on your computer in your backups. Computer operating systems incorporate a back-up function that can be invoked manually or sometimes on a specified schedule. Options include backing up to floppy disk, magnetic tape cartridge, or recordable CD-ROM.
- *Safety-proof your backups.* Keep backups of vital information in fireproof safes or in an off-site location. Safes are available at office and business supply stores. Most safes provide protection to vital documents from temperatures of up to several thousand degrees Fahrenheit as well as some security against theft.
- *Get assistance.* Subscribe to a service that stores electronic files for your company off site. This is a relatively new service which is available in most metropolitan areas. Check your phone directory for services near you.
- *Perform preventive maintenance.* Your equipment should be checked and cleaned on a regular basis. Dirt and dust are the

primary causes of electronic equipment failure. Excessive heat is the second most common culprit.

- *Plan for contingencies.* Purchase an older computer for emergency use if your primary system fails. You will retain minimum capabilities during down time at about 10 percent of the cost of a new system. You will also develop a new respect for the speed and versatility of your primary computer system should it become necessary to use the older system.

Lighting

Providing adequate lighting for your office space is an important consideration. The quantity, quality, and efficiency of various light sources will affect your decisions. Also, different tasks require different qualities and intensities of light. Finally, your age is a determining factor. Older workers require as much as 50 percent more light than younger workers for the same task.

Choosing the correct lighting is vital to preventing eyestrain and promoting maximum efficiency.

Choosing the correct lighting is vital to preventing eyestrain and promoting maximum efficiency. The best source of light for all tasks is daylight. An open, airy office featuring lots of natural light is ideal for many businesses. Ready sources of daylight include windows, conventional skylights, and special tube type skylights that reflect light gathered from a hemispherical collector on the roof.

Not all offices have the advantage of access to natural light, nor is daylight always available. The solution, then, is to use artificial light from incandescent, fluorescent, or halogen sources. These light sources each possess differing characteristics.

Incandescent light is the most common. Bulbs are inexpensive and produce a soft, pale yellow light that is warm and localized. The localized nature of incandescent light bulbs makes them most suitable as task lights providing spot illumination for paperwork, reading, or other close, detailed work. Incandescent lights are energy-inefficient, however, producing a great deal of heat as a byproduct. The bulbs wear out after as little as several hundred hours of use.

Halogen light bulbs are similar to incandescent light bulbs, but produce a whiter light. Halogen bulbs cost several times more than incandescent bulbs, but use about 10 percent less electricity and last four to six times longer. They have the advantage of fitting into existing incandescent fixtures without modification. Also, you can easily adjust the output of both incandescent and halogen fixtures by installing a dimmer switch in the circuit.

Fluorescent fixtures are the most energy-efficient, producing the same amount of light as incandescent fixtures for approximately half the electricity. Fluorescent light is also diffuse, making it suitable for lighting large areas, but unsuitable for illuminating tasks. Fixtures are expensive, can have a noticeable flicker, and cannot be easily dimmed. However, numerous types of tubes are available, producing remarkably different qualities of light that are suitable for different purposes. If yours is a homebased business, a full-spectrum daylight tube will probably serve you best in your home office. Fluorescent lighting has the added advantage of being long lasting. Tubes are rated from 3,000 to 7,000 hours between failure.

Fluorescent lighting has the added advantage of being long lasting.

The best lighting conditions for your office will depend on the tasks that you perform there. However, the following general guidelines apply to most workspaces:

- *Consistency.* Prevent eyestrain resulting from adjusting to varying light levels by maintaining all lighting in the room at or near the same intensity.
- *Glare.* Eliminate glare and reflections from shiny objects. Position fixtures so that the light doesn't shine directly in your eyes.
- *Shadows.* Illuminate computer workstations by reflecting light from the ceiling and walls. Reflected light is more diffuse and produces fewer shadows and reflections from computer monitor screens.
- *Fluorescent bulbs.* Illuminate the room with indirect fluorescent lighting. Illuminate tasks with direct light from an incandescent or halogen source.

Select the Best Location

Location! Location! Location! You have probably heard this phrase when discussing real estate issues. But did you know that location, location, location applies even more so when it comes to selecting a place from which to operate your business?

Location is the most important ingredient for success for any business that depends on customers finding it. You might have the highest-quality product or the most reliable service in your area. But the truth is: if you don't locate your business appropriately, you will lose potential customers traveling on foot or by car.

The reasons to locate in a certain place vary depending on your type of business. For example, if you are going to open a restaurant or retail business, you want to locate ideally in an area where there is a lot of available parking, a good flow of walk-in and drive-by traffic, and little competition. If you are a manufacturer or wholesaler, you will be more interested in a site that is close to major transportation services, has a large pool of skilled labor available, and has sufficient access to water, sewer, and other vital services. Lastly, if you are going to be one of the millions of people who are starting their businesses out of their homes, then your location considerations are basically concerned with knowing zoning and land use restrictions in your neighborhood. You will need to know what you can and cannot do in terms of shipping and receiving, signage, business activity, and remodeling in your particular residential area.

To select the best site for your business involves taking a serious look at four factors that will ultimately influence your business.

Know the City

First, understand the dynamics of the city in which you wish to locate. This knowledge entails familiarizing yourself with the relationship of the surrounding cities, the road system and configurations within the city, the traffic patterns of the people who live, work, play, and travel in the city, and what causes people to travel in specific routes. In short, you must understand the traffic patterns of your potential customers and what generates these traffic patterns.

Decide whether your product or service is suited for the type of city you want to locate in.

Identify Your Trading Area

Decide whether your product or service is suited for the type of city you want to locate in—whether it be downtown, urban, suburban, or rural. Study the ways the parts of the city connect with each other and how these connections or lack thereof affect the size, shape, and density of your trading area. Believe it or not: you will learn a lot about your trading area—and the people who make up your trading area—by studying the grocery stores in the area in which you want to serve.

Essential Characteristics

Consider the top location characteristics—accessibility, visibility, convenience, and high density. How visible, accessible, and convenient is your site? The flow of traffic or lack of flow will affect your customers' decisions to visit your business. Also, your customers' perceptions of safety and whether or not they have adequate parking will influence their decisions to return to your business place. How dense is the population? High density of the population in the area you want to serve is an ideal situation. The law of numbers will work in your favor.

Know Your Market Position

You have probably already done most of this research for your sales and marketing plan. However, the point cannot be overemphasized: have a thorough knowledge of your industry and your product or service, your customers, and your competitors. The first three location suggestions are worth nothing if you haven't clearly identified your market position.

The more organized you are in the planning phase, the better you will be once your business is up and running.

Chapter Wrap-Up

Whether you start your business out of your home or purchase land to build a new office suite or production center, you will need to set up your business for maximum efficiency. This entails a thorough evaluation of your operations to find out what you need to maintain your business—both on the administrative and production ends. Among other things, seriously consider the following:

- *How to handle incoming mail and incoming phone calls.* What type of phone system will you need for the services you offer?
- *How to arrange your workspace and your employees' workspaces.* How many chairs and desks will you require? What type of lighting will best suite your operation? Are there any special equipment requirements?
- *Which city or road is the best area in which to locate your business.* Which areas will provide maximum accessibility and visibility while at the same time be within a short distance from your target market?

The key to setting up your operation is organization. The more organized you are in the planning phase, the better you will be once your business is up and running.

CHAPTER 13

Welcome to Utah

With 14 well-known ski areas, Utah boasts of having "the greatest snow on earth"—an average snowfall of 500 inches at the major resort areas. Perhaps that is why Salt Lake City, Utah was selected as the home of the 2002 Winter Olympics. But, if you are not a ski bunny, there is much, much more to attract you to this highly diversified state.

Rich in natural resources, Utah is a leading producer of copper, gold, silver, lead, zinc, molybdenum, and oil. Utah has large deposits of low sulfur coal and oil shale. The state's leading crops include alfalfa, winter wheat, and beans. Utah's traditional industries of mining and agriculture are enhanced by a growing tourism business, and companies involved in aerospace, computers, and biomedicine are setting up shop as well.

The region was first explored by Spanish friars in 1776. American frontiersman Jim Bridger discovered the Great Salt Lake in 1824. Other famous pioneers to explore Utah include John C. Freemont, Kit Carson, and Jedediah Smith who lead the first overland expedition to California in 1826.

Fleeing religious persecution, the Mormons traveled west and reached the Great Salt Lake in 1847. The Utah region was acquired by the United States in 1848 in the treaty ending the

Mexican War. But, Mormon difficulties with the federal government about polygamy continued until the Mormon Church renounced the practice in 1890, six years before Utah achieved statehood.

The Union Pacific and Central Pacific railroads met on May 10, 1869 at Promontory Summit, creating the first transcontinental railroad. This event was celebrated with the driving of the famous golden railroad spike.

Utah encompasses 84,916 square miles of some of the most beautiful landscapes in the nation. A great vacationland with 11,000 miles of fishing streams, 147,000 acres of lakes and reservoirs and numerous national parks, Utah has something for everyone. More discussion about Utah's parks, ski resorts, rivers, and lakes will follow later in this chapter.

If you are looking for a great place to start or relocate your business, you should take a good look at Utah. The state's tax structure offers a relatively low individual and corporate tax rate and extends other incentives to business owners. The state's central-western location provides easy access to domestic and foreign markets. You can find friendly people, great educational and social opportunities, and a wonderful lifestyle for your family right here in the "Beehive State."

Demographics, or the vital statistics of human populations, should be of great interest to any prospective or existing small business owner.

Get to Know the Demographics of Utah

Demographics, or the vital statistics of human populations, should be of great interest to any prospective or existing small business owner. Things like size, growth, density, and distribution of the populations of the major counties and cities in Utah will affect the way you do business—from your marketing strategy to how you will obtain financing. The major source of demographic research is the United States Census Bureau.

Take a moment to understand the influence of the demographic makeup of Utah on your proposed business. Start with a look at three main factors: population, major industries, and income and consumption rates.

Population Statistics

Utah is one of the fastest growing states in the country, ranking 35th in the nation in population growth. This rapid growth can be attributed to both the area's high birth rate and to positive in-migration. The majority of people moving to and from Utah do so for employment-related reasons. Utah's population reached 2.2 million in 2000, a positive increase every year since 1990. The state expects to have a boost in population to nearly 3 million by 2025.

Utah currently has the youngest population in the nation with a median age in 2003 of just 27.1 years, well below the national figure of 35.2 years. This trend is projected to continue well into the next decade.

Utah's households are not only young, they are densely populated as well. The state is 1st in the nation in the number of persons per household at 3.13, compared to the national average of 2.62. The number of people per family in this state is 3.67, compared to the national figure of 3.16.

Utah currently has the youngest population in the nation with a median age in 2003 of just 27.1 years.

TABLE 1: POPULATION STATISTICS

		Utah	United States
Resident population	1990	1,723,000	248,791,000
	2000	2,233,169	281,421,906
Resident population change	1990–2000	29.6%	13.1%
Percent under 18 yrs old	2000	32.2%	25.7%
Percent 65 yrs or older	2000	8.5%	12.4%
Foreign born persons	2000	7.1%	11.1%
High school graduates, age 25+	2000	87.7%	80.4%
Households	2000	701,281	105,480,101
Land area (square miles)	2000	82,144	3,537,438
Persons per square mile	2000	27.2	79.6
Population projections	2015	2,670,000	310,160,000
	2025	2,883,000	329,048,000

Source: U.S. Census Bureau

Business and Employment

Like many other states, Utah experienced a downturn both in its economy and employment numbers from 2000–2002. This was due in large part to the collapse of the dot-com bubble followed by the aftermath of 9/11. However, there are signs of recovery in 2003 being led by gains in the services industries, particularly health and education, and the financial sector. The trade, transportation and utilities sector continues to employ the largest number of Utah residents, followed by government, professional and business services, and manufacturing.

In 2003, the largest employer in Utah was Intermountain Health Care with over 20,000 employees. It was followed by the State of Utah, Brigham Young University, Hill Air Force Base, Wal Mart Associates, Granite and Jordan School Districts, and Convergys. Agricultural workers comprise about 2 percent of the state's total workforce.

TABLE 2: BUSINESS AND EMPLOYMENT STATISTICS

		Utah	United States
Private nonfarm establishments	1999	53,809	7,008,444
Private nonfarm employment	1999	889,355	110,705,661
Private nonfarm employment change	1990–1999	55.8%	18.4%
Manufacturers shipments ($1,000)	1997	24,014,379	3,842,061,405
Retail sales ($1,000)	1997	19,964,601	2,460,886,012
Retail sales per capita	1997	$9,666	$9,190
Civilian population employed	1990	67.6%	62.8%
	2000	65.3%	59.7%
Average annual pay	1990	$20,074	$23,602
	2001	$30,074	$36,214

Source: U.S. Census Bureau

Utah's general income is somewhat lower than the U.S. average but is slowly increasing.

Income and Consumption Rates

Utah's general income is somewhat lower than the U.S. average but is slowly increasing. The median household income, however, is on par with the rest of the country. Homeownership rates in Utah are higher than the national average and this seems to be a continuing trend. Energy consumption by Utah residents is close to mid range, ranking 31st in the nation in 1999.

TABLE 3: INCOME AND CONSUMPTION STATISTICS

		Utah	United States
Personal income per capita	1990	$14,983	$18,572
	2001	$24,180	$30,472
Median household income ('98 $s)	1990	$37,591	$37,343
	1999	$45,726	$41,994
Persons below poverty level	1999	9.4%	12.4%
Energy consumption per capita (million BTUs)	1990	315	326
	1999	326	351
Homeownership rates	1990	70.1%	63.9%
	2001	72.4%	67.8%

Source: U.S. Census Bureau

Utah State Data Center

To break much of this census data down into manageable pieces, the Bureau of the Census created the State Data Center (SDC) Program. Since 1978, state data centers have provided training and technical assistance in accessing and using census data for research, administration, planning, and decisionmaking. Users of this information have ranged from state, county, and local governments to the business community to university researchers. Further, in 1988, the SDC expanded its services through its Business and Industry Data Center (BIDC) Program. The BIDC Program directly serves businesses through a variety of government, academic, and nonprofit organizations.

Since 1978, state data centers have provided training and technical assistance in accessing and using census data.

Utah has four agencies that provide census data. The lead center is the Utah Office of Planning and Budget at the state capitol in Salt Lake City. Each agency can provide printouts, extracts, tape copies, and online data services. They provide newsletters, technical journals, and Census maps. Contact the lead center for information about the agency nearest you. Refer to Appendix C for contact information or to learn the center's Web site.

You can learn more about the SDK/BID programs by contacting the Customer Liaison Office of the U.S. Bureau of the Census. Refer to Appendix B for the address and phone number of this agency.

As you get to know the incentives for doing business in Utah, notice how using this statistical information can give you the edge on understanding the potential market and customer for your product or service. The statistics here just begin to scratch the surface. For more detailed analyses and surveys of the makeup of Utah, contact your state data center.

Incentives for Doing Business in Utah

Utah is a forward-looking state and its government recognizes the importance of the contribution small businesses make to the financial stability of the state. The requirements for establishing a new business in Utah are very much the same as in all other states. But, Utah is striving to simplify the process and has established a single point of contact to help you get your business up an running. The One-Stop Online Business Registration Center is operated by the Division of Corporations and Commercial Code in Utah's Department of

Commerce. The center can provide most of the forms needed for registering your business with state and federal agencies.

Utah's individual and corporate tax structure is more favorable than many other states. More details about Utah's taxes are provided later in this chapter.

Utah offers a cost of living that falls below the national levels for most indicators. Educational opportunities in Utah are outstanding and there are plenty of cultural and recreational activities. Health care is excellent, and it is said that Utah's residents enjoy lower disease rates—significantly lower cancer rates—and longer life expectancies. Also important to your family is the crime rate in Utah is lower than it is in 43 other states.

Educational opportunities in Utah are outstanding and there are plenty of cultural and recreational activities.

Overall Business Climate

For the past 15 years the Corporation for Enterprise Development has graded each of the 50 states in terms of their overall business climate. The grading system is A to F (F being the lowest rank) for three indexes called Performance, Business Vitality, and Development Capacity. The three indices are further subdivided into additional indices that rank the states in comparison to one another and offer a seven-year history of the rankings. In 2002, Utah received grades in the specific indices as follows:

- *Performance Index* measures how well the state is providing a shared and sustainable standard of living. It measures the degree to which the economy is proving jobs, how well the workforce is compensated, how widely shared the economic growth is distributed, and the quality of life. Grade: B
- *Business Vitality Index* measures the well-being of businesses currently operating in the state. Businesses spawn new businesses, they grow and attract other businesses. Therefore, the health of existing businesses is important to the state's ability to attract and grow businesses. Grade: B
- *Development Capacity Index* measures capacity-building investments such as the development of an educated and skilled workforce, and the creation and maintenance of a physical infrastructure. Grade: A

The full report of the Corporation for Enterprise Development can be viewed at its Web site, http://drc.cfed.org.

Access to Markets

Utah's mid-west location is an equal distance to all major western markets. Utah is served by an international airport, two railroads, and an east-west, north-south interstate highway system, all providing easy access to domestic and foreign markets.

> Utah's mid-west location is an equal distance to all major western markets.

AIRPORTS

The Salt Lake City International Airport is located ten minutes west of metropolitan Salt Lake City. The nation's 25th busiest airport in passenger traffic with more than 18 million passengers served in 2002 and it is a full-service customs port of entry. Salt Lake City International has 12 commercial airlines that provide daily flights to major U.S. cities and other communities in Utah. Some of the airlines operating out of Salt Lake City International include: America West Airlines, Continental Airlines, Delta Air Lines, Northwest Airlines, Southwest Airlines, and United Airlines, just to name a few.

Looking to the future, Salt Lake City International has acquired sufficient property to allow for expansion of the facility. This should ensure the quality of air service in Utah without the problems and delays associated with congestion and overcrowding that plagues many large airports.

RAILROADS

Utah's rail service has approximately 1,700 miles of track and a Class I railroad—the combined Union Pacific and Southern Pacific lines—provides freight service in and out of Utah. Utah's strategic location makes it an excellent switching route for coast-to-coast shipments without having to back haul shipments. Amtrak provides passenger service to major U.S. cities.

HIGHWAYS

Utah's transportation network includes more than 43,000 miles of federal, state, and local highways and roads. Three interstate highways provide efficient transportation of goods and materials throughout the state and across the nation. Interstate Highway I-70 provides an east-west route through the central part of the state. Interstate I-15 links the north and south. Interstate I-80 is a coast-to-coast artery that runs through Salt Lake City. Other important links are I-84, northbound to the Pacific Northwest, and I-215 which is the Salt Lake County belt route.

In addition to the interstate highway system, Utah's primary and secondary state highways provide easy access to rural areas of the state.

More than 2,300 interstate and intrastate motor freight carriers have operations in Utah. This provides same-day or one- to two-day service to major metropolitan markets in the Western United States. Ten cities in Utah are designated as ports of entry. These cities include Daniels, Echo, Kanab, Loma, Monticello, Peerless, Perry, St. George, Wendover, and Salt Lake City—POE headquarters.

For your convenience, a map showing Utah's interstate highway system is included at the end of this chapter.

Labor Force Outlook

According to statistics provided by the Utah Department of Workforce Services, approximately 98 percent of Utah's workers were employed in nonagricultural industries in 2003; of these, about 7.5 percent were self employed. Nearly 2 percent of Utah's workers were employed in agriculture.

Thanks to Utah's high birth rate, Utah is one of the few states with a growing indigenous labor force—one that is predicted to grow at twice the national average rate. The pool of available young workers is expected to increase by 60 percent by the year 2020.

Utah is currently ranked fourth in the nation in percentage of adults who have completed high school and the overall literacy rate is high.

Utah's workforce is young, healthy, and well educated. In fact, it is the youngest labor force of any state and Utah has the lowest death rate for cancer and second-lowest rate for heart disease in the nation. Studies have also shown that the Utah workforce has a low absenteeism rates when compared with other states. Utah is currently ranked fourth in the nation in percentage of adults who have completed high school and the overall literacy rate is high as well.

Demographic projections indicate that non-farm payroll employment for Utah will increase from 1,075,600 in 2000 to almost 1.8 million in 2030; an increase of 722,000 jobs over the projections period. The supply of labor is aided by the high labor force participation rate. Among males over 16, some 81.8 percent participated in the labor force in 2000, compared to the national average of 74.7 percent. Utah's female participation rate is also above the national average, 63.3 percent compared to 60.0 percent nationally.

Tax Incentives

The individual and corporate tax structure in Utah is tied to the federal tax system with a top rate of 7 percent levied on taxable income greater than $7,500. Utah does not require quarterly prepayments of income taxes for self-employed individuals, but provides for this method for those who choose to prepay. The tax system allows for several credits and exemptions. For example:

- Farmers and ranchers may claim a tax credit for tax paid for gasoline and diesel fuel used in agricultural operations.
- Utah businesses that install renewable commercial energy systems may claim the Utah Renewable Energy Tax Credit.
- Certain types of manufacturing businesses operating within designated rural Enterprise Zones in the state may be eligible for expanded state income or Utah corporate franchise tax incentives.
- Utah permits businesses to take a credit of 20 percent of the cost of rehabilitation of historic buildings for residential use.
- Employers who hire disabled workers may be eligible for a significant tax credit.
- Individuals and corporations in a recycling development zone may be eligible for tax credits for the purchase of equipment or facilities for certain recycling activities.

Other taxes that may affect your Utah business include sales and use tax, city or county sales tax, and property tax.

Utah businesses that install renewable commercial energy systems may claim the Utah Renewable Energy Tax Credit.

Lifestyle

Residents of Utah enjoy a four-season climate with temperatures ranging from an average of 37 degrees in January to 93 degrees in July. Annual precipitation varies from less than 5 inches in the Great Salt Lake Desert to more than 60 inches in the northern mountain ranges. Snow accumulates to 10 feet or more at some Wasatch Mountain ski resorts and at some locations, the season-long snow total can be up to 50 feet.

The state's altitude ranges from a low of 2,200 feet in Washington County to 13,528 feet at King's Peak, Utah's highest point. There are seven major rivers in Utah. They are the Bear, Colorado, Green, Provo, Sevier, San Juan, and Weber rivers.

The cost of living in Utah compares favorably with the nation as a whole. A cost of living index created by the American Chamber of Commerce's Research Association compared Salt Lake City to 11 western metropolitan cities for costs associated with housing, groceries, utilities, and health care. It was found that Salt Lake City is typically at or below the national average for all such costs.

SPORTS AND RECREATION

Utah's five national parks include: Arches, Bryce Canyon, Canyonlands, Capitol Reef, and Zion National Park—all quite different and all quite breathtaking. Utah also boasts of seven national monuments: Cedar Breaks, Dinosaur, Grand Staircase-Escalante, Hovenweep, Natural Bridges, Rainbow Bridge, and Timpanogos Cave. If that's not enough to impress you, the state encompasses 7 national forests, 45 state parks, and 22 major lakes. What's more, there are 14 Alpine and 10 Nordic ski resorts and 850 miles of groomed snowmobiling trails. Utah's ski season runs from mid-November through the first of May.

Utah encompasses 7 national forests, 45 state parks and 22 major lakes.

If you are a sports fan, you are not out in the cold in Utah—in spite of all the snow. The Utah Jazz competes in the National Basketball Association's exciting seasons. Hockey lovers can cheer for the Utah Grizzlies, or if you prefer, take in a AAA baseball game with the Salt Lake Stingers. Women's sports are growing in popularity and the Utah Predators score high in women's volleyball as do the Utah Starzz of the Women's National Basketball Association. In addition to these professional teams, Utah is well represented in college sports by the Cougars of BYU, the Aggies of Utah State University, or the Running Utes of the University of Utah.

ARTS

If your tastes run more to the performing arts, Utah has much to offer. There is an opera company, a symphony orchestra, and several ballet, modern dance and theater companies. Major performing arts organizations include: Ballet West, Ririe Woodbury Dance Company, the Utah Opera Company, Repertory Dance Theatre and the internationally renown Mormon Tabernacle Choir. In addition, the Utah Symphony, housed in Maurice Abravanel Hall, performs more than 70 concerts at home each year and travels to Wyoming, Nevada, Idaho, and other communities in Utah on a regular basis. A fully professional theater is in residence at the University of Utah's Pioneer Theatre Company and produces seven plays from September through May.

EDUCATION

Higher education is readily available for Utah's residents. The University of Utah is a major urban state university with significant programs in research, graduate, professional, and undergraduate education, and degree programs including law and medicine. Utah

State University is a primary center of university research and of graduate, professional, and undergraduate education in many fields of study. Other major institutions in the state include: Weber State University, Southern Utah University, Westminster College, Dixie College, Utah Valley State College, and Brigham Young University, just to name a few.

High-quality medical care is available throughout Utah. There are 52 hospitals with more than 6,300 beds. The University of Utah Health Sciences Center is well-known for its patient care and teaching facilities. The center includes the University Hospital, the School of Medicine, and the School of Nursing. The center is widely recognized for its burn care center, trauma center, newborn intensive care unit, the John Moran Eye Center, and more. Also located at the University of Utah in Salt Lake City is the Huntsman Cancer Institute—opened in 1999—a world-class cancer research and treatment center. According to the U.S. Department of Health and Human Services, Utah's residents enjoy the fourth longest life expectancy in the nation.

The Utah Technology Finance Corporation provides financial assistance to small companies, particularly those involved in the field of information technology.

Research and Development, Financing, and Support Services

To assist in the incubation and growth of new and emerging high technology business, the Utah Technology Finance Corporation provides financial assistance to small companies, particularly those involved in the field of information technology. UTFC provides subordinated debt financing up to $250,000.

For more information about its services, contact the Utah Technology Finance Corporation at the address included in Appendix C.

Chapter Wrap-Up

Utah's economic, social, and cultural advantages make it a very desirable place to live. Low humidity and lots of sunshine are two favorable aspects of Utah's weather. Relatively low individual and corporate taxes and a business-friendly government make Utah an attractive location for new and expanding businesses. A well-educated, dependable, and comparatively young workforce is another feature available in Utah. If you choose to establish your roots in Utah, you too will sing the praises of Utah—and probably louder than the Mormon Tabernacle Choir.

Map of Utah

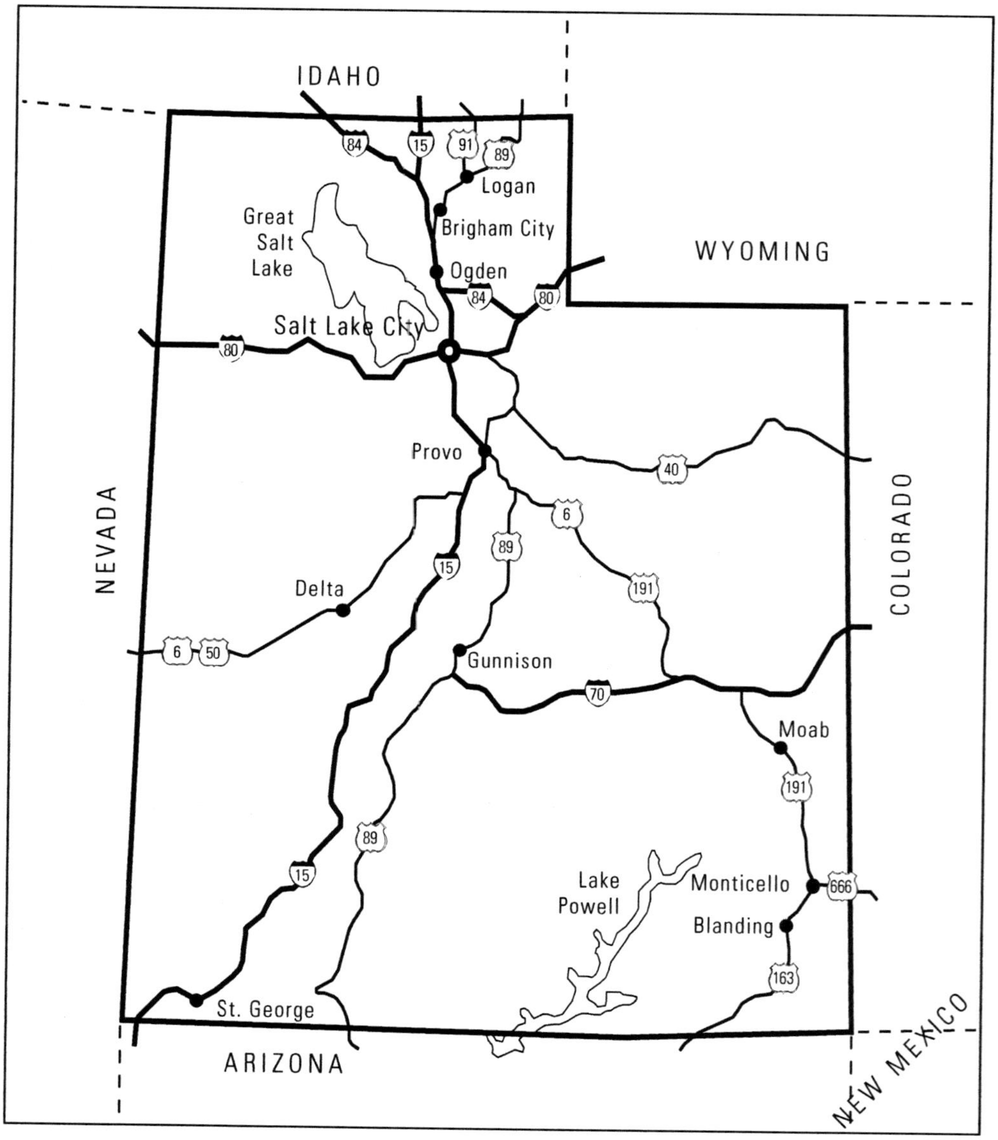
IDAHO
WYOMING
NEVADA
COLORADO
ARIZONA
NEW MEXICO
Great Salt Lake
Logan
Brigham City
Ogden
Salt Lake City
Provo
Delta
Gunnison
Moab
Lake Powell
Monticello
Blanding
St. George
84
15
91
89
80
40
6
50
191
70
666
163

Forms You'll Need to Get Started

This appendix contains many of the referenced forms. The table identifies the chapter in which each form is mentioned and the page on which it is located in Appendix A. The government forms reproduced here must not be used for submission. Obtain full-sized forms from the appropriate government agency for that purpose.

Form 2553. Election by a Small Business Corporation

Form **2553**
(Rev. October 2001)
Department of the Treasury
Internal Revenue Service

Election by a Small Business Corporation
(Under section 1362 of the Internal Revenue Code)
▶ See Parts II and III on back and the separate instructions.
▶ The corporation may either send or fax this form to the IRS. See page 2 of the instructions.

OMB No. 1545-0146

Notes: 1. *Do not file Form 1120S, U.S. Income Tax Return for an S Corporation, for any tax year before the year the election takes effect.*
2. *This election to be an S corporation can be accepted only if all the tests are met under* ***Who May Elect*** *on page 1 of the instructions; all shareholders have signed the consent statement; and the exact name and address of the corporation and other required form information are provided.*
3. *If the corporation was in existence before the effective date of this election, see* ***Taxes an S Corporation May Owe*** *on page 1 of the instructions.*

Part I Election Information

Please Type or Print		
	Name of corporation (see instructions)	**A** Employer identification number
	Number, street, and room or suite no. (If a P.O. box, see instructions.)	**B** Date incorporated
	City or town, state, and ZIP code	**C** State of incorporation

D Check the applicable box(es) if the corporation, after applying for the EIN shown in **A** above, changed its name ☐ or address ☐

E Election is to be effective for tax year beginning (month, day, year) . . . . ▶ / /

F Name and title of officer or legal representative who the IRS may call for more information

G Telephone number of officer or legal representative
( )

H If this election takes effect for the first tax year the corporation exists, enter month, day, and year of the **earliest** of the following: (1) date the corporation first had shareholders, (2) date the corporation first had assets, or (3) date the corporation began doing business . . . . ▶ / /

I Selected tax year: Annual return will be filed for tax year ending (month and day) ▶

If the tax year ends on any date other than December 31, except for an automatic 52-53-week tax year ending with reference to the month of December, you **must** complete Part II on the back. If the date you enter is the ending date of an automatic 52-53-week tax year, write "52-53-week year" to the right of the date. See Temporary Regulations section 1.441-2T(e)(3).

J Name and address of each shareholder; shareholder's spouse having a community property interest in the corporation's stock; and each tenant in common, joint tenant, and tenant by the entirety. (A husband and wife (and their estates) are counted as one shareholder in determining the number of shareholders without regard to the manner in which the stock is owned.)	**K** Shareholders' Consent Statement. Under penalties of perjury, we declare that we consent to the election of the above-named corporation to be an S corporation under section 1362(a) and that we have examined this consent statement, including accompanying schedules and statements, and to the best of our knowledge and belief, it is true, correct, and complete. We understand our consent is binding and may not be withdrawn after the corporation has made a valid election. (Shareholders sign and date below.)		**L** Stock owned		**M** Social security number or employer identification number (see instructions)	**N** Share-holder's tax year ends (month and day)
	Signature	Date	Number of shares	Dates acquired		

Under penalties of perjury, I declare that I have examined this election, including accompanying schedules and statements, and to the best of my knowledge and belief, it is true, correct, and complete.

Signature of officer ▶ **Title ▶** **Date ▶**

For Paperwork Reduction Act Notice, see page 4 of the instructions. Cat. No. 18629R Form **2553** (Rev. 10-2001)

Form 2553. Election by a Small Business Corporation, continued

Form 2553 (Rev. 10-2001) Page **2**

Part II **Selection of Fiscal Tax Year** (All corporations using this part must complete item O and item P, Q, or R.)

O Check the applicable box to indicate whether the corporation is:

1. ☐ A new corporation adopting the tax year entered in item I, Part I.
2. ☐ An existing corporation retaining the tax year entered in item I, Part I.
3. ☐ An existing corporation changing to the tax year entered in item I, Part I.

P Complete item P if the corporation is using the expeditious approval provisions of Rev. Proc. 87-32, 1987-2 C.B. 396, to request **(1)** a natural business year (as defined in section 4.01(1) of Rev. Proc. 87-32) or **(2)** a year that satisfies the ownership tax year test in section 4.01(2) of Rev. Proc. 87-32. Check the applicable box below to indicate the representation statement the corporation is making as required under section 4 of Rev. Proc. 87-32.

1. Natural Business Year ▶ ☐ I represent that the corporation is retaining or changing to a tax year that coincides with its natural business year as defined in section 4.01(1) of Rev. Proc. 87-32 and as verified by its satisfaction of the requirements of section 4.02(1) of Rev. Proc. 87-32. In addition, if the corporation is changing to a natural business year as defined in section 4.01(1), I further represent that such tax year results in less deferral of income to the owners than the corporation's present tax year. I also represent that the corporation is not described in section 3.01(2) of Rev. Proc. 87-32. (See instructions for additional information that must be attached.)

2. Ownership Tax Year ▶ ☐ I represent that shareholders holding more than half of the shares of the stock (as of the first day of the tax year to which the request relates) of the corporation have the same tax year or are concurrently changing to the tax year that the corporation adopts, retains, or changes to per item I, Part I. I also represent that the corporation is not described in section 3.01(2) of Rev. Proc. 87-32.

Note: *If you do not use item P and the corporation wants a fiscal tax year, complete either item Q or R below. Item Q is used to request a fiscal tax year based on a business purpose and to make a back-up section 444 election. Item R is used to make a regular section 444 election.*

Q Business Purpose—To request a fiscal tax year based on a business purpose, you must check box Q1 and pay a user fee. See instructions for details. You may also check box Q2 and/or box Q3.

1. Check here ▶ ☐ if the fiscal year entered in item I, Part I, is requested under the provisions of section 6.03 of Rev. Proc. 87-32. Attach to Form 2553 a statement showing the business purpose for the requested fiscal year. See instructions for additional information that must be attached.

2. Check here ▶ ☐ to show that the corporation intends to make a back-up section 444 election in the event the corporation's business purpose request is not approved by the IRS. (See instructions for more information.)

3. Check here ▶ ☐ to show that the corporation agrees to adopt or change to a tax year ending December 31 if necessary for the IRS to accept this election for S corporation status in the event (1) the corporation's business purpose request is not approved and the corporation makes a back-up section 444 election, but is ultimately not qualified to make a section 444 election, or (2) the corporation's business purpose request is not approved and the corporation did not make a back-up section 444 election.

R Section 444 Election—To make a section 444 election, you must check box R1 and you may also check box R2.

1. Check here ▶ ☐ to show the corporation will make, if qualified, a section 444 election to have the fiscal tax year shown in item I, Part I. To make the election, you must complete **Form 8716,** Election To Have a Tax Year Other Than a Required Tax Year, and either attach it to Form 2553 or file it separately.

2. Check here ▶ ☐ to show that the corporation agrees to adopt or change to a tax year ending December 31 if necessary for the IRS to accept this election for S corporation status in the event the corporation is ultimately not qualified to make a section 444 election.

Part III **Qualified Subchapter S Trust (QSST) Election Under Section 1361(d)(2)***

Income beneficiary's name and address	Social security number
Trust's name and address	Employer identification number

Date on which stock of the corporation was transferred to the trust (month, day, year) . . . . ▶ / /

In order for the trust named above to be a QSST and thus a qualifying shareholder of the S corporation for which this Form 2553 is filed, I hereby make the election under section 1361(d)(2). Under penalties of perjury, I certify that the trust meets the definitional requirements of section 1361(d)(3) and that all other information provided in Part III is true, correct, and complete.

Signature of income beneficiary or signature and title of legal representative or other qualified person making the election Date

*Use Part III to make the QSST election only if stock of the corporation has been transferred to the trust on or before the date on which the corporation makes its election to be an S corporation. The QSST election must be made and filed separately if stock of the corporation is transferred to the trust after the date on which the corporation makes the S election.

Form **2553** (Rev. 10-2001)

Form SS-4. Application for Employer Identification Number

Form **SS-4** (Rev. December 2001) Department of the Treasury Internal Revenue Service

Application for Employer Identification Number

(For use by employers, corporations, partnerships, trusts, estates, churches, government agencies, Indian tribal entities, certain individuals, and others.)

▶ See separate instructions for each line. ▶ Keep a copy for your records.

EIN

OMB No. 1545-0003

Type or print clearly.

1 Legal name of entity (or individual) for whom the EIN is being requested

2 Trade name of business (if different from name on line 1)
3 Executor, trustee, "care of" name

4a Mailing address (room, apt., suite no. and street, or P.O. box)
5a Street address (if different) (Do not enter a P.O. box.)

4b City, state, and ZIP code
5b City, state, and ZIP code

6 County and state where principal business is located

7a Name of principal officer, general partner, grantor, owner, or trustor
7b SSN, ITIN, or EIN

8a **Type of entity** (check only one box)
- ☐ Sole proprietor (SSN) ______
- ☐ Partnership
- ☐ Corporation (enter form number to be filed) ▶ ______
- ☐ Personal service corp.
- ☐ Church or church-controlled organization
- ☐ Other nonprofit organization (specify) ▶ ______
- ☐ Other (specify) ▶
- ☐ Estate (SSN of decedent) ______
- ☐ Plan administrator (SSN) ______
- ☐ Trust (SSN of grantor) ______
- ☐ National Guard
- ☐ Farmers' cooperative
- ☐ REMIC
- ☐ State/local government
- ☐ Federal government/military
- ☐ Indian tribal governments/enterprises

Group Exemption Number (GEN) ▶ ______

8b If a corporation, name the state or foreign country (if applicable) where incorporated | State | Foreign country

9 **Reason for applying** (check only one box)
- ☐ Started new business (specify type) ▶ ______
- ☐ Hired employees (Check the box and see line 12.)
- ☐ Compliance with IRS withholding regulations
- ☐ Other (specify) ▶
- ☐ Banking purpose (specify purpose) ▶ ______
- ☐ Changed type of organization (specify new type) ▶ ______
- ☐ Purchased going business
- ☐ Created a trust (specify type) ▶ ______
- ☐ Created a pension plan (specify type) ▶ ______

10 Date business started or acquired (month, day, year)
11 Closing month of accounting year

12 First date wages or annuities were paid or will be paid (month, day, year). **Note:** *If applicant is a withholding agent, enter date income will first be paid to nonresident alien. (month, day, year)* . . . . ▶

13 Highest number of employees expected in the next 12 months. **Note:** *If the applicant does not expect to have any employees during the period, enter "-0-."* . . . . ▶

Agricultural	Household	Other

14 Check **one** box that best describes the principal activity of your business.
- ☐ Health care & social assistance
- ☐ Wholesale-agent/broker
- ☐ Construction
- ☐ Rental & leasing
- ☐ Transportation & warehousing
- ☐ Accommodation & food service
- ☐ Wholesale-other
- ☐ Retail
- ☐ Real estate
- ☐ Manufacturing
- ☐ Finance & insurance
- ☐ Other (specify)

15 Indicate principal line of merchandise sold; specific construction work done; products produced; or services provided.

16a Has the applicant ever applied for an employer identification number for this or any other business? . . . . ☐ **Yes** ☐ **No**
Note: *If "Yes," please complete lines 16b and 16c.*

16b If you checked "Yes" on line 16a, give applicant's legal name and trade name shown on prior application if different from line 1 or 2 above.
Legal name ▶ Trade name ▶

16c Approximate date when, and city and state where, the application was filed. Enter previous employer identification number if known.

Approximate date when filed (mo., day, year)	City and state where filed	Previous EIN

Third Party Designee

Complete this section **only** if you want to authorize the named individual to receive the entity's EIN and answer questions about the completion of this form.

Designee's name | Designee's telephone number (include area code) ( )

Address and ZIP code | Designee's fax number (include area code) ( )

Under penalties of perjury, I declare that I have examined this application, and to the best of my knowledge and belief, it is true, correct, and complete.

Name and title (type or print clearly) ▶ | Applicant's telephone number (include area code) ( )

Signature ▶ Date ▶ | Applicant's fax number (include area code) ( )

For Privacy Act and Paperwork Reduction Act Notice, see separate instructions. Cat. No. 16055N Form **SS-4** (Rev. 12-2001)

Form SS-4. Application for Employer Identification Number, continued

Form SS-4 (Rev. 12-2001) Page 2

Do I Need an EIN?

File Form SS-4 if the applicant entity does not already have an EIN but is required to show an EIN on any return, statement, or other document.[1] **See also the separate instructions for each line on Form SS-4.**

IF the applicant...	AND...	THEN...
Started a new business	Does not currently have (nor expect to have) employees	Complete lines 1, 2, 4a–6, 8a, and 9–16c.
Hired (or will hire) employees, including household employees	Does not already have an EIN	Complete lines 1, 2, 4a–6, 7a–b (if applicable), 8a, 8b (if applicable), and 9–16c.
Opened a bank account	Needs an EIN for banking purposes only	Complete lines 1–5b, 7a–b (if applicable), 8a, 9, and 16a–c.
Changed type of organization	Either the legal character of the organization or its ownership changed (e.g., you incorporate a sole proprietorship or form a partnership)[2]	Complete lines 1–16c (as applicable).
Purchased a going business[3]	Does not already have an EIN	Complete lines 1–16c (as applicable).
Created a trust	The trust is other than a grantor trust or an IRA trust[4]	Complete lines 1–16c (as applicable).
Created a pension plan as a plan administrator[5]	Needs an EIN for reporting purposes	Complete lines 1, 2, 4a–6, 8a, 9, and 16a–c.
Is a foreign person needing an EIN to comply with IRS withholding regulations	Needs an EIN to complete a Form W-8 (other than Form W-8ECI), avoid withholding on portfolio assets, or claim tax treaty benefits[6]	Complete lines 1–5b, 7a–b (SSN or ITIN optional), 8a–9, and 16a–c.
Is administering an estate	Needs an EIN to report estate income on Form 1041	Complete lines 1, 3, 4a–b, 8a, 9, and 16a–c.
Is a withholding agent for taxes on non-wage income paid to an alien (i.e., individual, corporation, or partnership, etc.)	Is an agent, broker, fiduciary, manager, tenant, or spouse who is required to file **Form 1042,** Annual Withholding Tax Return for U.S. Source Income of Foreign Persons	Complete lines 1, 2, 3 (if applicable), 4a–5b, 7a–b (if applicable), 8a, 9, and 16a–c.
Is a state or local agency	Serves as a tax reporting agent for public assistance recipients under Rev. Proc. 80-4, 1980-1 C.B. 581[7]	Complete lines 1, 2, 4a–5b, 8a, 9, and 16a–c.
Is a single-member LLC	Needs an EIN to file **Form 8832,** Classification Election, for filing employment tax returns, **or** for state reporting purposes[8]	Complete lines 1–16c (as applicable).
Is an S corporation	Needs an EIN to file **Form 2553,** Election by a Small Business Corporation[9]	Complete lines 1–16c (as applicable).

[1] For example, a sole proprietorship or self-employed farmer who establishes a qualified retirement plan, or is required to file excise, employment, alcohol, tobacco, or firearms returns, must have an EIN. **A partnership, corporation, REMIC (real estate mortgage investment conduit), nonprofit organization (church, club, etc.), or farmers' cooperative must use an EIN for any tax-related purpose even if the entity does not have employees.**

[2] However, **do not** apply for a new EIN if the existing entity only **(a)** changed its business name, **(b)** elected on Form 8832 to change the way it is taxed (or is covered by the default rules), or **(c)** terminated its partnership status because at least 50% of the total interests in partnership capital and profits were sold or exchanged within a 12-month period. (The EIN of the terminated partnership should continue to be used. See Regulations section 301.6109-1(d)(2)(iii).)

[3] Do not use the EIN of the prior business unless you became the "owner" of a corporation by acquiring its stock.

[4] However, IRA trusts that are required to file **Form 990-T,** Exempt Organization Business Income Tax Return, must have an EIN.

[5] A plan administrator is the person or group of persons specified as the administrator by the instrument under which the plan is operated.

[6] Entities applying to be a Qualified Intermediary (QI) need a QI-EIN even if they already have an EIN. **See Rev. Proc. 2000-12.**

[7] See also *Household employer* on page 4. (**Note:** State or local agencies may need an EIN for other reasons, e.g., hired employees.)

[8] Most LLCs **do not** need to file Form 8832. See **Limited liability company (LLC)** on page 4 for details on completing Form SS-4 for an LLC.

[9] An existing corporation that is electing or revoking S corporation status should use its previously-assigned EIN.

Form SS-4. Instructions for Form SS-4

Instructions for Form SS-4

(Rev. December 2001)

Department of the Treasury
Internal Revenue Service

Application for Employer Identification Number

Section references are to the Internal Revenue Code unless otherwise noted.

General Instructions

Use these instructions to complete **Form SS-4,** Application for Employer Identification Number. Also see **Do I Need an EIN?** on page 2 of Form SS-4.

Purpose of Form

Use Form SS-4 to apply for an employer identification number (EIN). An EIN is a nine-digit number (for example, 12-3456789) assigned to sole proprietors, corporations, partnerships, estates, trusts, and other entities for tax filing and reporting purposes. The information you provide on this form will establish your business tax account.

CAUTION *An EIN is for use in connection with your business activities only. Do **not** use your EIN in place of your social security number (SSN).*

File only one Form SS-4. Generally, a sole proprietor should file only one Form SS-4 and needs only one EIN, regardless of the number of businesses operated as a sole proprietorship or trade names under which a business operates. However, if the proprietorship incorporates or enters into a partnership, a new EIN is required. Also, each corporation in an affiliated group must have its own EIN.

EIN applied for, but not received. If you do not have an EIN by the time a **return** is due, write "Applied For" and the date you applied in the space shown for the number. **Do not** show your social security number (SSN) as an EIN on returns.

If you do not have an EIN by the time a **tax deposit** is due, send your payment to the Internal Revenue Service Center for your filing area as shown in the instructions for the form that you are are filing. Make your check or money order payable to the **"United States Treasury"** and show your name (as shown on Form SS-4), address, type of tax, period covered, and date you applied for an EIN.

Related Forms and Publications

The following **forms** and **instructions** may be useful to filers of Form SS-4:

- **Form 990-T,** Exempt Organization Business Income Tax Return
- **Instructions for Form 990-T**
- **Schedule C (Form 1040),** Profit or Loss From Business
- **Schedule F (Form 1040),** Profit or Loss From Farming
- **Instructions for Form 1041 and Schedules A, B, D, G, I, J, and K-1,** U.S. Income Tax Return for Estates and Trusts
- **Form 1042,** Annual Withholding Tax Return for U.S. Source Income of Foreign Persons
- **Instructions for Form 1065,** U.S. Return of Partnership Income
- **Instructions for Form 1066,** U.S. Real Estate Mortgage Investment Conduit (REMIC) Income Tax Return
- **Instructions for Forms 1120 and 1120-A**
- **Form 2553,** Election by a Small Business Corporation
- **Form 2848,** Power of Attorney and Declaration of Representative
- **Form 8821,** Tax Information Authorization
- **Form 8832,** Entity Classification Election

For more **information** about filing Form SS-4 and related issues, see:

- **Circular A,** Agricultural Employer's Tax Guide (Pub. 51)
- **Circular E,** Employer's Tax Guide (Pub. 15)
- **Pub. 538,** Accounting Periods and Methods
- **Pub. 542,** Corporations
- **Pub. 557,** Exempt Status for Your Organization
- **Pub. 583,** Starting a Business and Keeping Records
- **Pub. 966,** EFTPS: Now a Full Range of Electronic Choices to Pay All Your Federal Taxes
- **Pub. 1635,** Understanding Your EIN
- **Package 1023,** Application for Recognition of Exemption
- **Package 1024,** Application for Recognition of Exemption Under Section 501(a)

How To Get Forms and Publications

Phone. You can order forms, instructions, and publications by phone 24 hours a day, 7 days a week. Just call 1-800-TAX-FORM (1-800-829-3676). You should receive your order or notification of its status within 10 workdays.

Personal computer. With your personal computer and modem, you can get the forms and information you need using the IRS Web Site at **www.irs.gov** or File Transfer Protocol at **ftp.irs.gov.**

CD-ROM. For small businesses, return preparers, or others who may frequently need tax forms or publications, a CD-ROM containing over 2,000 tax products (including many prior year forms) can be purchased from the National Technical Information Service (NTIS).

To order **Pub. 1796,** Federal Tax Products on CD-ROM, call **1-877-CDFORMS** (1-877-233-6767) toll free or connect to **www.irs.gov/cdorders.**

Cat. No. 62736F

Form SS-4. Instructions for Form SS-4, continued

Tax Help for Your Business

IRS-sponsored Small Business Workshops provide information about your Federal and state tax obligations. For information about workshops in your area, call 1-800-829-1040 and ask for your Taxpayer Education Coordinator.

How To Apply

You can apply for an EIN by telephone, fax, or mail depending on how soon you need to use the EIN.

Application by Tele-TIN. Under the Tele-TIN program, you can receive your EIN by telephone and use it immediately to file a return or make a payment. To receive an EIN by telephone, IRS suggests that you complete Form SS-4 so that you will have all relevant information available. Then call the Tele-TIN number at 1-866-816-2065. (International applicants must call 215-516-6999.) Tele-TIN hours of operation are 7:30 a.m. to 5:30 p.m. time. The person making the call must be authorized to sign the form or be an authorized designee. See **Signature** and **Third Party Designee** on page 6. Also see the **TIP** below.

An IRS representative will use the information from the Form SS-4 to establish your account and assign you an EIN. Write the number you are given on the upper right corner of the form and sign and date it. Keep this copy for your records.

If requested by an IRS representative, mail or fax (facsimile) the signed Form SS-4 (including any Third Party Designee authorization) **within 24 hours** to the Tele-TIN Unit at the service center address provided by the IRS representative.

TIP *Taxpayer representatives can use Tele-TIN to apply for an EIN on behalf of their client and request that the EIN be faxed to their **client** on the same day. (**Note:** By utilizing this procedure, you are authorizing the IRS to fax the EIN without a cover sheet.)*

Application by Fax-TIN. Under the Fax-TIN program, you can receive your EIN by fax within 4 business days. Complete and fax Form SS-4 to the IRS using the Fax-TIN number listed below for your state. A long-distance charge to callers outside of the local calling area will apply. Fax-TIN numbers can only be used to apply for an EIN. **The numbers may change without notice.** Fax-TIN is available 24 hours a day, 7 days a week.

Be sure to provide your fax number so that IRS can fax the EIN back to you. (**Note:** By utilizing this procedure, you are authorizing the IRS to fax the EIN without a cover sheet.)

Do not call Tele-TIN for the same entity because duplicate EINs may be issued. See **Third Party Designee** on page 6.

Application by mail. Complete Form SS-4 at least 4 to 5 weeks before you will need an EIN. Sign and date the application and mail it to the service center address for your state. You will receive your EIN in the mail in approximately 4 weeks. See also **Third Party Designee** on page 6.

Call 1-800-829-1040 to verify a number or to ask about the status of an application by mail.

If your principal business, office or agency, or legal residence in the case of an individual, is located in:	Call the Tele-TIN or Fax-TIN number shown or file with the "Internal Revenue Service Center" at:
Connecticut, Delaware, District of Columbia, Florida, Georgia, Maine, Maryland, Massachusetts, New Hampshire, New Jersey, New York, North Carolina, Ohio, Pennsylvania, Rhode Island, South Carolina, Vermont, Virginia, West Virginia	Attn: EIN Operation Holtsville, NY 00501 Tele-TIN 866-816-2065 Fax-TIN 631-447-8960
Illinois, Indiana, Kentucky, Michigan	Attn: EIN Operation Cincinnati, OH 45999 Tele-TIN 866-816-2065 Fax-TIN 859-669-5760
Alabama, Alaska, Arizona, Arkansas, California, Colorado, Hawaii, Idaho, Iowa, Kansas, Louisiana, Minnesota, Mississippi, Missouri, Montana, Nebraska, Nevada, New Mexico, North Dakota, Oklahoma, Oregon, Puerto Rico, South Dakota, Tennessee, Texas, Utah, Washington, Wisconsin, Wyoming	Attn: EIN Operation Philadelphia, PA 19255 Tele-TIN 866-816-2065 Fax-TIN 215-516-3990
If you have no legal residence, principal place of business, or principal office or agency in any state:	Attn: EIN Operation Philadelphia, PA 19255 Tele-TIN 215-516-6999 Fax-TIN 215-516-3990

Specific Instructions

Print or type all entries on Form SS-4. Follow the instructions for each line to expedite processing and to avoid unnecessary IRS requests for additional information. Enter "N/A" (nonapplicable) on the lines that do not apply.

Line 1—Legal name of entity (or individual) for whom the EIN is being requested. Enter the legal name of the entity (or individual) applying for the EIN exactly as it appears on the social security card, charter, or other applicable legal document.

Individuals. Enter your first name, middle initial, and last name. If you are a sole proprietor, enter your individual name, not your business name. Enter your business name on line 2. Do not use abbreviations or nicknames on line 1.

Trusts. Enter the name of the trust.

Estate of a decedent. Enter the name of the estate.

Partnerships. Enter the legal name of the partnership as it appears in the partnership agreement.

-2-

Form SS-4. Instructions for Form SS-4, continued

Corporations. Enter the corporate name as it appears in the corporation charter or other legal document creating it.

Plan administrators. Enter the name of the plan administrator. A plan administrator who already has an EIN should use that number.

Line 2—Trade name of business. Enter the trade name of the business if different from the legal name. The trade name is the "doing business as" (DBA) name.

CAUTION *Use the full legal name shown on line 1 on all tax returns filed for the entity. (However, if you enter a trade name on line 2 and choose to use the trade name instead of the legal name, enter the trade name on **all returns** you file.) To prevent processing delays and errors, **always** use the legal name only (or the trade name only) on **all** tax returns.*

Line 3—Executor, trustee, "care of" name. Trusts enter the name of the trustee. Estates enter the name of the executor, administrator, or other fiduciary. If the entity applying has a designated person to receive tax information, enter that person's name as the "care of" person. Enter the individual's first name, middle initial, and last name.

Lines 4a-b—Mailing address. Enter the mailing address for the entity's correspondence. If line 3 is completed, enter the address for the executor, trustee or "care of" person. Generally, this address will be used on all tax returns.

TIP *File **Form 8822**, Change of Address, to report any subsequent changes to the entity's mailing address.*

Lines 5a-b—Street address. Provide the entity's physical address **only** if different from its mailing address shown in lines 4a-b. **Do not** enter a P.O. box number here.

Line 6—County and state where principal business is located. Enter the entity's primary **physical** location.

Lines 7a-b—Name of principal officer, general partner, grantor, owner, or trustor. Enter the first name, middle initial, last name, and SSN of **(a)** the principal officer if the business is a corporation, **(b)** a general partner if a partnership, **(c)** the owner of an entity that is disregarded as separate from its owner (disregarded entities owned by a corporation enter the corporation's name and EIN), or **(d)** a grantor, owner, or trustor if a trust.

If the person in question is an **alien individual** with a previously assigned individual taxpayer identification number (ITIN), enter the ITIN in the space provided and submit a copy of an official identifying document. If necessary, complete **Form W-7,** Application for IRS Individual Taxpayer Identification Number, to obtain an ITIN.

You are **required** to enter an SSN, ITIN, or EIN unless the only reason you are applying for an EIN is to make an entity classification election (see Regulations section 301.7701-1 through 301.7701-3) and you are a nonresident alien with no effectively connected income from sources within the United States.

Line 8a—Type of entity. Check the box that best describes the type of entity applying for the EIN. If you are an alien individual with an ITIN previously assigned to you, enter the ITIN in place of a requested SSN.

CAUTION *This is not an election for a tax classification of an entity. See **"Limited liability company (LLC)"** on page 4.*

Other. If not specifically mentioned, check the "Other" box, enter the type of entity and the type of return, if any, that will be filed (for example, "Common Trust Fund, Form 1065" or "Created a Pension Plan"). Do not enter "N/A." If you are an alien individual applying for an EIN, see the **Lines 7a-b** instructions above.

- **Household employer.** If you are an individual, check the "Other" box and enter "Household Employer" and your SSN. If you are a state or local agency serving as a tax reporting agent for public assistance recipients who become household employers, check the "Other" box and enter "Household Employer Agent." If you are a trust that qualifies as a household employer, you do not need a separate EIN for reporting tax information relating to household employees; use the EIN of the trust.
- **QSub.** For a qualified subchapter S subsidiary (QSub) check the "Other" box and specify "QSub."
- **Withholding agent.** If you are a withholding agent required to file Form 1042, check the "Other" box and enter "Withholding Agent."

Sole proprietor. Check this box if you file Schedule C, C-EZ, or F (Form 1040) and have a qualified plan, or are required to file excise, employment, or alcohol, tobacco, or firearms returns, or are a payer of gambling winnings. Enter your SSN (or ITIN) in the space provided. If you are a nonresident alien with no effectively connected income from sources within the United States, you do not need to enter an SSN or ITIN.

Corporation. This box is for any corporation **other than a personal service corporation.** If you check this box, enter the income tax form number to be filed by the entity in the space provided.

CAUTION *If you entered **"1120S"** after the "Corporation" checkbox, the corporation **must** file Form 2553 **no later than the 15th day of the 3rd month of the tax year the election is to take effect.** Until Form 2553 has been received and approved, you will be considered a Form 1120 filer. See the Instructions for Form 2553.*

Personal service corp. Check this box if the entity is a personal service corporation. An entity is a personal service corporation for a tax year only if:

- The principal activity of the entity during the testing period (prior tax year) for the tax year is the performance of personal services substantially by employee-owners, and
- The employee-owners own at least 10% of the fair market value of the outstanding stock in the entity on the last day of the testing period.

Personal services include performance of services in such fields as health, law, accounting, or consulting. For more information about personal service corporations,

-3-

Form SS-4. Instructions for Form SS-4, continued

see the Instructions for Forms 1120 and 1120-A and Pub. 542.

Other nonprofit organization. Check this box if the nonprofit organization is other than a church or church-controlled organization and specify the type of nonprofit organization (for example, an educational organization).

CAUTION *If the organization also seeks tax-exempt status, you **must** file either Package 1023 or Package 1024. See Pub. 557 for more information.*

If the organization is covered by a group exemption letter, enter the four-digit **group exemption number (GEN).** (Do not confuse the GEN with the nine-digit EIN.) If you do not know the GEN, contact the parent organization. Get Pub. 557 for more information about group exemption numbers.

Plan administrator. If the plan administrator is an individual, enter the plan administrator's SSN in the space provided.

REMIC. Check this box if the entity has elected to be treated as a real estate mortgage investment conduit (REMIC). See the Instructions for Form 1066 for more information.

Limited liability company (LLC). An LLC is an entity organized under the laws of a state or foreign country as a limited liability company. For Federal tax purposes, an LLC may be treated as a partnership or corporation or be disregarded as an entity separate from its owner.

By **default,** a domestic LLC with only one member is **disregarded** as an entity separate from its owner and must include all of its income and expenses on the owner's tax return (e.g., **Schedule C (Form 1040)**). Also by default, a domestic LLC with two or more members is treated as a partnership. A domestic LLC may file Form 8832 to avoid either default classification and elect to be classified as an association taxable as a corporation. For more information on entity classifications (including the rules for foreign entities), see the instructions for Form 8832.

CAUTION ***Do not** file Form 8832 if the LLC accepts the default classifications above. **However, if the LLC will be electing S Corporation status, it must timely file both Form 8832 and Form 2553.***

Complete Form SS-4 for LLCs as follows:

- A single-member, domestic LLC that accepts the default classification (above) does not need an EIN and generally should not file Form SS-4. Generally, the LLC should use the name and EIN of its **owner** for all Federal tax purposes. However, the reporting and payment of employment taxes for employees of the LLC may be made using the name and EIN or **either** the owner or the LLC as explained in Notice 99-6, 1999-1 C.B. 321. You can find Notice 99-6 on page 12 of Internal Revenue Bulletin 1999-3 at **www.irs.gov. (Note:** If the LLC-applicant indicates in box 13 that it has employees or expects to have employees, the owner (whether an individual or other entity) of a single-member domestic LLC will also be assigned its own EIN (if it does not already have one) even if the LLC will be filing the employment tax returns.)
- A single-member, domestic LLC accepts the default classification (above) and wants an EIN for filing employment tax returns (see above) or non-Federal purposes, such as a state requirement, must check the "Other" box and write "Disregarded Entity" or, when applicable, "Disregarded Entity—Sole Proprietorship" in the space provided.
- A multi-member, domestic LLC that accepts the default classification (above) must check the "Partnership" box.
- A domestic LLC that will be filing Form 8832 to elect corporate status must check the "Corporation" box and write in "Single-Member" or "Mult-Member" immediately below the "form number" entry line.

Line 9—Reason for applying. Check only **one** box. Do not enter "N/A."

Started new business. Check this box if you are starting a new business that requires an EIN. If you check this box, enter the type of business being started. **Do not** apply if you already have an EIN and are only adding another place of business.

Hired employees. Check this box if the existing business is requesting an EIN because it has hired or is hiring employees and is therefore required to file employment tax returns. **Do not** apply if you already have an EIN and are only hiring employees. For information on employment taxes (e.g., for family members), see Circular E.

CAUTION *You may be required to make electronic deposits of all depository taxes (such as employment tax, excise tax, and corporate income tax) using the Electronic Federal Tax Payment System (EFTPS). See section 11, Depositing Taxes, of Circular E and Pub. 966.*

Created a pension plan. Check this box if you have created a pension plan and need an EIN for reporting purposes. Also, enter the type of plan in the space provided.

TIP *Check this box if you are applying for a trust EIN when a new pension plan is established. In addition, check the "Other" box in line 8a and write "Created a Pension Plan" in the space provided.*

Banking purpose. Check this box if you are requesting an EIN for banking purposes only, and enter the banking purpose (for example, a bowling league for depositing dues or an investment club for dividend and interest reporting).

Changed type of organization. Check this box if the business is changing its type of organization for example, the business was a sole proprietorship and has been incorporated or has become a partnership. If you check this box, specify in the space provided (including available space immediately below) the type of change made. For example, "From Sole Proprietorship to Partnership."

Purchased going business. Check this box if you purchased an existing business. **Do not** use the former owner's EIN unless you became the "owner" of a corporation by acquiring its stock.

-4-

Form I-9. Employment Eligibility Verification

U.S. Department of Justice
Immigration and Naturalization Service

OMB No. 1115-0136

Employment Eligibility Verification

INSTRUCTIONS

PLEASE READ ALL INSTRUCTIONS CAREFULLY BEFORE COMPLETING THIS FORM.

Anti-Discrimination Notice. It is illegal to discriminate against any individual (other than an alien not authorized to work in the U.S.) in hiring, discharging, or recruiting or referring for a fee because of that individual's national origin or citizenship status. It is illegal to discriminate against work eligible individuals. Employers **CANNOT** specify which document(s) they will accept from an employee. The refusal to hire an individual because of a future expiration date may also constitute illegal discrimination.

Section 1 - Employee. All employees, citizens and noncitizens, hired after November 6, 1986, must complete Section 1 of this form at the time of hire, which is the actual beginning of employment. **The employer is responsible for ensuring that Section 1 is timely and properly completed.**

Preparer/Translator Certification. The Preparer/Translator Certification must be completed if Section 1 is prepared by a person other than the employee. A preparer/translator may be used only when the employee is unable to complete Section 1 on his/her own. However, the employee must still sign Section 1.

Section 2 - Employer. For the purpose of completing this form, the term "employer" includes those recruiters and referrers for a fee who are agricultural associations, agricultural employers or farm labor contractors.

Employers must complete Section 2 by examining evidence of identity and employment eligibility within three (3) business days of the date employment begins. If employees are authorized to work, but are unable to present the required document(s) within three business days, they must present a receipt for the application of the document(s) within three business days and the actual document(s) within ninety (90) days. However, if employers hire individuals for a duration of less than three business days, Section 2 must be completed at the time employment begins. **Employers must record: 1)** document title; **2)** issuing authority; **3)** document number, **4)** expiration date, if any; and **5)** the date employment begins. Employers must sign and date the certification. Employees must present original documents. Employers may, but are not required to, photocopy the document(s) presented. These photocopies may only be used for the verification process and must be retained with the I-9. **However, employers are still responsible for completing the I-9.**

Section 3 - Updating and Reverification. Employers must complete Section 3 when updating and/or reverifying the I-9. Employers must reverify employment eligibility of their employees on or before the expiration date recorded in Section 1. Employers **CANNOT** specify which document(s) they will accept from an employee.

- If an employee's name has changed at the time this form is being updated/ reverified, complete Block A.
- If an employee is rehired within three (3) years of the date this form was originally completed and the employee is still eligible to be employed on the same basis as previously indicated on this form (updating), complete Block B and the signature block.
- If an employee is rehired within three (3) years of the date this form was originally completed and the employee's work authorization has expired **or** if a current employee's work authorization is about to expire (reverification), complete Block B and:
  - examine any document that reflects that the employee is authorized to work in the U.S. (see List A **or** C),
  - record the document title, document number and expiration date (if any) in Block C, and
  - complete the signature block.

Photocopying and Retaining Form I-9. A blank I-9 may be reproduced, provided both sides are copied. The Instructions must be available to all employees completing this form. Employers must retain completed I-9s for three (3) years after the date of hire or one (1) year after the date employment ends, whichever is later.

For more detailed information, you may refer to the INS Handbook for Employers, (Form M-274). You may obtain the handbook at your local INS office.

Privacy Act Notice. The authority for collecting this information is the Immigration Reform and Control Act of 1986, Pub. L. 99-603 (8 USC 1324a).

This information is for employers to verify the eligibility of individuals for employment to preclude the unlawful hiring, or recruiting or referring for a fee, of aliens who are not authorized to work in the United States.

This information will be used by employers as a record of their basis for determining eligibility of an employee to work in the United States. The form will be kept by the employer and made available for inspection by officials of the U.S. Immigration and Naturalization Service, the Department of Labor and the Office of Special Counsel for Immigration Related Unfair Employment Practices.

Submission of the information required in this form is voluntary. However, an individual may not begin employment unless this form is completed, since employers are subject to civil or criminal penalties if they do not comply with the Immigration Reform and Control Act of 1986.

Reporting Burden. We try to create forms and instructions that are accurate, can be easily understood and which impose the least possible burden on you to provide us with information. Often this is difficult because some immigration laws are very complex. Accordingly, the reporting burden for this collection of information is computed as follows: **1)** learning about this form, 5 minutes; **2)** completing the form, 5 minutes; and **3)** assembling and filing (recordkeeping) the form, 5 minutes, for an average of 15 minutes per response. If you have comments regarding the accuracy of this burden estimate, or suggestions for making this form simpler, you can write to the Immigration and Naturalization Service, HQPDI, 425 I Street, N.W., Room 4034, Washington, DC 20536. OMB No. 1115-0136.

EMPLOYERS MUST RETAIN COMPLETED FORM I-9
PLEASE DO NOT MAIL COMPLETED FORM I-9 TO INS

Form I-9 (Rev. 11-21-91)N

Form I-9. Employment Eligibility Verification, continued

U.S. Department of Justice
Immigration and Naturalization Service

OMB No. 1115-0136

Employment Eligibility Verification

Please read instructions carefully before completing this form. The instructions must be available during completion of this form. ANTI-DISCRIMINATION NOTICE: It is illegal to discriminate against work eligible individuals. Employers CANNOT specify which document(s) they will accept from an employee. The refusal to hire an individual because of a future expiration date may also constitute illegal discrimination.

Section 1. Employee Information and Verification. To be completed and signed by employee at the time employment begins.

Print Name: Last ____ First ____ Middle Initial ____ Maiden Name ____

Address *(Street Name and Number)* ____ Apt. # ____ Date of Birth *(month/day/year)* ____

City ____ State ____ Zip Code ____ Social Security # ____

I am aware that federal law provides for imprisonment and/or fines for false statements or use of false documents in connection with the completion of this form.

I attest, under penalty of perjury, that I am (check one of the following):
- ☐ A citizen or national of the United States
- ☐ A Lawful Permanent Resident (Alien # A____________
- ☐ An alien authorized to work until ___/___/___ (Alien # or Admission #)____________

Employee's Signature ____ Date *(month/day/year)* ____

Preparer and/or Translator Certification. *(To be completed and signed if Section 1 is prepared by a person other than the employee.) I attest, under penalty of perjury, that I have assisted in the completion of this form and that to the best of my knowledge the information is true and correct.*

Preparer's/Translator's Signature ____ Print Name ____

Address *(Street Name and Number, City, State, Zip Code)* ____ Date *(month/day/year)* ____

Section 2. Employer Review and Verification. To be completed and signed by employer. Examine one document from List A OR examine one document from List B and one from List C, as listed on the reverse of this form, and record the title, number and expiration date, if any, of the document(s)

List A	OR	List B	AND	List C
Document title: ____________		____________		____________
Issuing authority: ____________		____________		____________
Document #: ____________		____________		____________
Expiration Date *(if any)*: ___/___/___		___/___/___		___/___/___
Document #: ____________				
Expiration Date *(if any)*: ___/___/___				

CERTIFICATION - I attest, under penalty of perjury, that I have examined the document(s) presented by the above-named employee, that the above-listed document(s) appear to be genuine and to relate to the employee named, that the employee began employment on *(month/day/year)* ___/___/___ **and that to the best of my knowledge the employee is eligible to work in the United States. (State employment agencies may omit the date the employee began employment.)**

Signature of Employer or Authorized Representative ____ Print Name ____ Title ____

Business or Organization Name ____ Address *(Street Name and Number, City, State, Zip Code)* ____ Date *(month/day/year)* ____

Section 3. Updating and Reverification. To be completed and signed by employer.

A. New Name *(if applicable)* ____ B. Date of rehire *(month/day/year) (if applicable)* ____

C. If employee's previous grant of work authorization has expired, provide the information below for the document that establishes current employment eligibility.

Document Title:____________ Document #: ____________ Expiration Date (if any): ___/___/___

I attest, under penalty of perjury, that to the best of my knowledge, this employee is eligible to work in the United States, and if the employee presented document(s), the document(s) I have examined appear to be genuine and to relate to the individual.

Signature of Employer or Authorized Representative ____ Date *(month/day/year)* ____

Form I-9 (Rev. 11-21-91)N Page 2

Sample Income Statement (Profit & Loss Statement)

For Year: ________________	January	February	March	April	May
INCOME					
Gross Sales					
Less returns and allowances					
Net Sales					
Cost of Goods					
Gross Profit					
GENERAL & ADMINISTRATIVE (G&A) EXPENSES					
Salaries and wages					
Employee benefits					
Payroll taxes					
Sales commissions					
Professional services					
Rent					
Maintenance					
Equipment rental					
Furniture and equipment purchase					
Depreciation and amortization					
Insurance					
Interest expenses					
Utilities					
Telephone					
Office supplies					
Postage and shipping					
Marketing and advertising					
Travel					
Entertainment					
Other					
Other					
TOTAL G&A EXPENSES					
Net income before taxes					
Provision for taxes on income					
NET INCOME AFTER TAXES (Net Profit)					

Sample Income Statement, continued

June	July	August	September	October	November	December	TOTAL

Sample Cash Flow Statement

For the period of: ___________	January	February	March	April	May
SALES Cash sales					
CREDIT SALES COLLECTIBLE For this month					
From last month					
From prior months					
OTHER CASH INFLOWS Sale of equipment					
Loan proceeds					
TOTAL INFLOWS					
PURCHASES Accounts payable that will be paid this month					
Salaries, wages, and benefits					
Other operating costs					
Tax payments					
Loan fees, principal, interest					
Equipment purchases					
Dividends					
Other ______________					
Total Outflows					
INFLOWS MINUS OUTFLOWS EQUALS NET CASH					
COMPANY CASH BUDGET					
Opening cash balance					
Cash inflows					
Cash available					
Cash outflows					
Net end of month cash					

Sample Cash Flow Statement, continued

June	July	August	September	October	November	December	TOTAL

Sample Balance Sheet

Company Name: ______________________

Balance Sheet as of: ______________________

ASSETS:		LIABILITIES:		
Cash	________	Accounts payable		________
Marketable securities	________	Sales tax payable		________
Accounts receivable	________	Payroll payable		________
Inventory	________	Payroll taxes payable		________
Prepaid expenses	________	Income taxes payable		________
________	________	Accruals		________
TOTAL CURRENT ASSETS	________	TOTAL CURRENT LIABILITIES		________
Land	________	Notes Payable		
Buildings	________	________		________
Equipment	________	________		________
Accumulated depreciation	________	________		________
Leasehold improvements	________	________		________
Amortization of leasehold improvements	________	________		________
TOTAL FIXED ASSETS	________	TOTAL LONG-TERM LIABILITIES		________
Deposits	________	Draws		________
Long-term investments	________	Paid-in capital		________
Deferred Assets	________	Retained earnings prior		________
________	________	Retained earnings current		________
LONG-TERM ASSETS	________	TOTAL EQUITY		________
TOTAL ASSETS	$ ________	TOTAL EQUITY & LIABILITIES		$ ________

Note: Total Assets must equal Total Equity and Liabilities.

Sample Purchase Order

Purchase Order Number ______________________

From ______________________ Phone ______________________

Address ______________________

____

Vendor	Ship to
______________________	______________________
______________________	______________________
______________________	______________________
______________________	______________________
____	

Job Reference # ______________________ Ship Via ______________________

Delivery Date ______________________ Terms ______________________

Quantity	Item Number	Description	Unit Cost	Extended Price
________	________	________	________	________
________	________	________	________	________
________	________	________	________	________
________	________	________	________	________
________	________	________	________	________
________	________	________	________	________
________	________	________	________	________

Conditions:

Our purchase order number must appear on all invoices, bills of lading, shipping memos, and packing lists. Goods are subject to our inspection and approval. If shipment will be delayed for any reason, advise us immediately and state all necessary facts. To avoid errors, note specifications carefully and let us know if unable to complete orders as written.

Subtotals	$________
Freight	$________
Tax	$________
Total	$________

Approved by ______________________ Date______________________

Sample Invoice

Invoice Number ____________

From ____________ Phone ____________

Address ____________

____________ Order Taken by ____________

To ____________ Phone ____________

Address ____________ Date of Order ____________

____________ Purchase Order # ____________

Job Location ____________ Ordered by

____________ Starting Time

Quantity	Material	Price	Amount

Description of Work

Date	Hours	Rate	Amount

Total Labor $____________

Other Charges

Recap of Job Invoice

Terms ____________

Date Completed ____________

I hereby acknowledge the satisfactory completion of the above work.

Authorized Signature ____________

Total Materials $____________

Total Labor $____________

Total Other Charges $____________

Tax $____________

Total Due ____________

Sample Job Description

POSITION MINIMUM REQUIREMENTS:

Education ______________________________
____
____

Experience ______________________________
____
____

Responsibility ______________________________
____
____

Initiative ______________________________
____
____

Skills ______________________________
____
____

Physical Requirements ______________________________
____
____

Mental Requirements ______________________________
____
____

Supervision ______________________________
____
____

Equipment Used ______________________________
____
____

Other Supervision ______________________________
____
____

Prepared by______________________ Date ______________________

Approved by ______________________ Date ______________________

Sample Job Application

Our policy is to provide equal employment opportunity to all qualified persons without regard to race, creed, color, religious belief, sex, age, national origin, physical or mental disability, or veteran status.

PERSONAL INFORMATION

Name ______________________________

Home Address ______________________________

Day Phone ______________ Evening Phone ______________

Social Security Number ______________________________

Are you a citizen or authorized by INS to work? (Documentation may be required.) ☐ Yes ☐ No

Have you ever been convicted of a felony? (This will not necessarily affect your application.) ☐ Yes ☐ No

EMPLOYMENT DESIRED

Have you ever applied for employment here? ☐ Yes ☐ No

When? ______________________________

Have you ever been employed by this company? ☐ Yes ☐ No

When? ______________ Where? ______________

Are you presently employed? ☐ Yes ☐ No

May we contact your employer? ☐ Yes ☐ No

Are you available for full-time work? ☐ Yes ☐ No

Are you available for part-time work? ☐ Yes ☐ No

Will you relocate? ☐ Yes ☐ No

Are you willing to travel? ☐ Yes ☐ No If yes, what percent? ______________

Date you can start: ______________________________

Desired position: ______________________________

Desired starting salary: ______________________________

Please list applicable skills: ______________________________

EDUCATION

School	Location	Major	Degree	Grade Average

Please list any scholastic honors received and offices held in school: ______________________________

____

Are you planning to continue your studies? ☐ Yes ☐ No

If yes, where and what courses of study? ______________________________

____

Sample Job Application, continued

WORK EXPERIENCE

Please list employment from the last ten years, starting with the most recent employer.

Company Name ______________________________

Address ______________________________

Job Title ______________________________

Responsibilities ______________________________

____

Dates of Employment — From ______________ To ______________

Reason for Leaving ______________________________

Company Name ______________________________

Address ______________________________

Job Title ______________________________

Responsibilities ______________________________

____

Dates of Employment — From ______________ To ______________

Reason for Leaving ______________________________

Company Name ______________________________

Address ______________________________

Job Title ______________________________

Responsibilities ______________________________

____

Dates of Employment — From ______________ To ______________

Reason for Leaving ______________________________

Company Name ______________________________

Address ______________________________

Job Title ______________________________

Responsibilities ______________________________

____

Dates of Employment — From ______________ To ______________

Reason for Leaving ______________________________

Attach additional sheet if necessary.

Sample Job Application, continued

REFERENCES

List three personal references, not related to you, whom have known you more than one year:

Name ____________ Phone ____________ Years Known ________

Address ____________________________

Name ____________ Phone ____________ Years Known ________

Address ____________________________

Name ____________ Phone ____________ Years Known ________

Address ____________________________

EMERGENCY CONTACT

In case of emergency, please notify: ____________________

Name ____________________ Phone ____________

Address ____________________________

Name ____________________ Phone ____________

Address ____________________________

PLEASE READ BEFORE SIGNING

I certify that all information provided by me on this application is true and complete to the best of my knowledge and that I have withheld nothing which, if disclosed, would alter the integrity of this application.

I authorize my previous employers, schools or persons listed as references to give any information regarding my employment or educational record. I agree that this company and my previous employers will not be held liable in any respect if a job is not extended, or is withdrawn, or employment is terminated because of false statements, omissions or answers made by myself on this application. In the event of any employment with this company I will comply with all rules and regulations as set by the company in any communication distributed to the employees.

In compliance with the Immigration Reform and Control Act of 1986, I understand that I am required to provide approved documentation to the company, which verifies my right to work in the United States on the first day of employment. I have received from the company a list of approved documents which are required.

I understand that employment at this company is "at will" which means that either I or this company can terminate the employment relationship at any time, with or without prior notice, and for any reason not prohibited by statute. All employment is continued on that basis. I hereby acknowledge that I have read and understand the above statements.

Signature ____________________ Date ____________

Sample Job Application, continued

LISTS OF ACCEPTABLE DOCUMENTS

LIST A		LIST B		LIST C
Documents that Establish Both Identity and Employment Eligibility	**OR**	**Documents that Establish Identity**	**AND**	**Documents that Establish Employment Eligibility**
1. U.S. Passport (unexpired or expired) 2. Certificate of U.S. Citizenship *(INS Form N-560 or N-561)* 3. Certificate of Naturalization *(INS Form N-550 or N-570)* 4. Unexpired foreign passport, with *I-551 stamp or* attached *INS Form I-94* indicating unexpired employment authorization 5. Alien Registration Receipt Card with photograph *(INS Form I-151 or I-551)* 6. Unexpired Temporary Card *(INS Form I-688)* 7. Unexpired Employment Authorization Card *(INS Form I-688A)* 8. Unexpired Reentry Permit *(INS Form I-327)* 9. Unexpired Refugee Travel Document *(INS Form I-571)* 10. Unexpired Employment Authorization Document issued by the INS which contains a photograph *(INS Form I-688B)*		1. Driver's license or ID card issued by a state or outlying possession of the United States provided it contains a photograph or information such as name, date of birth, sex, height, eye color and address 2. ID card issued by federal, state or local government agencies or entities, provided it contains a photograph or information such as name, date of birth, sex, height, eye color and address 3. School ID card with a photograph 4. Voter's registration card 5. U.S. Military card or draft record 6. Military dependent's ID card 7. U.S. Coast Guard Merchant Mariner Card 8. Native American tribal document 9. Driver's license issued by a Canadian government authority **For persons under age 18 who are unable to present a document listed above:** 10. School record or report card 11. Clinic, doctor or hospital record 12. Day-care or nursery school record		1. U.S. social security card issued by the Social Security Administration *(other than a card stating it is not valid for employment)* 2. Certification of Birth Abroad issued by the Department of State *(Form FS-545 or Form DS-1350)* 3. Original or certified copy of a birth certificate issued by a state, county, municipal authority or outlying possession of the United States bearing an official seal 4. Native American tribal document 5. U.S. Citizen ID Card *(INS Form I-197)* 6. ID Card for use of Resident Citizen in the United States *(INS Form I-179)* 7. Unexpired employment authorization document issued by the INS *(other then those listed under List A)*

Illustrations of many of these documents appear in Part 8 of the Handbook for Employers (M-274)

Form I-9 (Rev. 11-21-91)N Page 3

Form W-4. Employee's Withholding Allowance Certificate

Form W-4 (2002)

Purpose. Complete Form W-4 so your employer can withhold the correct Federal income tax from your pay. Because your tax situation may change, you may want to refigure your withholding each year.

Exemption from withholding. If you are exempt, complete only lines 1, 2, 3, 4, and 7 and sign the form to validate it. Your exemption for 2002 expires February 16, 2003. See **Pub. 505,** Tax Withholding and Estimated Tax.

Note: *You cannot claim exemption from withholding if **(a)** your income exceeds $750 and includes more than $250 of unearned income (e.g., interest and dividends) and **(b)** another person can claim you as a dependent on their tax return.*

Basic instructions. If you are not exempt, complete the **Personal Allowances Worksheet** below. The worksheets on page 2 adjust your withholding allowances based on itemized deductions, certain credits, adjustments to income, or two-earner/two-job situations. Complete all worksheets that apply. **However, you may claim fewer (or zero) allowances.**

Head of household. Generally, you may claim head of household filing status on your tax return only if you are unmarried and pay more than 50% of the costs of keeping up a home for yourself and your dependent(s) or other qualifying individuals. See line E below.

Tax credits. You can take projected tax credits into account in figuring your allowable number of withholding allowances. Credits for child or dependent care expenses and the child tax credit may be claimed using the **Personal Allowances Worksheet** below. See **Pub. 919,** How Do I Adjust My Tax Withholding? for information on converting your other credits into withholding allowances.

Nonwage income. If you have a large amount of nonwage income, such as interest or dividends, consider making estimated tax payments using **Form 1040-ES,** Estimated Tax for Individuals. Otherwise, you may owe additional tax.

Two earners/two jobs. If you have a working spouse or more than one job, figure the total number of allowances you are entitled to claim on all jobs using worksheets from only one Form W-4. Your withholding usually will be most accurate when all allowances are claimed on the Form W-4 for the highest paying job and zero allowances are claimed on the others.

Nonresident alien. If you are a nonresident alien, see the **Instructions for Form 8233** before completing this Form W-4.

Check your withholding. After your Form W-4 takes effect, use Pub. 919 to see how the dollar amount you are having withheld compares to your projected total tax for 2002. See Pub. 919, especially if you used the **Two-Earner/Two-Job Worksheet** on page 2 and your earnings exceed $125,000 (Single) or $175,000 (Married).

Recent name change? If your name on line 1 differs from that shown on your social security card, call 1-800-772-1213 for a new social security card.

Personal Allowances Worksheet (Keep for your records.)

A Enter "1" for **yourself** if no one else can claim you as a dependent . . . . A ______

B Enter "1" if:
- You are single and have only one job; or
- You are married, have only one job, and your spouse does not work; or
- Your wages from a second job or your spouse's wages (or the total of both) are $1,000 or less.

. . B ______

C Enter "1" for your **spouse.** But, you may choose to enter "-0-" if you are married and have either a working spouse or more than one job. (Entering "-0-" may help you avoid having too little tax withheld.) . . . . C ______

D Enter number of **dependents** (other than your spouse or yourself) you will claim on your tax return . . . . D ______

E Enter "1" if you will file as **head of household** on your tax return (see conditions under **Head of household** above) . E ______

F Enter "1" if you have at least $1,500 of **child or dependent care expenses** for which you plan to claim a credit . . F ______

(**Note:** *Do **not** include child support payments. See **Pub. 503,** Child and Dependent Care Expenses, for details.*)

G **Child Tax Credit** (including additional child tax credit):
- If your total income will be between $15,000 and $42,000 ($20,000 and $65,000 if married), enter "1" for each eligible child plus **1 additional** if you have three to five eligible children or **2 additional** if you have six or more eligible children.
- If your total income will be between $42,000 and $80,000 ($65,000 and $115,000 if married), enter "1" if you have one or two eligible children, "2" if you have three eligible children, "3" if you have four eligible children, or "4" if you have five or more eligible children.

G ______

H Add lines A through G and enter total here. **Note:** *This may be different from the number of exemptions you claim on your tax return.* ▶ H ______

For accuracy, complete all worksheets that apply.
- If you plan to **itemize or claim adjustments to income** and want to reduce your withholding, see the **Deductions and Adjustments Worksheet** on page 2.
- If you have **more than one job** or are **married and you and your spouse both work** and the combined earnings from all jobs exceed $35,000, see the **Two-Earner/Two-Job Worksheet** on page 2 to avoid having too little tax withheld.
- If **neither** of the above situations applies, **stop here** and enter the number from line H on line 5 of Form W-4 below.

Cut here and give Form W-4 to your employer. Keep the top part for your records.

Form **W-4**
Department of the Treasury
Internal Revenue Service

Employee's Withholding Allowance Certificate

▶ **For Privacy Act and Paperwork Reduction Act Notice, see page 2.**

OMB No. 1545-0010

2002

1 Type or print your first name and middle initial	Last name	2 Your social security number
Home address (number and street or rural route)	3 ☐ Single ☐ Married ☐ Married, but withhold at higher Single rate. **Note:** *If married, but legally separated, or spouse is a nonresident alien, check the "Single" box.*	
City or town, state, and ZIP code	4 **If your last name differs from that on your social security card, check here. You must call 1-800-772-1213 for a new card.** ▶ ☐	

5 Total number of allowances you are claiming (from line H above **or** from the applicable worksheet on page 2) | 5 |

6 Additional amount, if any, you want withheld from each paycheck . . . . | 6 | $

7 I claim exemption from withholding for 2002, and I certify that I meet **both** of the following conditions for exemption:
- Last year I had a right to a refund of **all** Federal income tax withheld because I had **no** tax liability **and**
- This year I expect a refund of **all** Federal income tax withheld because I expect to have **no** tax liability.

If you meet both conditions, write "Exempt" here . . . . ▶ | 7 |

Under penalties of perjury, I certify that I am entitled to the number of withholding allowances claimed on this certificate, or I am entitled to claim exempt status.

Employee's signature
(Form is not valid unless you sign it.) ▶ **Date** ▶

8 Employer's name and address (Employer: Complete lines 8 and 10 only if sending to the IRS.)	9 Office code (optional)	10 Employer identification number

Cat. No. 10220Q

Form W-4. Employee's Withholding Allowance Certificate, continued

Form W-4 (2002) Page 2

Deductions and Adjustments Worksheet

Note: *Use this worksheet only if you plan to itemize deductions, claim certain credits, or claim adjustments to income on your 2002 tax return.*

1 Enter an estimate of your 2002 itemized deductions. These include qualifying home mortgage interest, charitable contributions, state and local taxes, medical expenses in excess of 7.5% of your income, and miscellaneous deductions. (For 2002, you may have to reduce your itemized deductions if your income is over $137,300 ($68,650 if married filing separately). See **Worksheet 3** in Pub. 919 for details.) . . . 1 $________

2 Enter: { $7,850 if married filing jointly or qualifying widow(er); $6,900 if head of household; $4,700 if single; $3,925 if married filing separately } . . . . 2 $________

3 **Subtract** line 2 from line 1. If line 2 is greater than line 1, enter "-0-" . . . . 3 $________

4 Enter an estimate of your 2002 adjustments to income, including alimony, deductible IRA contributions, and student loan interest 4 $________

5 **Add** lines 3 and 4 and enter the total. Include any amount for credits from **Worksheet 7** in Pub. 919. . 5 $________

6 Enter an estimate of your 2002 nonwage income (such as dividends or interest) . . . . 6 $________

7 **Subtract** line 6 from line 5. Enter the result, but not less than "-0-" . . . . 7 $________

8 **Divide** the amount on line 7 by $3,000 and enter the result here. Drop any fraction . . . . 8 ________

9 Enter the number from the **Personal Allowances Worksheet,** line H, page 1 . . . . 9 ________

10 **Add** lines 8 and 9 and enter the total here. If you plan to use the **Two-Earner/Two-Job Worksheet,** also enter this total on line 1 below. Otherwise, **stop here** and enter this total on Form W-4, line 5, page 1 . 10 ________

Two-Earner/Two-Job Worksheet

Note: *Use this worksheet only if the instructions under line H on page 1 direct you here.*

1 Enter the number from line H, page 1 (or from line 10 above if you used the **Deductions and Adjustments Worksheet**) 1 ________

2 Find the number in **Table 1** below that applies to the **lowest** paying job and enter it here . . . . . 2 ________

3 If line 1 is **more than or equal to** line 2, subtract line 2 from line 1. Enter the result here (if zero, enter "-0-") and on Form W-4, line 5, page 1. **Do not** use the rest of this worksheet . . . . 3 ________

Note: *If line 1 is **less than** line 2, enter "-0-" on Form W-4, line 5, page 1. Complete lines 4–9 below to calculate the additional withholding amount necessary to avoid a year end tax bill.*

4 Enter the number from line 2 of this worksheet . . . . 4 ________

5 Enter the number from line 1 of this worksheet . . . . 5 ________

6 **Subtract** line 5 from line 4 . . . . 6 ________

7 Find the amount in **Table 2** below that applies to the **highest** paying job and enter it here . . . . . 7 $________

8 **Multiply** line 7 by line 6 and enter the result here. This is the additional annual withholding needed . . 8 $________

9 Divide line 8 by the number of pay periods remaining in 2002. For example, divide by 26 if you are paid every two weeks and you complete this form in December 2001. Enter the result here and on Form W-4, line 6, page 1. This is the additional amount to be withheld from each paycheck . . . . 9 $________

Table 1: Two-Earner/Two-Job Worksheet

Married Filing Jointly				All Others			
If wages from **LOWEST** paying job are—	Enter on line 2 above	If wages from **LOWEST** paying job are—	Enter on line 2 above	If wages from **LOWEST** paying job are—	Enter on line 2 above	If wages from **LOWEST** paying job are—	Enter on line 2 above
$0 - $4,000	0	44,001 - 50,000	8	$0 - $6,000	0	75,001 - 95,000	8
4,001 - 9,000	1	50,001 - 55,000	9	6,001 - 11,000	1	95,001 - 110,000	9
9,001 - 15,000	2	55,001 - 65,000	10	11,001 - 17,000	2	110,001 and over	10
15,001 - 20,000	3	65,001 - 80,000	11	17,001 - 23,000	3		
20,001 - 25,000	4	80,001 - 95,000	12	23,001 - 28,000	4		
25,001 - 32,000	5	95,001 - 110,000	13	28,001 - 38,000	5		
32,001 - 38,000	6	110,001 - 125,000	14	38,001 - 55,000	6		
38,001 - 44,000	7	125,001 and over	15	55,001 - 75,000	7		

Table 2: Two-Earner/Two-Job Worksheet

Married Filing Jointly		All Others	
If wages from **HIGHEST** paying job are—	Enter on line 7 above	If wages from **HIGHEST** paying job are—	Enter on line 7 above
$0 - $50,000	$450	$0 - $30,000	$450
50,001 - 100,000	800	30,001 - 70,000	800
100,001 - 150,000	900	70,001 - 140,000	900
150,001 - 270,000	1,050	140,001 - 300,000	1,050
270,001 and over	1,150	300,001 and over	1,150

Privacy Act and Paperwork Reduction Act Notice. We ask for the information on this form to carry out the Internal Revenue laws of the United States. The Internal Revenue Code requires this information under sections 3402(f)(2)(A) and 6109 and their regulations. **Failure to provide a properly completed form will result in your being treated as a single person who claims no withholding allowances; providing fraudulent information may also subject you to penalties.** Routine uses of this information include giving it to the Department of Justice for civil and criminal litigation, to cities, states, and the District of Columbia for use in administering their tax laws, and using it in the National Directory of New Hires.

You are not required to provide the information requested on a form that is subject to the Paperwork Reduction Act unless the form displays a valid OMB control number. Books or records relating to a form or its instructions must be retained as long as their contents may become material in the administration of any Internal Revenue law. Generally, tax returns and return information are confidential, as required by Code section 6103.

The time needed to complete this form will vary depending on individual circumstances. The estimated average time is: **Recordkeeping,** 46 min.; **Learning about the law or the form,** 13 min.; **Preparing the form,** 59 min. If you have comments concerning the accuracy of these time estimates or suggestions for making this form simpler, we would be happy to hear from you. You can write to the Tax Forms Committee, Western Area Distribution Center, Rancho Cordova, CA 95743-0001. **Do not** send the tax form to this address. Instead, give it to your employer.

Sample Performance Review

Name ____

Job Title ____

Department ____

Supervisor ____

Date Hired ________________ Last Review Date ______________ Today's Date __________

The following definitions apply to each factor rated below. (See page 4 for full explanation)

Level 6 — Far exceeds job requirements
Level 5 — Consistently exceeds job requirements
Level 4 — Meets and usually exceeds job requirements
Level 3 — Consistently meets job requirements
Level 2 — Inconsistent in meeting job requirements
Level 1 — Does not meet job requirements
(Circle appropriate number.)

Quantity of Work Level 1 2 3 4 5 6

Volume of work regularly produced. Speed and consistency of output.

Comments: ____

____

____

____

Quality of Work Level 1 2 3 4 5 6

Extent to which employee can be counted upon to carry out assignments to completion.

Comments: ____

____

____

____

Job Cooperation Level 1 2 3 4 5 6

Amount of interest and enthusiasm shown in work.

Comments: ____

____

____

____

Sample Performance Review, continued

Ability to work with others Level 1 2 3 4 5 6

Extent to which employee effectively interacts with others in the performance of his/her job.

Comments: ______________________________

____

____

____

Adaptability Level 1 2 3 4 5 6

Extent to which employee is able to perform a variety of tasks within the scope of his/her job.

Comments: ______________________________

____

____

____

Job Knowledge Level 1 2 3 4 5 6

Extent of job information and understanding possessed by employee.

Comments: ______________________________

____

____

____

Initiative Level 1 2 3 4 5 6

Extent to which employee is a self starter in attaining objectives of the job.

Comments: ______________________________

____

____

____

Overall Performance Evaluation Level 1 2 3 4 5 6

Comments: ______________________________

____

____

____

____

____

____

Sample Performance Review, continued

Attendance ☐ Problem ☐ No Problem

Volume of work regularly produced. Speed and consistency of output

Comments: ______________________________

____

____

____

EMPLOYEE'S CAREER DEVELOPMENT

Strengths: ______________________________

____

____

____

____

Development Needs: ______________________________

____

____

____

____

Development Plan (include Long Range): ______________________________

____

____

____

EMPLOYEE'S COMMENTS (optional)

General comments about your performance: ______________________________

____

____

____

____

Read and Acknowledged by:

Employee ______________________________ Date ______________

Approvals

Supervisor ______________________________ Date ______________

Department Manager ______________________________ Date ______________

Personnel ______________________________ Date ______________

Owner or CEO ______________________________ Date ______________

Federal Agency Contacts

Federal Information Center
www.info.gov/
(800) FED-INFO (333-4636)
Purpose: A one-stop phone number to help you reach other federal numbers.

U.S. Small Business Administration (SBA) Field Offices
www.sba.gov
Purpose: Free financial assistance and counseling on creating a marketing plan to developing a business plan.

Utah District Office
125 South State Street, Room 2227
Salt Lake City, UT 84138
(801) 524-3209

SBA Online Library
www.sba.gov/library

SBA Answer Desk
(800) UASK-SBA
www.sba.gov.answerdesk.html

Purpose: For 24-hour information relating to small business.

U.S. Business Advisor
Office of Technology
Mail Code 6470
409 3rd Street, SW
Washington, DC 20416
(202) 205-6450
(202) 205-7754
www.business.gov
Purpose: Electronic one-stop center for making electronic links to all government business sites.

Business Information Center (BICs)
Purpose: To get counseling and training for your new or expanding business.

Utah Business Information Center
310 South Main Street, North Mezzanine
Salt Lake City, UT 84191
(801) 746-2269 (SCORE and information)
(801) 746-2273 (FAX and TDD)

Ogden Business Information Center
2444 Washington Boulevard
Ogden, UT 84401
(801) 629-8604
(801) 392-0604 (FAX)

National Business Incubation Association (NBIA)
www.nbia.org
Purpose: Will help you locate the nearest business incubator.

NBIA Headquarters
20 East Circle Drive, Suite 190
Athens, OH 45701-3751
(740) 593-4331
(740) 593-1996 (FAX)

U.S. Department of Commerce
www.doc.gov
Purpose: Serves as the umbrella agency for a variety of programs geared toward business.
Headquarters

1401 Constitution Avenue, NW
Washington, DC 20230
(202) 482-2000
(202) 482-5270 (FAX)

Bureau of Economic Analysis (BEA)
Public Information Office
1441 L Street
Washington, DC 20230
(202) 606-9900
(202) 606-5355 (TDD)

For information on services:
STAT-USA
(202) 482-1986
www.bea.gov

U.S. Census Bureau—Denver Region (serving Utah)
6900 West Jefferson Avenue, Suite 100
Denver, CO 80235
(303) 969-6750
(303) 969-6777 (FAX)
www.census.gov

Economic Development Administration (EDA)
14th and Constitution Avenue
Washington, DC 20230
(202) 482-5081
www.doc.gov/eda

Denver EDA Regional Office (serving Utah)
1244 Speer Boulevard, Room 670
Denver, CO 80204
(303) 844-4714

International Trade Administration (ITA)
Trade Information Center
(800) USA-TRADE (872-8723)
(800) TDD-TRADE (833-8723)
(202) 482-6097 (FAX)
tic@ita.doc.gov (e-mail)
www.ita.doc.gov

Minority and Business Development Agency (MBDA)
U.S. Department of Commerce
14th and Constitution Avenue, NW
Room 5053
Washington, DC 20230
(202) 482-0404
(202) 482-2678 (FAX)
help@mbda.gov (e-mail)
www.mbda.gov

Dallas Regional MBDA Center (serving Utah)
1100 Commerce Street
Dallas, TX 75242
(214) 767-8001
(214) 767-0613 (FAX)

U.S. Department of Labor
www.dol.gov
Purpose: Information about retirement, safety and health, and wage, hour and work standards.

U.S. Department of Labor/OSHA
www.osha.gov
Purpose: To obtain information about the Occupational Safety and Health Act.

Denver Regional Office (serving Utah)
1999 Broadway, Suite 1690
Denver, CO 80202-5716
(303) 844-1600

U.S. Chamber of Commerce
www.uschamber.org
Purpose: Provides a link between small business and government, and is the main center for a nationwide network of local chambers of commerce.

Chamber Headquarters
1615 H Street, NW
Washington, DC 20062-2000
(202) 659-6000

Internal Revenue Service (IRS)
www.irs.ustreas.gov
Purpose: Where to register to pay withholding tax (FUTA, unemployment, SSI, FICA), income, and corporate taxes.

Taxpayer Education Coordinator (serving Utah)
600 17th Street
Stop 6610DEN
Denver, CO 80202
(303) 446-1659
Live telephone assistance
(800) 829-1040

Tele-TIN
EIN Operations
Philadelphia IRS Center
Philadelphia, PA 19255
(800) 829-4933
(215) 516-3990 (fax-TIN)
Purpose: To apply for an employer identification number (EIN). Note: You must complete *Form SS-4* before you call.

Tele-Tax
(800) 829-4477 (nationwide)
Purpose: Provides recorded tax information, available 24 hours a day, on a wide variety of tax-related subjects.

Equal Employment Opportunity Commission (EEOC)
Purpose: To provide minimum wage posters and information about employer responsibilities under ADA.

EEOC Publications Information Center
P.O. Box 12549
Cincinnati, OH 45212-0549
(800) 669-3362
(800) 800-3302 (TDD)

EEOC Headquarters
1801 L Street, NW
Washington, DC 20507
(202) 663-4900
(202) 663-4494 (TDD)
(800) 669-4000 (connection to nearest EEOC field office)
(800) 669-6820 (TDD) (connection to nearest EEOC field office)

Phoenix EEOC District Office (serving Utah)
3300 North Central Avenue, Suite 690
Phoenix, AZ 85012
(602) 640-5000
(602) 640-5071 (FAX)
(800) 669-4000

Environmental Protection Agency
www.epa.gov
Purpose: To provide assistance for compliance with federal EPA requirements.

EPA Region 8 (serving Utah)
999 18th Street, Suite 300
Denver, CO 80202-2466
(303) 3112-6312
(800) 227-8917 (in Utah)

Federal Trade Commission (FTC)
www.ftc.gov
Purpose: Provides federal disclosure information on franchise opportunities.

FTC Headquarters
600 Pennsylvania Avenue, NW
Washington, DC 20580
(877) FTC-HELP (382-4357) (consumer response center)

Denver Regional Office (serving Utah)
1961 Stout Street
Suite 1523
Denver, CO 80284-0101
(303) 844-2271

Bureau of Consumer Protection
Division of Service Industry Practices
601 Pennsylvania Avenue, NW
Washington, DC 20580
(202) 326-3222 (general questions)
www.ftc.gov/bcp/bcp.htm

Bureau of Citizenship and Immigration Service (BCIS)
www.bcis.gov/graphics/services/employerinfo/oblhome.htm
Purpose: For information on the employment eligibility verification process and where to find the employer relations office nearest you for assistance with *Form I-9.*

Office of Business Liaison (OBL)
(800) 357-2099 (hotline)
(800) 375-5283 (National Customer Service Center)
(202) 305-2523 (fax, for complicated inquiries)

Employer Support of the Guard and Reserve
www.esgr.org
Purpose: To provide information and mediation for understanding and applying the law related to military leave.

National Committee
1555 Wilson Boulevard, Suite 200
Arlington, VA 22209-2405
(800) 336-4590
(703) 696-1411 (FAX)

U.S. Patent and Trademark Office
www.uspto.gov
Purpose: To provide federal trademarks, service marks, and trade names.

For new trademark applications:
Box NEW APP FEE
Assistant Commissioner for Trademarks
Crystal Plaza 3
Room 2C02
Arlington, VA 22202-3515
(800) 786-9199
(703) 308-HELP (4357)
(703) 305-7785 (TDD)
(703) 305-7786 (FAX)

Trademark Assistance Center
(703) 308-9000
(703) 308-7016 (FAX)

State and Private Agency Contacts

Utah Secretary of State
www.mycorporation.com/secretary-state/Utah.htm
Purpose: Answers questions on the formation of all types of businesses. Registers all corporations and limited liability companies.

Department of Commerce
160 East 300 South, 2nd Floor
P.O. Box 146701
Salt Lake City, UT 84114
(801) 530-6431
(801) 530-6446 (FAX)

Utah Department of Commerce
www.commerce.utah.gov
Purpose: Contact the appropriate agency to register your business, apply for a sales and use tax number, a withholding account, business name or trademark registration, or required license.

Division of Public Utilities
160 East 300 South, 4th Floor

Salt Lake City, UT 84111
(801) 530-7622

Division of Corporations and
Commercial Code
160 East 300 South
Salt Lake City, UT 84111
(801) 530-4849
(801) 530-6111 (FAX)
(877) 526-3994 (toll free in Utah)

Division of Occupational and
Professional Licensing
P.O. Box 146741
Salt Lake City, UT 84114-6741
(801) 530-6628
(801) 530-6511 (FAX)
(866) 275-3675 (toll free in Utah)

Utah Department of Workforce Services
www.jobs.utah.gov/
Purpose: Contact the appropriate agency to register your business and pay unemployment insurance taxes, or to file new hire reports.

Employer Accounts
140 East 300 South
P.O. Box 45288
Salt Lake City, UT 84145-0288
(801) 526-9400 (register your business)
(800) 222-2857 (toll free in Utah)

Utah New Hire Registry
P.O. Box 45247
Salt Lake City, UT 84145-0247
(801) 526-4361
(801) 526-4391 (FAX)

Utah State Tax Commission
www.tax.utah.gov/
Purpose: Contact to register your business for a sales and use tax license, a withholding tax account, a cigarette license, or to pay other applicable taxes.

210 North 1950 West
Salt Lake City, UT 84134
(801) 297-2200
(800) 662-4335 (nationwide)

Utah Labor Commission
www.labor.state.ut.us
Purpose: Contact the appropriate division for information about minimum wage, child labor laws, health and safety regulations, or workers' compensation insurance.

160 East 300 South, 3rd Floor
Salt Lake City, UT 84114-6650
(801) 530-6800

Employment Standards Bureau (minimum wage, child labor laws)
P.O. Box 146630
Salt Lake City, UT 84114-6630
(801) 530-6801
(800) 222-1238

UOSH Division (safety and health regulations)
P.O. Box 146650
Salt Lake City, UT 84114-6650
(801) 530-6901

Division of Industrial Accidents (workers' compensation insurance)
P.O. Box 146610
Salt Lake City, UT 84114-6610
(801) 530-6800

Utah Department of Environmental Quality
www.eq.state.ut.us

Purpose: Contact for information about environmental protection regulations and for compliance assistance.

168 North 1950 West
Salt Lake City, UT 84116
(801) 536-4400
(801) 536-4278 (Small Business Ombudsman)
(800) 458-0145

State Ombudsman
168 North 1950 West
Salt Lake City, UT 84114
(801) 536-4478

DEQ Office of Planning and Public Affairs
(Pre-Design Program)
(801) 536-4476
(801) 536-0061 (FAX)

Small Business Development Center (SBDC)
www.sba.gov/sbdc/
Purpose: This lead center will direct you to the nearest SBDC counselor for free training and start-up assistance.

Salt Lake Community College (Lead Center)
1623 South State Street
Salt Lake City, UT 84115
(801) 957-3480
(801) 957-3489 (FAX)

Utah State Data Center
www.census.gov/
Purpose: To provide the most up to date census data for the state.

Office of Planning and Budget
116 State Capitol
Salt Lake City, UT 84114
(801) 538-1027
(801) 538-1547 (FAX)
www.overnor.state.ut.us/dea/

Utah Technology Finance Corporation
www.utfc.org
Purpose: Contact for information about assistance offered to new and expanding high technology businesses.

699 East South Temple, Suite 220
Salt Lake City, UT 84102
(801) 741-4200
(801) 741-4249 (FAX)

State Business Publication

Utah Business Magazine
1245 East Brickyard Road, Suite 90
Salt Lake City, UT 84106
(801) 568-0114
www.utahbusiness.com/

National Federation of Independent Businesses (NFIB)
www.nfib.com
Purpose: A nonprofit small business advocacy group that lobbies at both the state and federal level.

Membership Services Office—NFIB
53 Century Boulevard, Suite 250
Nashville, TN 37214
(800) NFIB-NOW

National Association for the Self-Employed® (NASE)
www.nase.org
Purpose: A membership organization for small business owners; gives advice and valuable competitive information.

NASE Headquarters
P.O. Box 612067
DFW Airport
Dallas, TX 75261-2067
(800) 232-NASE
(800) 551-4446 (FAX)

Society of Risk Management Consultants (SRMC)
www.srmcsociety.org
Purpose: An organization that can assist in finding a professional and ethical insurance consultant.

SRMC Headquarters
P.O. Box 510228
Milwaukee, WI 53203
(800) 765-SRMC

National Venture Capital Association (NVCA)
www.nvca.org
Purpose: To find sources of venture capital.

NVCA Headquarters
1655 North Fort Myer Drive, Suite 850
Arlington, VA 22209
(703) 524-2549
(703) 524-3940 (FAX)

National Association of Small Business Investment Companies (NASBIC)
www.nasbic.org
Purpose: Central contact agency to find SBICs throughout the nation.

NASBIC Headquarters
666 11th Street, NW, Suite 750
Washington, DC 20001
(202) 628-5055
(202) 628-5080 (FAX)

National Association of Women Business Owners (NAWBO)
www.nawbo.org
Purpose: Provides networking and business assistance to women-owned businesses.

NAWBO Headquarters
8405 Greensboro Drive, Suite 800
McLean, VA 22102
(703) 506-3268
(800) 55-NAWBO (nationwide)
(703) 506-3266 (FAX)

State Loan Programs

Utah has several state agencies to help you find assistance and financing for your business. Most of the state loan or bond programs fall into one of the following general categories:

- *Loan guarantee programs.* Programs in which a public agency guarantees a loan made by a private lending institution by agreeing to repay a percentage of it, lessening the lender's risk and making it easier for your business to obtain the loan. You can expect to be charged a fee by the guarantying entity.
- *Direct loans and grants.* Loans and grants can be made available to your business to finance projects that will further the objectives of the public entity making the loan or grant.

Venture Capital Funds

A venture capital fund is used for equity financing and is professionally managed money that seeks a high rate of return for its investors. This is usually done by investing in new business startups that demonstrate the possibility of very rapid growth.

For more information, contact:

Utah Ventures
2755 East Cottonwood Parkway, Suite 520
Salt Lake City, Utah 84121
(801) 365-0233
or
Wasatch Venture Fund
One Main Street, Suite 1660
Salt Lake City, Utah 84133
(801) 524-8939

Certified Development Companies (CDC)

CDCs are private companies that are licensed by the U.S. Small Business Administration to provide long-term financing under the SBA 504 Program. A percentage of the loan must be provided by the borrower and the remainder of the project's cost is furnished by a private lender. There are two such CDCs in Utah. They are:

Northern Utah Capital Corporation
2404 Washington Boulevard, Suite 1100
Ogden, Utah 84401
(801) 627-1333
(801) 329-7609 (FAX)

Deseret Certified Development Company
2595 East 3300 South
Salt Lake City, Utah 84109
(801) 474-3232
(801) 493-0111 (FAX)

Utah Microenterprise Loan Fund

The Utah Microenterprise Loan Fund offers loans up to $10,000 for terms up to five years to owners of new or established firms who do not qualify for traditional funding sources—usually business owners who are socially or economically disadvantaged. This fund is a nonprofit, tax-exempt corporation. The interest rate is prime plus 3 percent fixed, and your business must be located in Salt Lake County. For more information, contact:

Utah Microenterprise Loan Fund
3595 South Main Street

Salt Lake City, Utah 84115
(801) 269-8408
(801) 269-1063 (FAX)

Utah Technology Finance Corporation (UTFC)

The UTFC is an independent corporation of the state that makes investments in Utah businesses to foster their creation, growth, and success. State and federal funds are available through programs such as Early Technology Business Capital, Utah Rural Loan Program, MicroLoan Program, Utah Loan Fund, Bank Participation Loan Program, and Defense Conversion Program. Utah exporters can access export finance assistance programs offered by ExIm Bank through the UTFC. For more information, contact:

Utah Technology Finance Corporation
699 East Temple,
Suite 220
Salt Lake City, Utah 84102
(801) 714-4200
(801) 714-4249 (FAX)
www.utfc.state.ut.us

Public Offering of Securities

Raising capital through the public markets can be successful. But, due to the legal complexities, you should consult an attorney with securities expertise before making your decision. Individuals offering or selling securities in Utah must be licensed in the state in accordance with the Utah Uniform Securities Act. Federal registration of the security may also be required. Securities are legally defined as common and preferred stocks, note debentures, voting trust certificates, certificates of deposit, or warrants. There are several other types of securities. For complete details contact:

Utah Department of Commerce, Division of Securities
160 East 300 South
P.O. Box 146760
Salt Lake City, Utah 84114-6760
(801) 530-6431
(800) 530-6446
www.commerce.state.ut.us

Index